M

MAY 17 2002

DATE DUE

AUG 2 1 2002	
	AUG 1 9 2004
SEP - 8 2002	
OCT 2 0 2002	
NOV 1 6 2002	
DEC 1 8 2002	
AUG 1 9 2003	

DEMCO, INC. 38-2931

REINVENTING
THE
BAZAAR

REINVENTING THE BAZAAR

A Natural History of Markets

JOHN MCMILLAN

W. W. Norton & Company

NEW YORK   LONDON

For information about permission to reproduce selections from this book,
write to Permissions, W. W. Norton & Company, Inc., 500 Fifth Avenue,
New York, NY 10110

The text of this book is composed in Electra LH Regular OSF, with the
display set in Aperto
Composition by Gina Webster
Manufacturing by The Maple-Vail Book Manufacturing Group
Book design by Brooke Koven
Production manager: Andrew Marasia

Library of Congress Cataloging-in-Publication Data

McMillan, John.
Reinventing the bazaar : a natural history of markets / John
McMillan. — 1st ed.
p.   cm.
Includes bibliographical references and index.
ISBN 0-393-05021-1
1. Capitalism. 2. Economic history. 3. Evolutionary economics.
4. Capitalism — History. I. Title.
HB501 .M554 2002
330.12'2 — dc21

2002000521

W. W. Norton & Company, Inc., 500 Fifth Avenue,
New York, N.Y. 10110
www.wwnorton.com

W. W. Norton & Company Ltd., Castle House, 75/76 Wells Street,
London W1T 3QT

1 2 3 4 5 6 7 8 9 0

To my mother

C O N T E N T S

PREFACE

"What is a tenured professor going to teach me about the market economy?" asked Scott McNealy, the chairman and chief executive officer of Sun Microsystems, speaking before students at Stanford University's Graduate School of Business. Notably skeptical of tenured professors, McNealy meant his question to be taken rhetorically, but the challenge he posed deserves to be taken up.

The market economy is as ever-present as the air we breathe, not only for a superstar executive like McNealy but for everyone. We encounter markets every day in countless ways: in our buying and selling, working, and investing. We can glean insight, however, by taking a fresh angle on the familiar.

This book is a riposte to McNealy's challenge. Current research by economists is deepening our understanding of markets. New ideas in economics, and some old ones, are used in the chapters that follow to dissect exotic, innovative, and everyday marketplaces—some in physical space, others in cyberspace. How do markets work? What can they do? What can't they do? These are the questions I will address.

Markets are subtle organizations. The mechanisms that underpin transacting are intricate—and they are in everlasting flux. People are ingenious at finding ways to make exchanges that bring mutual gains.

Markets do what they are supposed to do, however, only if they are well structured. Any successful economy has an array of devices and procedures to enable markets to work smoothly. A workable platform has five elements: information flows smoothly; property rights are protected; people can be trusted to live up to their promises; side effects on third parties are curtailed; and competition is fostered.

The platform for a market in large part evolves by trial and error. The mechanisms for transacting develop from the bottom up, via innovations made by the participants. Spontaneous evolution is the main driver of markets. To reach their full potential, however, markets need help from the government. Markets and governments have an uneasy relationship. Markets coordinate the economy better than any centralized alternative; governments sometimes distort and even destroy markets. But help from the government is essential if the economy is to reach its full potential.

The strength of markets lies in their adaptability, their restless reinvention. Shaping markets for the twenty-first century is both a task for governments and an opportunity for entrepreneurs.

"Economists occasionally tell better stories than novelists, " remarked the novelist Mario Vargas Llosa.[1] My task is to try to live up to Vargas Llosa's observation. The raw material is rich. The story of markets is full of human ingenuity and creativity—as well as disappointment and failure.

REINVENTING
THE
BAZAAR

ONE

::::

The Only Natural Economy

Flowers in all their colors covering an area the size of 125 soccer fields are what you see if you visit the world's largest flower market, in the Dutch village of Aalsmeer. The scale is astounding. Seven million roses, three million tulips, two million chrysanthemums, and eight million other flowers and potted plants pass through on a typical morning. Some two thousand buyers bid U.S.$5 million for them.[1]

The flowers are flown in from as far away as Colombia, Kenya, and Zimbabwe. While shipping flowers to the Netherlands might seem akin to taking coals to Newcastle, the Dutch today are in the business of running the global flower trade. The marketplace is organized so expeditiously that the flowers are still fresh when they reach their ultimate destinations all around the world.

A worldwide market in cut flowers, delicate and perishable as they are, could not exist without modern technology. It was not until the late 1980s that countries like Kenya became significant suppliers. Efficient air transportation and telecommunications are needed to move roses from a grower near Nairobi to Aalsmeer and then on to a buyer, say, in Seoul, all in less than a day. Electronic devices keep track of the flowers as they move through the auction house. The "Dutch clock" method of bidding allows the thousands of auctions to run in a few hours. A gigantic clock, to which every bidder is wired, dominates the front of each auction hall. As each lot of flowers is towed by, the clock's hand starts at a high price and rotates through lower

3

prices until one of the bidders stops it with a push of a button. Computers then automatically organize the flowers' delivery to the buyer's address.

Sophisticated as its processes are, the core of the global flower market—competitive buying and selling—is as old as civilization. The Aalsmeer market marries high technology to the time-honored practices of the bazaar.

* * * *

On November 9, 1989, the people of Berlin joyously tore down the wall that for thirty years had divided their city. As the wall fell, so did communism and the planned economy. On April 30, 1995, the U.S. government ceased controlling the internet. As entrepreneurs devised procedures for online buying and selling, electronic commerce burgeoned. These two dates denote the beginnings of what has become, for good or for ill, the age of the market.

The reinvention of markets did not begin with the internet or the end of central planning. Markets have been around as long as history and have been incessantly reinvented. The first cities, in the Fertile Crescent (today's Iraq), built trading links. Donkeys and camels carried goods—precious stones, ivory, weapons, spices, frankincense, and myrrh—between cities such as Babylon and Ur. As a by-product of their trading activities, the merchants spread new ideas and inventions. Money, the hub of markets, appeared early. You can see the progress of civilization depicted in an archeological museum's collection of antique coins.

Culture developed alongside markets. Writing originated around five thousand years ago in the Fertile Crescent as a means of recording economic information. The earliest known written documents—marks baked in clay—are tallies of livestock, grain, and oil. These written records were used by tax collectors and merchants. Mathematics also was invented in the Fertile Crescent as an aid to buying and selling, arithmetic being needed to compute costs and set prices.

In the Agora, the central marketplace in ancient Athens, stallholders clustered together according to their wares. Sellers of fish were in one area, meat was sold in stalls grouped in another area, clothing in another. Sellers of more valuable items like perfumes and jewelry had a special building. Potters making the storage jars and tableware that we now see in museums had their own section, as did metalworkers crafting keys, bronze mirrors, tools, and bells. Beyond just a marketplace, the Agora was the heart of Athens, the site of athletic contests, political meetings, theatrical performances, and religious festivals.[3]

The colors, noises, and smells of the Agora were probably much as in any bazaar of today, an extravagant example of which is the camel fair held once a year in the small town of Pushkar in India's desert state Rajasthan. The fair began centuries ago as an adjunct to a Hindu religious pilgrimage, Pushkar being where Lord Brahma, the creator, is believed to have dropped a lotus blossom petal and miraculously formed a lake. More camels are for sale than you thought you could ever see in one place: fifty thousand or so. It is a bustling, dusty, noisy scene. Snake charmers, musicians, gypsy dancers, jugglers, acrobats, and fire-eaters entertain the crowds. Women in vibrant saris sell food and handicrafts. There is camel racing and camel polo, with gamblers raucously urging on their favorites. All the while thousands of camels, meticulously groomed for the occasion, are being haggled over.

The bazaars of today's global village are on the internet. Quickly and cheaply connecting people anywhere in the world, the internet has transformed markets by allowing exchanges between buyers and sellers who might not otherwise find each other. By logging on to the global electronic shopping mall, you can purchase almost anything you might want.

Governments overruled markets for much of the twentieth century, most notably in communist countries like the Soviet Union and China, replacing them with their antithesis, central planning. Bitter letdown followed, as these economies stagnated. The failure of the centrally planned economies has made governments around the world more modest about what they can do, recognizing that an economy works well only when much of it is left to markets. In Russia, China, and elsewhere, the economy has been painfully rebuilt, sometimes in ways that prompt us to reexamine what we thought we knew about markets.

✳   ✳   ✳   ✳

What do we mean by "a market"? A market for something exists if there are people who want to buy it and people who want to sell it. The dictionary defines a market as "a meeting together of people for the purpose of trade by private purchase and sale," and "a public place where a market is held."[4] This does not go deep enough, though. What characterizes a market transaction?

Decision-making autonomy is key. Participation in the exchange is voluntary; both buyer and seller are able to veto any deal. They are separate entities. Controlling their own resources, the participants in a market, in deciding how those resources are to be used, are not obliged to follow others' orders. They are free to make decisions—to buy, to sell, to exert effort, to invest—that reflect their own preferences. Their choices are not completely free though: they are constrained by the extent of their resources and by the rules of the marketplace.

If people lack autonomy, then their dealings are not, by this definition, market dealings. Where an authority relationship exists—one party is in charge of the other, or a higher authority is in charge of them both—then any transactions are of some other category; they are not market transactions.

For those who are poor, the freedom that is the essence of markets may be very circumscribed. "Let them eat cake" is unhelpful advice for those who cannot afford bread. Bargaining power between buyer and seller is sometimes quite unequal. Being able to veto any deal does convey some bargaining power, but not necessarily much. Nevertheless, the opportunity to agree to an exchange or to decline it is a kind of freedom. Some choice, even if it is narrow, is usually better than none.

Competition, while not a defining feature of a market, is usually present and adds to the autonomy. Competition curbs any individual participant's power and, in most markets, prevents anyone from having a decisive effect on overall outcomes. A consumer can say, "No, I'll shop elsewhere." A competitive market means that alternatives exist.

A definition of a market transaction, then, is *an exchange that is voluntary: each party can veto it, and (subject to the rules of the marketplace) each freely agrees to the terms.* A market is a forum for carrying out such exchanges.

In addition to markets, there is also *the market*, an abstraction as in "the market economy" or "the free market" or "the market system." The abstract market arises from the interaction of many actual markets. By "a market" or "a marketplace," I mean a specific physical place or cyberspace where goods are bought and sold. By "the market" (the context will make it clear), I mean the abstraction.

A lot of transactions are excluded by this definition of a market. Markets are never ubiquitous. Even in the most market-oriented economy, a majority of transactions do not actually go through markets. The reach of markets is delimited. Three categories of nonmarket activity are prevalent.

One is unpaid work inside households, such as care-giving, housework, and preparing food for the family. The economic value of home labor is hard to assess, but the average full-time homemaker in the United States, by one estimate, produces outputs that if priced would be worth about $17,000 per year.[5]

Government activities such as building roads and supplying schools and the police force make up another nonmarket category. Government consumption (which means all government activities other than transferring money between people) amounts to a fifth or more of national income in modern economies.

The business taking place inside firms is yet another major nonmarket category. In the United States and similar economies, more transactions occur within firms than through markets. When General Motors procures an order of steering wheels, it makes a difference whether the steering wheel supplier is an independent firm or a GM division. Ownership does not change when goods move from one part of a firm to another, unlike when they move between firms or from firm to consumer. In market transactions, autonomous agents follow their own separate interests. Intrafirm deals, by contrast, are mediated not by the market but by the firm's rulebook, and are carried out—or at least are supposed to be carried out—in a manner that promotes not the individual goals of the decision-makers but the overall goals of the organization.

Why then is it called a "market economy," given that a majority of transactions, those inside households, firms, and government, are actually outside the market? It is a market economy because even these nonmarket transactions take place within the context of markets. The market transactions mold the economy overall.

No one is in charge of a market—or, rather, everyone is in charge. This decentralization brings dynamism. Markets empower people. The Czech playwright Vaclav Havel, a courageous dissident under communism and then president of his country as it dismantled its planned economy, has unique credentials to compare the market with its alternatives. "Though my heart may be left of center, I have always known that the only economic system that works is a market economy," he said. "This is the only natural economy, the only kind that makes sense, the only one that leads to prosperity, because it is the only one that reflects the nature of life itself. The essence of life is infinitely and mysteriously multiform, and therefore it cannot be contained or planned for, in its fullness and variability, by any central intelligence."[6]

*   *   *   *

Some have invoked the supernatural to explain what they find extraordinary: that markets can work with no one in charge. The Reverend Richard Whately, a professor of political economy at Oxford University in the eighteenth century, believed the coherence of the market to be proof that God exists. If no human planner is guiding the market to the optimal outcome, God must be. The invisible hand is the hand of God.

A religious fervor characterizes some of today's fans of the free market. "The true spirit capital of the current capitalist economy is not material. It is moral, intellectual, and spiritual," declared George Gilder, an evangelist for libertarianism. He also said that entrepreneurship "most deeply springs from religious faith and culture" and that entrepreneurs "embody and fulfill the sweet and mysterious consolations of the Sermon on the Mount." Ronald Reagan liked to use the catchphrase "the magic of the market"—inadvertently bearing out the jibes about his "voodoo economics."

Carlos Fuentes, the novelist, derided what he calls economic fundamentalism, "with its religious conviction that the market, left to its own devices, is capable of resolving all our problems." Mocking market zealots, Harvey Cox, who happens to be a professor of divinity, said that for its true believers the market is like God in "the mystery that enshrouds it and the reverence it inspires." Like God, the market is avowed by its proselytizers to be "omnipotent (possessing all power), omniscient (having all knowledge), and omnipresent (existing everywhere)." These divine attributes, Cox continued, "are not always completely evident to mortals but must be trusted and affirmed by faith."7

Faith is not needed. The "hand" that guides the market may be invisible, but it is not actually supernatural. The market is not omnipotent, omnipresent, or omniscient. It is a human invention with human imperfections. It does not necessarily work well. It does not work by magic or, for that matter, by voodoo. It works through institutions, procedures, rules, and customs. One of my aims in this book is to demystify the market.

Textbook economic theory does not dispel the markets-are-magical notion, for it says little about how markets go about doing their job. Although economics is in large part the study of markets, the textbooks depict them abstractly. The supply-and-demand diagram, expounded in countless Economics 101 lectures, is a bloodless account of exchange. It leaves unexplained much of what needs to be explained. It tells us what prices can do, but is silent on how they are set. Supply and demand bypasses questions of how buyers and sellers get together, what other dealings they have, how buyers evaluate what they are buying, and how agreements are enforced. Three Nobel laureates noted this oddity. George Stigler found it "a source of embarrassment that so little attention has been paid to the theory of markets." Douglass North noted the "peculiar fact" that economics "contains so little discussion of the central institution that underlies neoclassical economics—the market." Ronald Coase complained that the market has a "shadowy role" in economic theory, and "discussion of the market itself has entirely disappeared."

The Nobel laureates' critique has now been addressed. Modern economics has a lot to say about the workings of markets. Theorists have opened up the black box of supply and demand and peered inside. Game theory has been brought to bear on the processes of exchange. Examining markets up close, the new economics emphasizes market frictions and how they are kept in check. In 2001, this work received recognition with the award of the Nobel Prize in economics to George Akerlof, Michael Spence, and Joseph Stiglitz for laying the foundation, as the Nobel citation said, "for a general theory of markets with asymmetric information." Expressed in mathematics and impenetrable jargon, these new ideas reside obscurely in the technical journals. They have, however, a deeply practical content.[8]

*   *   *   *

Exchange is "one of the purest and most primitive forms of human socialization," the sociologist Georg Simmel wrote in 1900; it creates "a society, in place of a mere collection of individuals."[9] A market is a social construction. If it is to work smoothly, it must be well built. The term *market design* refers to the methods of transacting and the devices that serve to allow transacting to proceed smoothly.

Market design consists of the mechanisms that organize buying and selling; channels for the flow of information; state-set laws and regulations that define property rights and sustain contracting; and the market's culture, its self-regulating norms, codes, and conventions governing behavior. While the design does not control what happens in the market—as already noted, free decision-making is key—it shapes and supports the process of transacting.[10]

A workable market design keeps in check transaction costs—the various frictions in the process of making exchanges. These costs include the time, effort, and money spent in the process of doing business—both those incurred by the buyer in addition to the actual price paid, and those incurred by the seller in making the sale.[11] Transaction costs are many and varied.

Transaction costs can arise before any business is done. Locating potential trading partners may be costly and time-consuming. Comparing alternative sellers and choosing among them takes effort by the buyer. The quality of the goods for sale is often not immediately apparent, and the buyer may have to go to some trouble to evaluate it. If it cannot be reliably checked, the buyer might be reluctant to purchase.

In putting an agreement together, there are further transaction costs. Negotiations can be drawn out. Bargainers sometimes overreach in trying to squeeze out a good bargain, causing an impasse and spoiling what could have been a mutually beneficial deal.

After the fact, there are still other transaction costs. Monitoring work costs time and money. The enforcement of contracts and the prevention and settling of disputes do not come for free. If agreements are not watertight, productive opportunities may be forgone. A manufacturer making components like computer chips or car seats may make a uniform item and sell it to several firms rather than customizing to a single firm's specific needs, because customizing its production, though it would create more value, would leave it vulnerable to the sole customer's whims.

Transaction costs use up resources in ways that are unrelated to the actual value of the business to be done. In the extreme, transaction costs can cause markets to be dysfunctional. If market information is so inadequate that a buyer is unable to locate more than one seller, then that seller can exploit the fact that the buyer is locked in by charging an exorbitant price. A still more extreme market malfunction occurs if the costs of transacting are so high as to swamp any potential benefits from the deal. Transaction costs can thwart exchanges that would otherwise be worthwhile. Unemployment exists, for example, not simply because there are too few jobs, but also because transaction costs in the labor market prevent some employers and job seekers from connecting with each other. A new way of doing business that lowers transaction costs can benefit everyone.

Modern markets are sophisticated organizations. Markets for multifaceted products like automobiles and computers, and for labor and financial services, must solve a range of problems that might not arise with simpler items like clothing and food. One such issue is that a market works well only if information flows smoothly through it. An uneven distribution of information hinders negotiations and limits what can be contracted. Information transmission requires devices that ensure the communications are reliable. Another such issue is that a market works well only if people can trust each other. Trust requires mechanisms to bolster it since, regrettably, not everyone is inherently trustworthy. Many goods have hidden characteristics, so there must be some way of assuring buyers of the goods' quality. Trust is needed also in transactions that take time to complete. People are reluctant to invest in the absence of some assurance that the others' promises will be kept. For these and other reasons, a modern market economy needs a platform sturdy enough to support highly complex dealings.

When things work well, we take a market's design for granted. Where the costs of transacting are low, the devices that are serving to curb them are almost invisible. By contrast, an inadequate design is easily observed, the symptom being a dysfunctional market. I will examine markets around the world. Looking at poor countries, where for one reason or another transaction costs are often high, we can see what is missing. Looking at affluent countries, we can watch new ways of doing business arising in response to new technologies.

Some of the pieces of a market's design are devised by the market participants themselves; other pieces are devised by the government. It is by spontaneous change, for the most part, that the rules of the market game develop, with the market participants designing better ways to transact. (I will refer to this aspect of market design as *informal* or *bottom-up*.) However, lowering transaction costs is a task not only for entrepreneurs, but also for public policy. The government has the responsibility to establish and maintain an environment within which markets can work efficiently. (I will refer to this aspect of market design as *formal* or *top-down*.)

A basic part of the government's role in market design is the defining of property rights. The surest way to destroy a market is to undermine people's belief in the security of their own property. But the government's role goes far beyond just assigning property rights.

Government actions to underpin markets began early. In the fifth century B.C., Croesus (the king of Lydia, in what is now Turkey, who gave us the expression "as rich as Croesus") issued gold and silver coins of guaranteed purity. Ensuring the fidelity of money aided the spreading of commerce through the ancient world. Today, speeding the economic growth of poor countries in Africa, Asia, and Latin America requires, among other things, revamping their market-supporting institutions, such as laws of contract, so as to lower transaction costs. Underdevelopment results, I will argue, from markets not doing their job properly. Even in affluent countries, the government must be ready to adapt the rules of the market game to accommodate new technologies. The new forms of communication over the internet, for example, have necessitated a reconsideration of the laws of copyright: should the law allow people to use the internet to send each other recorded music for free, or does unrestricted copying impair the market for recordings? In well-functioning economies such as those of North America and Western Europe, the state actively supplies laws and regulatory overview.

Biological evolution works, in Richard Dawkins's phrase, like a blind watchmaker.[12] Organisms like the human eye, being so wondrously complex, might appear to have been designed by a master watchmaker, but in fact were "designed" by goalless, gradual, unplanned natural selection.

Economic systems evolve in a similar way. A market develops via trial and error, through the market participants' everyday actions. There are two differences, though. The components of the evolving economic system are intelligent actors, not dumb molecules. The direction of change is consciously affected by forward-looking market participants, who help design the system. In addition, parts of any economic system, such as the laws, are imposed by the state or some other organization—in effect, by a sighted watchmaker, though not always a skilled one. Even the most decentralized economy has some central management: from the legislature, the courts, and regulatory agencies. No one is in overall charge, but some are guiding it.

* * * *

The history of football is a model for the development of a market. Football in its variants—soccer, rugby, American football—traces its lineage to games of folk football played in England since medieval days. Folk football had few rules. What rules there were had emerged spontaneously: they rested on custom and varied from village to village. Any number of people could play. Spectators could join the fray if they felt inclined. There was no referee, just a kind of social control by the players themselves.

Little skill was on display, just muscle. The aim was to get the ball, a stuffed pig's bladder, to the opponent's end of the field, using any means. At the start of play, the ball would be seized by some of the strongest players. "The rest of the players immediately close in upon them, and a solid mass is formed," reported a spectator at an 1829 game between the Derbyshire parishes of All Saints and St. Peters. "The struggle to obtain the ball, which is carried in the arms of those who have possessed themselves of it, is then violent, and the motion of human tide heaving to and fro without the least regard to consequences is tremendous." Players often fell, "owing to the intensity of the pressure, fainting and bleeding beneath the feet of the surrounding mob."

For hundreds of years, folk football developed incrementally. Then quite suddenly it metamorphosed into soccer and rugby. These changes came not, as in the preceding centuries, from the local level, but from the top down. National governing bodies, the Football Association in 1863 and the Rugby Football Union in 1871, were formed to codify the rules. Soccer and rugby began when a formal design was overlaid on the patterns of play that had evolved.

The players' skills, and not just their brawn, now came to be emphasized. Folk football had been a popular but somewhat discreditable pastime for

English village people and schoolboys. In its new, structured forms, football swept the world. Soccer became the beautiful game it is today and the world's biggest sport. Rugby became a game of speed and strategy. By a further process of spontaneous evolution plus purposeful rule-setting, rugby in turn gave rise to the chesslike game of American football.[2] It was the explicit, enforceable rules that made the difference between folk football and its wildly successful descendants.

A typical market is born and grows like football. It evolves spontaneously, driven by its participants. It can operate with little or no formal structure — but only up to a point. To reach a degree of sophistication, its procedures need to be clarified and an authority given the power to enforce them. Only when the informal rules are supplemented by some formal rules can a market reach its full potential, with transactions being conducted efficiently and complex dealings being feasible.

An absolutely free market is like folk football, a free-for-all brawl. A real market is like American football, an ordered brawl.

✻   ✻   ✻   ✻

Markets provoke clashing opinions. Some people revile them as the source of exploitation and poverty. Others extol them as the font of liberty and prosperity. There is the dogma that markets are inherently harmful, so they should be routinely overridden by the state; and the dogma that markets are unambiguously beneficial, so we can leave everything to the free market. "For every problem there is a solution," said H. L. Mencken, "that is simple, direct, and wrong." Both of the simple, direct solutions regularly offered for all kinds of societal ills — "suppress the market" and "leave everything to the market" — more often than not are wrong.

"Find me a one-armed economist," President Herbert Hoover reportedly ordered, out of frustration with economic advisers who kept saying, "On the one hand . . . On the other hand . . ." Honest answers to the big questions in economics, however, are rarely free of caveats. On the merits of markets, most economists are unapologetically two-armed.

Markets are too important to be left to the ideologues. In fact, markets are the most effective means we have of improving people's well-being. For poor countries they offer the most reliable path away from poverty. For affluent countries they are part of what is needed to sustain their living standards.

Markets, then, are the most potent antipoverty engine there is — but only where they work well. The caveat is crucial. Over a billion Africans and Asians, according to the World Bank, eke out a living of sorts on one dollar or less a day.[13] That is more people than live in the affluent West. For a great many, it would seem, markets are not doing much good.

Governments in poor countries sometimes intervene excessively, to be sure, stifling markets and exacerbating the poverty. But that is not the entire story. If the state were to cease its counterproductive interventions, those countries would remain poor. In Calcutta, Cairo, or Tijuana, you see markets operating everywhere. You cannot steer clear of peddlers eager to sell you things. The problem in developing countries is not that markets are absent; it is that they are working badly.

Left to themselves, markets can fail. To deliver their full benefits, they need support from a set of rules, customs, and institutions. They cannot operate efficiently in a vacuum. If the rules of the market game are inadequate, as often they are, it is difficult and time-consuming to set them right. Many countries, to their citizens' detriment, have not yet been able to do so.

Markets are not miraculous. There are problems they cannot address. If their platform is unsound, they do not even solve the problems they are supposed to solve. Viewed as tools, markets need not be revered or reviled—just allowed to operate where they are useful.

In Russia in 1992, amid the ruins of communism, the state abruptly ceased controlling the economy. A few years later, when the country's progress toward a market economy had bogged down and the country was in a sorry state, a joke circulated on the streets of Moscow:

Q: How many people does it take to change a light bulb under communism?

A: Five: one to hold the light bulb, four to rotate the table he is standing on.

Q: Under capitalism, how many does it take?

A: None, the market will take care of it.

The Russian sarcasm underlines a key point. While markets can do a lot, they do not work automatically. Unaided, the market will not take care of things.

*   *   *   *

"God is in the details," declared the architect Ludwig Mies van der Rohe. Tradespeople building to architects' plans would habitually grumble that "the Devil is in the details," and Mies van der Rohe was inverting their complaint. For markets no less than for buildings, it is the details of design that determine whether or not they work well. Both God and the Devil are in the details.

T W O

⁜

Triumphs of Intelligence

On a sidewalk in Hanoi in 1995, a policeman accosts a peddler. Methodically wielding his truncheon, he squashes the melons she had been selling and smashes her wooden cart. A crowd gathers and watches in eerie silence. None of the bystanders tries to intercede: they know not to tangle with the Vietnamese police. Completing his task, the policeman struts off, leaving a mess on the sidewalk. The peddler resignedly picks up a few splintered bits from the wreckage. It is not her first encounter with a sadistic policeman, nor her last. But she has to scrape together a living so she will persevere.

Hanoi's sidewalk peddlers — mostly peasant women in conical straw hats, often with small children in tow — sell fruit and vegetables and small household items. The city people dub the stalls "frog markets" because of the peddlers' agility in fleeing the police, carrying their goods in carts or in baskets on poles slung across their shoulders. The unlucky ones who are caught watch helplessly as the police destroy or steal their merchandise. Those who escape lay out their wares on another street corner. A Communist Party newspaper called on the city government to "sweep those wandering people out of Hanoi." Unregulated trading was anathema to the authorities, but they were unable to suppress it. The vendors' stubbornness reaffirms a Vietnamese proverb: "Trying to stop a market is like trying to stop a river."

Rwandans in refugee camps in Zaire (now the Democratic Republic of Congo), having escaped their country's murderous civil war, immediately turned their home in exile into a locus of bustling commercial activity. Some eighty-two thousand businesses mushroomed in the camps by 1995, according to a report by the United Nations High Commissioner for Refugees. The squalor and terror and disease in the camps were rendered slightly less unbearable by the makeshift food markets, general stores, bars, restaurants, bus services, hairdressers, tailors, butchers, photographers, movie theaters, and pharmacies.

Markets sprang up, similarly, in prisoner-of-war camps during the Second World War. The prisoners traded their Red Cross rations of food, cigarettes, and clothing, according to R. A. Radford, a Briton captured by the Germans. In place of money, cigarettes were the medium of exchange and store of value. Prices fluctuated with supply and demand. Food prices rose whenever a new group of hungry prisoners arrived. In the early days, prices fell at the time of the weekly food delivery, but later the prisoners began to hold stocks of food, which smoothed the variations in supply. Some prisoners set themselves up as middlemen, buying in parts of the camp where prices were low and selling where prices were higher; their activities equalized prices. There was even a labor market, with prisoners offering services like laundering and portrait painting, and a rudimentary financial market, with sellers offering credit to buyers.[1]

These improvised marketplaces encapsulate some key features of markets in general. Markets are resilient; a refugee camp or a prison camp may seem improbable locations for a thriving market system. Markets generate gains from trade; one of the most important observations in all of economics is that buying and selling creates value. The Rwandan refugees focused their labor. Some scavenged meat, others grew vegetables; some gathered firewood, others worked as tailors or cooks. Then they traded what they produced. In the prison camp, nonsmokers sold cigarettes to buy food, while vegetarian Indians exchanged canned beef for jam and margarine. The ability to trade meant the refugees and prisoners were better off than if, like Robinson Crusoe, they could consume only their own allocations.

Markets have a way of breaking out. They can operate in hard times. Markets can grow like weeds and work effectively—at least when transactions are straightforward. When their livelihoods are on the line, people are ingenious at finding ways to improve their lot by creating new markets or designing better ones.

*   *   *   *

Even the simplest markets reveal surprising subtleties when looked at up close. Consider the Makola marketplace in the center of Accra, Ghana, as described by Claire Robertson, an Africanist scholar. The stallholders, who are mostly women, sell fish, vegetables, grains, canned foods, and basic household items. They operate on a tiny scale, a typical day's turnover being just a few dollars. The marketplace, housed in several large dirt-floor sheds, is overcrowded and dusty. The press of people, the noise, and the smell of fish overwhelm a visitor.

First impressions are misleading. Primitive as it may look, the Makola market is an intricate system. The stallholders are not just retailers but also wholesalers: they buy in bulk to sell small quantities to consumers, and they aggregate small purchases for resale to other sellers. They organize the transportation of goods—not a simple matter in a country with inadequate roads and railroads—serving as intermediaries between widely scattered producers and consumers. They do some rudimentary manufacturing: crafting with beads and processing raw materials into foodstuffs, condiments, and cosmetics. They find recycling uses for cans, bottles, and newspapers. Assessing their customers' creditworthiness and granting some of them credit, they take on the role of banks.

Being illiterate, the stallholders must keep their business records in their heads, using impressive powers of memory. They make precise calculations of their input costs so as to keep track of their profits. The price a vendor charges for a string of beads, for example, reflects the price she paid for the beads and thread, the time she or her employee spent stringing the beads, and her target profit margin.

The stallholders have developed their own miniature legal system. Informal property rights have arisen. Although they do not have legal title to their stall space, which is technically owned by the Accra city council, they act as though they do. Spaces are inherited. Often the current stallholder acquired the space from her mother or sister. Spaces are also rented, bought, and sold. Certain respected merchants, called "queen mothers," play the part of judges, arbitrating when disputes arise.

Gains from trade are generated. The vendors make others—as well as themselves—better off by making food available to the urban poor, and by providing income to farmers with which to buy necessities like clothing. Thus they exemplify Adam Smith's analysis of the merchant: "By pursuing his own interest he frequently promotes that of society more effectually than when he really intends to promote it."

The Makola marketplace has continued to operate despite periodic, sometimes violent attempts by the Ghanaian government to shut it down. These attempts reached a height of brutality in 1979 after the military gov-

ernment accused marketplace traders of violating its price controls. Soldiers
looted the stalls and then dynamited the marketplace. Later, in the town of
Kumasi, soldiers armed with machine guns raided the marketplace and beat
up the traders. Accusing one of profiteering, a soldier ripped her baby off her
back and shot her. Bulldozers then ground the marketplace stalls into the
dust. A soldier remarked, "That will teach Ghanaian women to stop being
wicked."

The Ghanaian government, invoking the "market women menace," was
using the merchants as a scapegoat for its own policy failures, which had led
to severe shortages and inflation. Newspapers parroted the government's line.
One described the market demolition as a "happy tragedy" which produced
"tears of joy in the worker, the common man," who was "helpless at the
hands of the unfeeling Makola conspirators" (that is, the vendors).

Within a week the merchants were back where their stalls had been, selling their fish and vegetables, though now without a roof over them. The
Makola traders' accomplishments, Robertson wrote, "have been triumphs of
intelligence, determination, and sometimes desperation."[2]

An American case of the spontaneous development of markets came
during Prohibition. From 1920 to 1933 it was illegal to sell alcohol in the
United States. In spite of the law—or perhaps because of it—the liquor trade
flourished, as respectable people flocked to illicit bars, or speakeasies.

Prohibition had its costs. Thirsty drinkers paid exorbitant prices, as the
need to do business covertly meant transaction costs were high. Prices were
pushed up threefold. Some of the liquor was toxic, manufactured from dubious ingredients. Gangsters like Al Capone tried to monopolize the liquor
trade, murdering their rivals and corrupting police officers.

Despite all its efforts, the government utterly failed to squelch the alcohol market. Alcohol consumption, toward the end of the Prohibition era, was
still about two-thirds its pre-Prohibition level. "Detesting the interference
with their liberties, sober and high-minded Americans, who had hardly ever
touched liquor before, now made it almost a point of honor," says Scottish
historian Sir Robert Bruce Lockhart, "to drink on all social occasions."[3] The
bizarre episode that was Prohibition brings to mind a line from Robert Burns:
"freedom and whisky go together."

*　　*　　*　　*

The marketplace for secondhand books has been transformed. Many millions of old books are available for sale via the internet. Search engines allow
you to quickly find whatever you are looking for, no matter how obscure.

Merely by setting up a web site, anyone can sell to the world. Musty book-shops are now global players.

Out-of-print books on the abstruse topic of New Zealand rugby are not easily found in the United States. From my home in California, however, I was able to assemble an extensive collection. Once this would have been difficult if not impossible; the internet made it easy. I tracked down the books not only in New Zealand but also in the United Kingdom, South Africa, France, Australia, and Canada. I found a rare copy of the best rugby book ever written, the 1906 classic *The Complete Rugby Footballer on the New Zealand System* by Dave Gallaher and Billy Stead, offered by a bookshop in Swansea, Wales. Without the internet, to obtain such a book would have taken innumerable letters and telephone calls, and I might not have bothered. Because of the internet, that Swansea bookshop had my business.

In other words, certain kinds of transaction costs have been lowered by the internet: the cost of acquiring information, the time, effort, and money needed to learn what is available where and at what price. The transaction costs of buying out-of-print books in pre-internet days were high. Now all you have to do is point and click.4

The internet has made possible global markets for all kinds of goods that previously had only local markets. In pre-internet days, if you collected eighteenth-century snuffboxes, to assuage your obsession you might have driven from small town to small town to rummage through dusty antique shops and flea markets. Only rarely would you have stumbled upon the object of your dreams. With the internet, locating snuffboxes anywhere in the world is no longer difficult.

The growth of the internet has spurred the quest for new methods of transacting. Drawing on the internet's speedy two-way communication, a myriad of mechanisms have been concocted to make buying and selling easier. At the internet auction site eBay, for example, bidders feverishly compete for everything from junk to high art.

It all began in 1995, when Pierre Omidyar set up a web site called AuctionWeb for people wanting to exchange information about collectibles and to make trades. Legend has it that his initial goal was to sell his girl-friend's collection of Pez dispensers. The site's services were initially offered free of charge, as a service to the public. After six months' explosive growth in usage, based on word-of-mouth recommendations, Omidyar began charging a fee, a small percentage of the sale price, to cover his costs of running the web site. Payment was left up to the honesty of the seller, but the checks rolled in. He gave up his day job and was joined in the firm by Jeffrey Skoll.

Together they developed the auction software and the customer-support infrastructure. "We would work virtually anywhere we could find an office," Skoll recalled. "We started off in Omidyar's living room, then we moved to my living room." They initially contemplated focusing on a particular market segment, such as coins or stamps. "In the early days, our strategy changed by the day," said Skoll. They finally decided not to specialize, but to let anyone sell anything.

With the auction system reengineered to handle the massive volume of traffic, they relaunched AuctionWeb as eBay in September 1997. Less than two years later eBay's stock market value reached $22 billion. The business press proclaimed eBay's reinvention of markets. *BusinessWeek* said that, with its online auctions, "eBay has single-handedly created a new market." According to the *Economist*, "Internet auctioneers such as eBay may be the instigators of a revolutionary leap forward in the efficiency of the price mechanism."[5]

The eBay web site is a high-tech flea market. It has over 42 million registered users; the typical user spends twenty minutes a day on the site. Around five million auctions are running on any given day, selling everything from cast-offs to fine art. As I write this, for example, there are nearly fifteen hundred items listed under the heading "Victorian tradecards"—which, it turns out, are a nineteenth-century version of junk mail.

eBay has created a global market for goods that previously had a purely local market. It has even created markets for goods that previously had none. Among the stranger items that have been listed are a bucketful of dirt from Texas, two hundred thousand pounds of assorted knit fabrics, a parking space for one week near downtown San Francisco, sand from *Baywatch*, and a tee-shirt saying "I sold my soul on eBay."

One of the secrets of eBay's success was in recognizing that the internet, by making it easy for buyers and sellers to get together, created new possibilities for trading knickknacks of all kinds. The other secret of its success was in building a user-friendly and flexible auction mechanism. Pre-internet auctions had the disadvantage that they required the potential buyers to assemble in one place. (Bids were sometimes made by telephone or fax, but this was clumsy.) Bidders in an eBay auction get together only in cyberspace.

eBay lowered the costs of transacting enough that people anywhere wanting to trade low-value items are able to deal directly with each other. Its popularity induced others to start offering internet auctions. Now, at hundreds of different auction sites, people bid for computer equipment, antiques, fine art, stamps, toys, jewelry, travel services, real estate, and wine. eBay showed that the internet and auctions were made for each other.

The internet auctions brought active trade in goods that had been traded rarely. Old bathing caps, painted plaster hula girls, and plastic lunchboxes suddenly acquired value. People who used to think of such paraphernalia as worthless clutter in their attics learned, through eBay, how much collectors were willing to pay for it. Usually this caused prices to rise, but not always. The prices of first editions of contemporary mass-market novels by authors like John Grisham, Anne Rice, and Tom Clancy collapsed.[6] Before internet auctions, a collector might have paid $75 in a used-book shop for a 1980 edition of Stephen King's *Firestarter*. Auctions on eBay and its competitors made ordinary readers aware of the value of their books gathering dust on their bookshelves. The market was flooded and the price of a book like *Firestarter* fell to around $30. Like any competitive market, the internet auctions generate information about the value of the goods traded, and sometimes there are surprises.

* * * *

What do the founders of eBay have in common with the Makola merchants? Each set up exchange mechanisms to generate gains from trade. Where markets are absent, mutual gains can be realized by establishing them. Where they are present, further gains are sometimes to be had by finding ways to make them work better.

People have forever been devising new markets and improving existing ones. Innovations in economic organization can be as productive as technological innovations. The two kinds of innovation sometimes go hand in hand. The Aalsmeer auction house, for example, made the worldwide trade in flowers feasible by using new information technology to automate its sales procedures and speed up the handling of the flowers.

While the internet has linked people more closely than ever before, this is not the first or even the biggest such transformation. Earlier advances in communications technology had a similar effect in broadening markets. "The telegraph and the printing-press," observed the magazine *Contemporary Review* in 1886, "have converted Great Britain into a vast agora, or assembly of the whole community." The postal service, the railroads, the telephone, and radio and television all in their own way transformed communications. In his 1847 *Principles of Communism* Friedrich Engels remarked of the industrial revolution, "big industry has brought all the people of the earth into contact with each other, has merged all local markets into one world market."

Engels was not enamored of the reinventing of markets, of course, but it is inexorable. Potential gains are missed if a transaction cost of some kind impedes buying and selling, so there is a profit opportunity in finding a way to lower that cost. Novel market devices appear. Someone may design a whole new marketplace. Or, through the separate actions of many, the market's rules and procedures gradually emerge or change.

Entire sectors of a modern economy are devoted to organizing transactions. The retail and wholesale trades and the advertising, insurance, and finance industries exist not to manufacture things but to facilitate transacting. These activities are a large part of any modern economy, accounting in the United States for one-fourth of the gross national product.[7] Innovating in any of these sectors means discovering a way to reduce the costs of transacting.

Resourceful entrepreneurs have long profited by finding ways to make markets more productive. Businesspeople often act as market designers. Their innovations are sometimes subtle, but they are sometimes very simple—or look so after the event. The shopkeeper who dreamed up the money-back guarantee, for example, made commerce work better for everyone by reducing consumers' uncertainty while also, no doubt, earning a return for himself on his bright idea. This innovation is sometimes credited to Potter Palmer, the founder of the retailer Marshall Field and Co., who in 1861 advertised in the *Chicago Tribune*, "Purchases made at my establishment that prove unsatisfactory either in price, quality or style, can be returned to the cashier's desk, for which the purchase money will be with pleasure returned."[8]

*   *   *   *

In eighteenth-century New York, stocks and bonds were traded haphazardly. Anyone wanting to buy or sell securities had to search for someone to trade with: by word of mouth, by advertising in a newspaper, or by just dallying in a coffeehouse until the right person appeared. In 1792, one John Sutton, sensing an opportunity, organized a securities exchange at 22 Wall Street, which was then a muddy lane. Sellers would bring in their stocks and bonds each morning, and at noon Sutton would auction them for a commission. Sutton's auction, which he called the Stock Exchange Office, sparked the growth of modern financial markets, for it grew to be the New York Stock Exchange.

The changeover was rapid. Sutton's auctions lost their effectiveness because other traders began to free-ride on them. The interlopers would attend the auctions merely to observe the going prices, then they would hold their own sales, offering the securities at lower commission rates and taking business away from Sutton. This practice soon became self-defeating, as it meant too few securities were passing through Sutton's auctions for the bids to be meaningful guides to the securities' true value.

To solve this problem, twenty-four of Wall Street's most prominent brokers agreed to form a new auction. They would trade securities at fixed fees. They would not buy or sell in other auctions but only among themselves. For a while they held their securities auctions in the street, then as winter approached, they moved into the Merchant's Coffee House. Later they constructed their own building.

They formulated from scratch the rules governing how securities were bought and sold, and set up methods of contract enforcement and dispute settlement. Membership in the stock exchange was restricted and lucrative, so the brokers were able to regulate themselves on the sanction of expulsion. Members who defaulted on contracts were barred. Nonmembers who reneged on contracts with members were blacklisted. Under its new rules, the market in securities flourished.[9]

A half-century before Sutton began his auction, rice merchants in Osaka, Japan, had already set up the world's first futures market. Rice was so important in Japan at the time that it was almost a form of currency in itself. The idea of forward trading—buying now goods that are to be delivered later—is said to have originated around 1620 when a Nagoya rice merchant named Chozaemon met a friend from Sendai, in the north of Japan, who was passing through Nagoya on a pilgrimage. The friend reported that the rice harvest in the north was going to be bad. Chozaemon promptly bought the future Nagoya-area rice harvest, paying the farmers 10 percent upfront and owing them the rest. After the harvest came in, he stored the rice for several months, selling it for a tidy profit once the north's poor harvest had driven prices up.

Learning from Chozaemon's example, the Osaka rice merchants over the next century instituted the sophisticated characteristics we now see in any modern futures market, like the Chicago Board of Trade. The association of traders governing the marketplace designed the rules. Contract terms came to be standardized, so the futures contracts could be readily traded: the contracts specified quantity, delivery date, and harvest location. Prices were set by auction. Trades were recorded in a market "book." The market was self-regulating; traders who broke the rules were expelled. Clearinghouses were formed to certify transactions. Acting simultaneously as seller to the contract buyer and buyer to the contract seller, the clearinghouses reduced the risks of default. There was even a financial news service: the daily price data were speeded around Japan by flag semaphore, carrier pigeons, and smoke signals.

The Osaka market had evolved to meet the needs of its participants. By trading futures contracts, cash-strapped growers could obtain funds before the rice was harvested, and cautious rice buyers could protect themselves against future price rises. It also provided a venue for investors to back their hunches, as the seventeenth-century novelist Ihara Saikaku recorded: "People bought and sold by speculating based on the condition of the sky, the evening winds, and the morning rains."[10]

Innovations in financial markets are ongoing. When a new company first goes public, via an initial public offering (IPO), the shares are conventionally sold at a fixed price. Since shares have not been traded before the offering, the investment bank setting the price has little on which to base its estimate of the company's value. In most cases, the price is set well below the level the stock market subsequently reveals the value to be. The ninety Silicon Valley companies that went public in 2000, for example, were listed for an average price of $16. The price at which they were trading at the end of the day of issue averaged $28. With the price rising immediately after the IPO by more than three-fourths, the investors fortunate enough to have purchased the initial offerings made remarkably quick and sizeable profits. William Hambrecht, head of the San Francisco firm W. R. Hambrecht and Co., believes there is a better way to price initial offerings. The investment banks deliberately induce a jump in the share price, he says, by underpricing the initial offering. They offer the shares to their favored clients, virtually guaranteeing them a healthy profit. They get a kickback in return, as the clients direct their future business to the investment bank. This way of running IPOs, in Hambrecht's view, is unfair to the firm's original owners and to small investors, who are excluded. He says, "There's a real scam going on."

In place of the fixed share price, Hambrecht's firm designed what it calls an open IPO, with an online auction of shares. The auction is a modified form of the Dutch auction, as used in the Aalsmeer flower market. Investors place bids for the number of shares they want to own and the price they want to pay. The price that emerges from this competitive market process aggregates the information and beliefs about the firm's value held by all investors interested enough to submit bids. The open IPO, Hambrecht says, "delivers a price that is a lot closer to the real market demand than an artificially negotiated price." While "the original business model was to see if we could put together the breadth and power of the web with an auction process," the difficult part of it was getting "a different pricing mechanism in a market that was used to negotiated pricing." The open IPO is "inherently a more efficient and cheaper process."

An early sign of the potential of IPO auctions was the enraged reaction from those doing business in the entrenched way. An industry observer remarked of Hambrecht, "Other investment banks act as though he's the anti-Christ."[11] While entering the IPO business and dissuading issuing firms from using the big-name investment banks was an arduous process, the new way of running IPOs won a few early converts, as firms like the online magazine Salon.com in 1999 and Peet's Coffee & Tea in 2001 chose to go public via open IPOs. The jury is still out, at the time of writing, on whether the auction IPO is a durable innovation in market design. The investment bankers argue that with the traditional form of IPO they perform a valuable service: by setting the share price, they are certifying the company's worth, saving investors the trouble of investigating for themselves. The traditional IPO, its defenders say, is efficiently adapted to the realities of the new-issue marketplace. The auction IPO may or may not pass the market test of survival. Either way, it exemplifies marketplace experimentation.

*   *   *   *

Rembrandt was an innovator not only in painting but also in commerce. He helped establish a full-fledged art market in seventeenth-century Amsterdam. "Rembrandt's obsession with the intricacies of the market system permeated his life and his work," according to the art historian Svetlana Alpers. Earlier, artists were not free agents but were dependent on rich and powerful patrons. Rembrandt determinedly worked to end the patronage system and to build in its place a market sustained by a broad range of art buyers. Part of his aim was higher prices for his work, but he also recognized that the competitive marketplace brought him more artistic autonomy than being beholden to a small number of patrons. Rembrandt, Alpers says, "was using the marketplace to add honor to art."

Composers in Germany a century or so later switched from being long-term employees of aristocratic patrons to producing for the open market. As employees, they wrote works as assigned, and their compositions belonged not to them but to their masters. Handel and Telemann were vocal in their dislike of being subject to their employers' whims, and they paved the way for Mozart and subsequent composers to work freelance. In a 1781 letter to his father, Mozart said, doubtless exaggerating somewhat, "Believe me, my sole purpose is to make as much money as possible; for after good health it is the best thing to have." Selling his compositions to sheet-music publishers, offer-

ing music lessons, and charging fees for the performance of his works in public concerts, Mozart earned his living as an entrepreneur in the marketplace.
In so doing, says the cognitive psychologist Howard Gardner, Mozart laid "a
foundation of independence and self-initiated creation."[12] Mozart saw the
market as offering him creative freedom.

The key feature of markets of all kinds is brought home when we look at
the growth of new market mechanisms. Benefiting both buyer and seller, any
transaction creates value. (Since either party can veto the deal, it must be
making both of them better off, in their own eyes, than not trading.) Buying
and selling is therefore a form of creation. Elementary as this point is, its
importance cannot be overstated. There are gains from trade, and people are
relentless in finding ways to realize them.

From fine art to finance, from eBay's online auctions to the Rwandan
refugee-camp commerce, new markets are continually being built from the
bottom up. Entrepreneurs, restlessly thinking up more efficient ways of transacting, play the part of market designers.

It is not just entrepreneurs who act as market designers. Market design
also comes from the top down, with the government taking the lead—sometimes, as we will see next, driven by pressure from their constituents.

THREE

∷∷∷

He Who Can't Pay Dies

A horrifying AIDS epidemic engulfed Africa toward the end of the twentieth century. Of the 33 million people infected worldwide as of 2000, 23 million were in Africa. Every single day, AIDS was killing an average of 5,500 Africans. The world had never before seen such high death rates among young adults. At the existing level of risk, in some African countries as many as a half of the fifteen-year-old boys were predicted to die of AIDS.[1]

Antiretroviral drugs successfully countered AIDS. U.S. deaths from AIDS fell 70 percent between 1996 and 1998. But success came mostly in North America and Western Europe. Priced at $10,000 to $15,000 for a year's dosage, the drugs were out of the reach of the majority of the disease's victims worldwide. "Some may think that, because better medicines have been found, the AIDS emergency is over. Alas, no," said United Nations Secretary General Kofi Annan in 2000. For most people living with AIDS, the annual price tag of an antiretroviral regime "belongs, quite simply, in another galaxy."

The drugs were priced at roughly ten times the manufacturing cost, the markup reflecting the companies' patent rights. "The poor have no consumer power, so the market has failed them," said Dr. James Orbinski, president of the aid organization Doctors Without Borders. "I'm tired of the logic that says, 'He who can't pay dies.'"[2]

By any humanitarian standard, the global pharmaceutical market as of the turn of the century was dysfunctional. It shows us markets at their very worst. At the same time, it shows us markets at their very best. It was market incentives, after all, that had spurred the development of the remarkable life-saving drugs.

A reinvention of the drug market began to occur step by step. Unlike the other market innovations we have looked at, the redesign of the market was pushed by public opinion.

✻   ✻   ✻   ✻

The high prices of the AIDS drugs were not the only reason for alarm. Little research was going into vaccines or cures for the awful diseases that killed millions each year in poor countries, like malaria, sleeping sickness, leish-maniasis, and tuberculosis. Meanwhile, vast sums were spent in a campaign for drugs to fight baldness and impotence. Even pets' needs did not go neglected: one company had developed an antidepressant for separation anxiety in dogs.

"Pharmaceutical companies will always aim for maximum profits by marketing a new obesity drug rather than pioneering a novel malaria treatment," said Dr. Bernard Pecoul of Doctors Without Borders, which was campaigning for better access to drugs in the developing world. "When new vaccines or medicines are developed, most of the world's population is left out of the picture." The search for new drugs is directed at the cosmetic afflictions of the rich while overlooking the fatal illnesses of the poor. Medicines against tropical diseases make up a minuscule 1 percent of new drug patents.[3] The pharmaceutical companies specialize in the maladies of the affluent.

A drug used for sleeping sickness, eflornithine, exemplifies the predicament, as recounted by the New York Times.[4] Sleeping sickness leads to death after an almost unbearable period of illness. Researchers looking for an anti-cancer drug discovered eflornithine's effectiveness against sleeping sickness accidently. The drug was so successful at bringing people out of otherwise fatal comas that in Africa it came to be called the "resurrection drug." It was unprofitable, however, so the patent holder ceased making it and stocks ran short. The patent holder's interest was reawakened when it found that eflornithine, used as an ingredient in face cream, could prevent the growth of facial hair in women. Because of this use as a cosmetic, its manufacture was restarted.

Salesmanship is the name of the game. Armies of salespeople hawk drugs to doctors. The industry's marketing costs in the United States are estimated to be more than $8,000 per physician. Far more is spent on marketing than on the search for new and better drugs. For instance, the Pharmacia Corp., maker of an eye drop for glaucoma, among other products, according to its published accounts spent 40 percent of its revenues on marketing and administration in 1999, twice as much as it spent on research. GlaxoSmithKline, the world's largest maker of AIDS drugs, spent 37 percent of its revenue in 2000 on marketing and administration, and 14 percent on research.[5]

In John le Carré's riveting novel *The Constant Gardener*, about a major drug company's dealings in Kenya, one of the characters calls its executives "the most secretive, duplicitous, mendacious, hypocritical bunch of corporate wide-boys it's been my dubious pleasure to encounter." In the name of "the god Profit," the fictive company, an "amoral monopoly that costs human lives every day," peddles dangerously inadequate drugs, tests its drugs unethically, bribes health officials, and intimidates scientists. "Drugs are the scandal of Africa," the novel's hero says. "If any one thing denotes the western indifference to African suffering it's the miserable shortage of the right drugs, and the disgracefully high prices that the pharmaceutical firms have been exacting over the last thirty years."

Le Carré told an interviewer that in writing the novel he had been driven by his "moral anger" at the pharmaceutical industry's "corporate cant, hypocrisy, corruption, and greed."[6] Vilification makes for gripping fiction. It can serve a useful purpose as a call to arms. But to do constructive economic analysis we need to step back and take a broader view. The novelist's subject is people and their character flaws; the economist's is institutions and how they shape behavior. Tempting as it may be to demonize the companies and their executives, damning the players gets in the way of diagnosing the structural problem.

In neglecting tropical diseases and in setting drug prices high, the pharmaceutical companies are responding to the system they are in: they are reacting to the incentives of the marketplace. It is the companies' fiduciary responsibility to act in their shareholders' interest. They invest where they see some prospect of a return. The resources they have available to devote to research, while large, are not unlimited, and they must make choices of where to direct them. "We can't deny that we try to focus on top markets: cardiovascular, metabolism, anti-infection, etc.," says an executive of the French-German company Aventis. "But we're an industry in a competitive environment. We have a commitment to deliver performance for shareholders."[7]

Innovation is a high-stakes dice roll. A blockbuster drug earns a billion dollars or more a year. Such returns do not come easily. Only three out of ten new drugs, according to the industry, make back their investment costs. Bringing a new drug to market is estimated to cost in the range of $200 to $500 million. (These numbers rest on guesswork, as the drug companies do not disclose their development costs for any individual drug.) Total spending on research in 1999, according to industry data, was over 20 percent of sales.[8]

The risk-taking, it must be said, is well rewarded. In profitability, the pharmaceutical industry ranked comfortably first in the 1999 Fortune 500 list of the top global companies. Its profits were 18 percent of revenues, putting it far ahead of the second-place industry, diversified financial firms, whose profits were 11 percent of revenues; the other industries' profits ranged all the way down to zero. These reported profits overstate the pharmaceutical industry's true profits because of the way the accounting is done (research costs are treated as current outlays, whereas it would make more sense to treat them as investments). Correcting for this accounting bias yields lower but still relatively high returns.[9] The drug industry is profitable.

The companies, nevertheless, are not the primary source of the global drug market's failings. They will do what it takes to maximize their profits. Let us take this as given and move on to the deeper issue of the design of the market.

To cover the costs of the research, expensive and uncertain as it is, any drug that is successfully developed must be priced well above its manufacturing cost. Enabling this is precisely what the patent laws, granting monopoly rights to the innovator, were intended to do. The global pharmaceutical market works exactly as it was designed to work. The challenge for those who believe it is flawed is to devise an alternative market design that would induce better outcomes.

*   *   *   *

The root of the shortcomings in the global pharmaceutical market is not companies' policies but countries' poverty. President Thabo Mbeki of South Africa, opening an international conference on AIDS, pointed to extreme poverty, rather than the disease, as the leading killer across Africa. Lowering the price of the AIDS antiretrovirals would make them accessible to more Africans, but most would still miss out.[10] Purchasing them in the amounts required, even at a far lower price, would bankrupt the health budgets of most African nations. At a 90 percent discount, a year's worth of antiretrovirals would cost more than the per capita income in many African nations.

Spending significant amounts on AIDS drugs would take money away from other urgent needs, like drugs against tuberculosis and pneumonia. And purchasing the AIDS drugs by itself would not solve the problem. Administering the antiretrovirals is complicated, and to be effective they require continuous supervision by a doctor, a level of care unavailable in most of Africa. Without an improvement in basic health services, the drugs' effects would be limited even if they were available. The only real solution, therefore, is to eliminate poverty.

Richer countries are healthier countries. There is a robust statistical relationship between health and per capita income.[11] With economic growth come the resources needed to attack disease. Societal changes that would lead to improved prevention, like a higher status for women and better education, are also a necessary part of any AIDS cure, and these improvements tend to follow increases in national income. Economic growth is the only reliable source of a cure for AIDS and the various tropical diseases. Obviously, though, growth is not easy to achieve, and in any case it is a long-term remedy. It would take decades to show effects and provides no hope for the current victims. Immediate remedies are also desperately needed.

Such remedies are not easy to devise. There is no alternative system that would do a better job in pharmaceutical innovation and delivery than the market system does. But the social value of a new vaccine against a tropical disease like malaria, from the many lives it would save, immeasurably exceeds what could be earned from selling the vaccine, given the low incomes of those who need it, so the incentives that come from the market are necessarily insufficient. The sales revenues would be so low that they would probably not cover the innovator's costs of doing the research. Poverty being the main problem, tinkering with the rules of the marketplace cannot solve it. But it might be able to help.

Is the design of the market part of the problem? Well, yes, in a way. It is clear where the research efforts will go when the market promises almost nothing for a cure for malaria and billions for a cure for erectile dysfunction.

Alongside these failings, however, the market system has some truly admirable triumphs: new pharmaceuticals that have prolonged and improved countless lives. The antiretrovirals have helped thousands who might otherwise have died from AIDS. Research has brought a host of other medical marvels, as pointed out by the Pharmaceutical Research and Manufacturers of America (PhRMA), an alliance of U.S. drug manufacturers.[12] Antibiotics and vaccines have almost eliminated diphtheria, syphilis, whooping cough, measles, and polio from the developed world. Deaths from influenza and pneumonia have been greatly reduced, as have deaths from heart disease, strokes, and ulcers. Millions live longer, more productively, and more comfortably.

Market incentives are what prompted the invention of these miracle drugs. Were it not for the profit motive, many of them would not exist. Adam Smith said self-interest can lead to beneficent outcomes: there is no more striking instance of this than the aggressive pursuit of profit giving rise to life-preserving medicines. No economic system that has ever been implemented, other than the market, has succeeded in consistently spawning major pharmaceutical innovations. The alternatives to the market—such as provision by international agencies or the state—have been far less successful than the drug companies in developing new pharmaceuticals. While government laboratories in the United States and Western Europe do important research, they lack the capacity and the incentives to turn basic science into usable medicines. Given the huge investments and the highly uncertain outcomes, the prospect of profits is needed to induce the continuing development of improved medicines on a large scale. Only the market can provide enough motivation.

Need we, then, be fatalistic? If there is no alternative to the market, is there nothing that can be done to get drugs to those who urgently need them?

*   *   *   *

To say that the drug companies respond to the rules of the marketplace is not the whole story. They do not passively take the market's rules as given, but actively try to shape them. They make sure they have their say on matters concerning market design. Their presence in the world's capitals is conspicuous. They subject the U.S. government to fierce lobbying, in part to counter accusations of price gouging. During the election campaign of 2000, the pharmaceutical industry's spending on lobbying, $167 million, exceeded that of any other industry.[13]

The vast sums the pharmaceutical companies spend on lobbying is a measure of the entanglement of state and market. The pharmaceutical market has never been a truly free market. Intellectual property could not exist without the state, for a sophisticated apparatus is required to define and enforce property rights in ideas. Governments have been essential in maintaining the existing pharmaceutical marketplace and will be essential to any attempt to improve it. That market incentives are needed to induce innovation in pharmaceuticals is not, therefore, an argument for laissez-faire. The market is an indispensable part of any solution, but only a part of it. The government is involved in two ways: supplying funds and designing the market.

Public health—preventing epidemics and the spread of disease, protecting against environmental hazards, promoting healthy behaviors, responding to disasters—is what economists call a public good. Like other public goods, as I will discuss later, it cannot be left to the market to supply. The control of communicable diseases brings gains that are widely shared. Those who receive vaccination against polio, for instance, benefit not just themselves but others as well. An individualistic reckoning of costs and benefits would result in too little use of vaccines. Public health is recognized in all the developed countries as a legitimate concern of the government. This rationale for state action applies not just within each separate country but also globally. Diseases such as Ebola, cholera, yellow fever, and meningitis spread across national borders. With modern air travel, they are spreading faster than ever. "A communicable disease occurring in one country," notes the World Health Organization, "can the next day find itself transmitted to another, anywhere in the world." The developed countries' sheer self-interest calls for them to fund international disease control.

Basic scientific knowledge also is a public good. The benefits from it are not captured by its discoverer, so markets induce little basic research. This is the reason why governments everywhere fund science. The U.S. government's expenditure on health-related research via the National Institutes of Health (NIH) and other federal agencies totaled $18 billion in 2000. Universities, foundations, and charities spent another $10 billion or so. These amounts add up to more than the research spending of all the U.S. pharmaceutical companies, which was $22.5 billion. Most of the major new drug patents awarded to the drug companies have their origins in government-funded research. Of the key discoveries cited in biomedical patents, just 17 percent came from industry, according to a study by the National Science Foundation. Much of the work that showed the effectiveness of AIDS antiretrovirals, for example, was done by the NIH and other public laboratories.[14] The productivity of the pharmaceutical companies' research rests on state funding.

Market incentives are generally needed to push ideas beyond pure science into usable applications. Converting a scientific breakthrough into a workable new drug is usually done most effectively in the private sector. But there are exceptions. Publicly funded research sometimes succeeds where the market fails. An outstanding example is the development of high-yielding grain varieties in the mid-1960s by an international network of research centers, including the International Center for the Improvement of Maize and Wheat in Mexico and the International Rice Research Institute in the Philippines. The research was funded by a consortium of governments, international agencies, and foundations. The new rice and wheat strains triggered the green revolution, almost doubling yields. Grains being the staple food of most of the world's people, the high-yielding grain varieties were, in terms of their impact on the very poor, among the most momentous inventions ever made. Following this impressive precedent, the International AIDS Vaccine Initiative, funded by governments, international agencies, and foundations, is searching for vaccines against AIDS, malaria, and tuberculosis.

A lot of money is needed to provide these international public goods. According to Dr. Peter Piot, the head of UNAIDS, a United Nations program, Africa needs $3 billion a year for basic measures to deal with AIDS and tens of billions of dollars more each year to provide Africans with the drugs used routinely in developed countries. Funds in the required amounts can come only from the developed world. "We need billions, not millions, to fight AIDS in the world," Dr. Piot said, "we can't fight an epidemic of this magnitude with peanuts."[15]

Beyond providing money, governments and international organizations have a role in rethinking the market's design, and in particular the rules governing intellectual property. A patent is a compromise solution to a problem that admits no ideal solution. It is an officially sanctioned monopoly. Offering the prospect of monopoly profits, a patent is a powerful incentive to innovate. The amazing pace of pharmaceutical advances in the past century attests to this. The prospect of patents helped induce the development, for instance, of the antiretrovirals as usable medicines.

But the patent system has a downside. The overpricing of the outputs that can result from the monopoly conferred by the patent, while rewarding the innovator, harms consumers. Patents successfully generate inventions while inhibiting their use.

Patent-induced overpricing occurs in any innovative industry but, because of the nature of demand, it is probably more marked in the pharmaceutical industry than elsewhere. The quantity purchased of a typical drug is relatively insensitive to its price. This is because the patient's need is great, decisions on use are made not by the user but by a physician, and the bill is often paid not by the user but by an insurance company or a government health plan. A study of the U.S. market for antiulcer drugs, in which four manufacturers competed, estimated that a 10 percent increase in price would have been followed by only a 7 percent decrease in demand.[16] This means (if you do the arithmetic) that an increase in the price would elicit an increase in the total revenue earned, implying that had there been a single supplier, as in many other pharmaceutical markets, the price would have been set much higher. When demand is inelastic, textbook economics says, a profit-maximizing monopolist prices far above its production cost. Where the buyers are not price-sensitive, charging what the market will bear means setting prices very high. Patents, for the invaluable purpose they serve, come with a real cost.

Since intellectual property laws are defined and enforced by the state, and since they represent an uneasy compromise between the needs of the innovator and the needs of the user, the rules of the pharmaceutical market are not cast in stone.

✻   ✻   ✻   ✻

Some developing countries initiated the redesigning of the pharmaceutical market unilaterally, setting their own intellectual property rules.

In India, the government chooses not to grant product patents in food and drugs, so manufacturers may sell copies of drugs patented by U.S. or European companies. Having to cover only the costs of manufacture and not any costs of research, and not being sheltered by patents, they set prices low. Unlike the developed nations with their patent-supported monopolies, India in 2000 had a pharmaceutical industry that contained some 20,000 companies and charged competitive prices. The difference between monopoly and competition is indicated by fluconazole, a drug used against fungal infections. In India it was unpatented and so was sold by several competing manufacturers, whereas in the United States the patent was upheld and the market was served by a single manufacturer. The price per pill was 25 cents in India and $10 in the United States.[17]

In Brazil, the manufacture of antiretrovirals without regard to patents has enabled large numbers of AIDS sufferers to receive treatment that would have been unaffordable at the patent-induced prices. In 1997 the Brazilian government began encouraging domestic firms to produce unlicensed copies of patented AIDS drugs. The government bought these copies and gave them to patients free of charge. The price of the antiretroviral cocktail was one-fourth its U.S. price. One of the antiretrovirals was a mere one-sixteenth its U.S. price. This policy has made Brazil a rare success story among the developing countries, as deaths from AIDS plummeted. Brazil's president, Fernando Henrique Cardoso, said, "This is a political and moral issue, a truly dramatic situation, that has to be viewed realistically and can't be solved just by the market."[18]

South Africa passed a law in 1997 to make essential medicines affordable by compulsory licensing. (This means appropriating the patent, manufacturing or importing copies of the drug, and paying the patent holder a royalty.) By cutting the licensing fees paid by African drug manufacturers, the government calculated it could reduce prices by between 50 and 90 percent, thus making the drugs much more widely available. Thailand followed South Africa in passing a law permitting drug patents to be circumvented.

The developing countries argued that they were permitted to ignore the patents and produce the drugs themselves under a provision in the rules of the World Trade Organization. Compulsory licensing is permissible in the event of a public health emergency. (The U.S. government itself sometimes decrees that a patent be compulsorily licensed, usually for antitrust reasons, ordering a company to share its technology in order to end a monopoly.)

The multinational pharmaceutical companies disagreed with the developing countries, charging that ignoring the patents was illegal. They lobbied for the U.S. government to impose trade sanctions on Brazil. A spokesman for PhRMA, the alliance of U.S. drug manufacturers, said of Brazil, "They are still part of the world order and need to work things out with our companies." PhRMA reacted similarly to South Africa's initiative. The legislation was "an abrogation of intellectual property," a spokesman charged, arguing that "if AIDS drugs get compulsory-licensed around the world, it will dampen research." South Africa's action, he said, was "piracy." The "knock-off companies in India and Brazil," wrote the columnist Andrew Sullivan, echoing the industry's line, "are at best copiers of American products and at worst thieves."[19]

The drug companies guarded their intellectual property zealously. In Ghana in 2000, for example, an Indian company, Cipla, began selling a generic version of an AIDS drug made by Glaxo-Wellcome, at one-tenth the multinational company's price. The African regional patent authority ruled Glaxo's patents were not valid in Ghana. Nevertheless, Cipla stopped selling it after Glaxo threatened to sue.

The developing countries said they needed to do away with patents to save lives. "How can we be denied access to drugs that prolong life," asked a Kenyan member of parliament, "when our people are dying?" The drug companies retorted that patents are necessary for innovation. "We need intellectual property protection across the board all around the world," a spokesman for Bristol-Myers Squibb said. "Without it, we would not have the incentive to develop new and more effective HIV/AIDS drugs."[20]

Which side was right? Patents being an imperfect device, it is not in principle wrong to overrule them. Since it is not a matter of principle, evaluating the contending claims simply entails comparing the costs and benefits.

There would be a cost of compulsory licensing: overriding the drug companies' intellectual property and making the drugs available at lower prices would mean lower profits and less research on new and better drugs. There would be a benefit: fewer deaths. Even if only a fraction of the Africans with AIDS could be saved (because it would take more than simply a price cut to get the drugs to most of the African sufferers), a fraction of tens of millions is a lot of lives.

The cost-benefit arithmetic in this particular case is easy to do—and it supports the developing countries' position. Since few of the AIDS drugs were sold in Africa at the high prices, there would be little lowering of profits and little or no cutback in research if Africa were allowed to free ride on the world's innovation. For the AIDS drug made by Glaxo-Wellcome, for example, just 10 percent of the $454 million in 1999 sales came from outside North America and Europe. Abrogating property rights, in this case, would have almost no direct cost. There could be indirect costs, via a thin-end-of-the-wedge effect, if a precedent were set that led to the overriding of other drug patents. Smuggling of the drugs back to the West could undermine the drug companies' pricing there. But the benefits—many lives saved or lengthened—are literally incalculable. Unless one believes, religiously, that property rights are sacrosanct, the benefits of overriding the patents in poor countries plainly outweighed the costs. The case for compulsory licensing of AIDS drugs as an emergency measure was overwhelming.

*   *   *   *

The U.S. government at first did not see things the developing countries' way. It sided with the drug companies, in the face of their munificent lobbying. The Clinton administration threatened trade sanctions against countries producing copies of patented drugs. Congress threatened to cut off aid. A 1999 State Department report to Congress said that "all relevant agencies of the U.S. government" were "engaged in an assiduous, concerted campaign to persuade the government of South Africa to withdraw or modify" its pharmaceuticals law. The United States filed a formal complaint against Brazil with the World Trade Organization, claiming that by allowing local firms to manufacture other firms' patented drugs Brazil was in violation of international trading rules.

Momentum gathered, nevertheless. International groups like Doctors Without Borders and Oxfam, the U.K. charity, rallied public opinion.

Newspapers frequently reported on the plight of AIDS sufferers. Activists pushed the issue onto the political agenda. They hounded Vice President Al Gore, noisily heckling his speeches during the early stages of his 2000 presidential election campaign. The group Act Up staged "die-ins" outside the Washington, D.C. headquarters of PhRMA, with mock tombstones, chalked body outlines, and slogans like "medication for every nation." Some shareholders of GlaxoSmithKline, concerned both about the issue in itself and about the damage a bad public image could do to the firm's share price, mounted a campaign to force it to make its drugs more accessible in poor countries. As a result of this broad-based public pressure, by 2001, a decade after public-health experts had begun warning the world of the impending AIDS crisis in poor countries, the tide had turned.

The Clinton administration reversed course and announced it would no longer threaten trade sanctions against developing countries that overruled AIDS drug patents. The World Bank and the United Nations built funds for such purposes. The European Union proposed a two-part plan: tiered pricing, with drug prices being lower in poorer countries, and a reform of international patent rules to make it easier for poor countries to import generic copies of drugs. Private philanthropy also was playing a role: for instance, the Global Fund for Children's Vaccines, run by Bill and Melinda Gates, was set up to cover the costs of immunizing children in developing countries. (The sums fell short, though, of the tens of billions of dollars that UNAIDS estimated were needed.)

When thirty-nine drug companies brought a suit to overturn the South African law allowing patents to be overridden, arguing the law violated international agreements on intellectual property, protesters outside the courtroom carried placards branding the drug company executives as "AIDS profiteers" who were "more deadly than the virus." The suit turned into a public-relations disaster for the companies, as they were accused of putting profits ahead of lives. In April 2001 they dropped it. "We needed to win this case otherwise many of us will die," said Nonthantla Maseko, a South African AIDS sufferer. "Our hope lay in winning this case. We had to win it."[21] By withdrawing their court action, the drug companies set a precedent that was generally interpreted to mean that poor countries could, for public-health reasons, override patents.

The five leading pharmaceutical companies agreed in 2000 to negotiate lower prices on their AIDS drugs for Africa and Asia. Then, in 2001, the major companies announced they would provide AIDS drugs to developing countries for what it cost to manufacture them, about one-tenth the price charged in the West. A stipulation, said Per Wold-Olsen, a Merck executive, was that "processes are put in place so that drugs are not re-exported to the developed world." He added that the governments of developed countries needed to help build health-care infrastructure and distribution systems for the developing countries. John McGoldrick of Bristol-Myers Squibb said, "We seek no profits on AIDS drugs in Africa and we will not let our patents be an obstacle."[22]

Ordinary market forces had pushed the drug companies to change their pricing, as they were starting to face competition from Indian generic pharmaceutical manufacturers. But the change was also a response to the activists' goading. The story of the AIDS drugs shows how consumers and their advocates—aid organizations like Doctors Without Borders and Oxfam, advocacy groups like Act Up, and the press—can push a market to be revamped. It is probably not coincidence that the countries that moved aggressively to change the market's rules—Brazil, South Africa, and Thailand—have governments that, being democratic, are susceptible to pressure from the public.

The solution of selling AIDS drugs at cost in the poor countries is not transferable, however, to drugs against many other diseases. AIDS drugs are a special case when we weigh the costs of lifting patent protection against the benefits, for their discovery was driven by the hugely lucrative market in developed countries. The poor countries would provide a tiny fraction of the global profits from AIDS drugs regardless of what pricing policies were adopted, so their failure to contribute to the research costs would not significantly dampen innovation incentives. With diseases that do not hit the developed world, by contrast, the weakening of incentives for research from overruling patents could be such a large drawback as to outweigh any benefits. Letting the poor nations free ride is of potential benefit only with diseases that strike the affluent countries and have the U.S. and European markets as an inducement to innovation. With tropical diseases, no patents would mean no research. Making innovations freely available would achieve nothing if it meant there were no innovations.

For developing drugs against the diseases that hit the poor countries alone, deeper changes in market design are needed. For such drugs, intellectual property protections need to be upheld if any research is to be done. Perhaps there are other ways, though, of running a patent system. How can research incentives be devised for new drugs against diseases in poor countries? Such drugs fail to be developed under the standard patent system because, despite their very high potential social value, the returns that could be earned from them would not cover their development costs.

Various alternatives and supplements to the patent system, all requiring action by governments and international agencies, have been explored by economist Michael Kremer, a leader in the search for workable ways to deliver drugs to the poor countries.[23] Lowering the cost of innovation by subsidizing the inputs drug companies use in their research, perhaps by means of tax credits, could make it profitable to develop drugs that have a low market value. Because it is hard to monitor research inputs, however, subsidizing inputs is in general less effective than rewarding success by paying for outputs. Another way of tipping the balance of costs and returns is revenue enhancement, under which the government or an international agency promises to top off the company's earnings once the new drug is being manufactured, by paying the company a prespecified sum for each dollar earned from its sales.

Given the poor countries' lack of buying power, this approach requires funding from the governments of Western Europe and North America and international agencies like the World Bank and the World Health Organization. With the $200 to $500 million cost to develop a new drug, these funds need to be very well endowed.

✻   ✻   ✻   ✻

The global pharmaceutical market highlights simultaneously the very worst aspects of markets and the very best. To drive the discovery of new drugs, market incentives are indispensable. There is more than one way, however, to design a market. The right design for a market varies with time and place. Any market is imperfect, and from time to time it may need to be redesigned.

Both entrepreneurs and governments, then, on occasion take on the role of market designer. Next we will look at what market design entails: the groundwork that is needed for markets to work well.

FOUR

::::

Information Wants to Be Free

The age-old Middle Eastern bazaar is the stuff of travel writing. In Marrakech, Morocco, you enter the bazaar through a tiled gate called Bab Doukkala into a maze of narrow streets teeming with shoppers. Your senses are bombarded by the pungent smell of spices, the gaudy colors of the goods for sale, the shouting of mule drivers. Vendors offer food: quinces, mint, cheese, meat. Craftspeople are grouped by their products: pottery, shoes, brassware, woodwork, engravings, clothing, baskets, mosaics.

Information in the bazaar "is poor, scarce, maldistributed, inefficiently communicated, and intensely valued," as the anthropologist Clifford Geertz put it. "The level of ignorance about everything from product quality and going prices to market possibilities and production costs is very high, and much of the way in which the bazaar functions can be interpreted as an attempt to reduce such ignorance for someone, increase it for someone, or defend someone against it." Prices are not posted for items beyond the most inexpensive. Trademarks do not exist. There is no advertising. Experienced buyers search extensively to try to protect themselves against being overcharged or being sold shoddy goods. The shoppers spend time comparing what the various merchants are offering, and the merchants spend time trying to persuade shoppers to buy from them. "The search for information is the central experience of life in the bazaar," said Geertz. It is "the really advanced art in the bazaar, a matter upon which everything turns."[1]

Bazaar merchants sometimes actively try to increase search costs by hiding price information. Negotiations are done discreetly, so that the merchant can offer a bargain to a favored customer without other shoppers learning the price. In Yemen, a merchant and customer sometimes conceal their bargaining, it is reported, by covering their hands with a cloth. They bargain by moving their fingers, using each finger to symbolize a number and using their eyes to indicate assent or disagreement.[2]

Picture yourself in Marrakech walking through that tiled gate into the bazaar. You want to buy a brass urn as a souvenir. The many sellers of brassware cluster in their own area. You can walk from one merchant to another in seconds, so comparison shopping is easy. But not costless. You are in Marrakech for just a couple of days and there are other places to visit. As you go from merchant to merchant, your travel companions start whining at you to make up your mind and just buy something so they can move along. Your cost of getting an extra price quote is not negligible.

You end up overpaying. As any visitor from the affluent West to a poor country sooner or later learns from bitter experience, a tourist is no match for a bazaar merchant. It is only partly a matter of technique. Bazaar merchants are tough, experienced bargainers. Furthermore, most tourists lack the general knowledge of normal price levels and the ability to judge quality of workmanship. But let us grant that you are a ruthless bargainer and an expert judge of value. Your costs of shopping around, small as they may be, are enough to prevent competition from breaking out among the merchants. You pay an exorbitant price.

※ ※ ※ ※

Let us examine the logic of this overpricing in more detail. Imagine that many sellers offer the identical brass urn that you want. You are willing to pay up to $10 for it and no more. (To keep the story simple, we will assume the sellers know your cutoff price; if they did not, you would have some bargaining power yourself.) The urn's cost to any of the merchants—wholesale price, plus rent, labor costs, and the minimal profit margin to stay in business—add up to $5. You have already obtained a price quote from the merchant you have been talking to. To get any further quotes you must talk to others. This means going slightly out of your way and using up a little more of your time; these costs are small but not zero. What price will each merchant quote?

As a benchmark, notice first that if there were just a single merchant selling the urn, you would be charged the monopoly price, right up to what you are willing to pay, $10. The merchant would rake in a profit of 100 percent.

As the opposite benchmark, suppose that there are many merchants and you are fully informed, so you can freely buy from whomever has the lowest price. In this case every merchant charges $5. Each would undercut its competitors in the quest for your business, driving the price down to where they are just covering their costs. The competitive process results in your getting a bargain.

But this does not occur when information is not free. Then the market settles down, with every merchant quoting the high price of $10. It is not that the merchants collude with each other. They do not have to. The price stays high merely because of the buyers' lack of information.

Imagine that all the merchants are quoting $10. Could one of them do better by undercutting this price? There is a downside to price-cutting: a reduction in revenue from any customers who would have bought from this merchant even at the higher price. If information were freely available, the price-cutter would get a compensating boost in sales as additional customers flocked in. When search costs exist, however, such extra sales may be negligible. If you incur a search cost of 10 cents or more for each merchant you sample, and there are fifty sellers offering the urn, then even if you know there is someone out there who is willing to sell it at cost, so you would save $5, it does not pay you to look for him. You would be looking for a needle in a haystack. If you visited one more seller, you would have a chance of one in fifty of that seller being the price-cutter, so the return on average from that extra price quote would be 10 cents (or $5 multiplied by 1/50), which is the same as your cost of getting one more quote. It does not pay to search. The price-cutter, getting little or no extra sales, raises his price back up.[3]

Pricing high, then, rests on the merchants' self-fulfilling expectations. The merchant you are bargaining with knows that you know that all the other merchants are quoting a high price. Knowing that you face a cost of going to another merchant, this merchant quotes you the same high price as everyone else. You are trapped; you pay the high price.

For competition to work, sellers must be rewarded for lowering their prices. This would occur if information were free. But when search costs lock customers in, sellers are penalized if they cut their prices. The cost of shopping around—even if it is tiny by comparison with the value of the purchase—can prevent competitive forces from breaking out. Each seller is a little monopolist. Because of the buyers' cost of searching, the merchants make a large profit. Big effects can come from small transaction costs.

❖　　❖　　❖　　❖

Today's economics has the problem of information at its core. The "biggest new concept in economics in the last thirty years," Kenneth Arrow said in 2000, "is the development of the importance of information, along with the dispersion of information."[4]

Two kinds of market frictions arise from the uneven supply of information. There are search costs: the time, effort, and money spent learning what is available where for how much. And there are evaluation costs, arising from the difficulties buyers have in assessing quality. A successful market has mechanisms that hold down the costs of transacting that come from the dispersion of information.

Search costs can cause markets to malfunction in large and small ways. The fun of the hunt aside, the time and money spent on acquiring information is better spent doing something else. In addition, transactions sometimes occur between the wrong people, or fail to occur at all. If search costs are high, shoppers will not search very far or might even give up looking. The difficulty of locating alternative sellers might mean you purchase from the seller you know, though there might be other sellers who would offer you a better deal or a different product that better fits your needs. Search costs can result in inappropriate matches of buyer and seller, sometimes preventing mutually beneficial transactions from being made. And search costs, as we saw, actually weaken the force of competition. The mere existence of choice does not in itself ensure that the market operates competitively. For there to be effective competition, buyers must be able to easily compare the choices.

Information is the lifeblood of markets. Knowledge of what is available where, and who wants it, is crucial. A market works badly if information does not flow through it. Rarely does information flow absolutely freely, but well-functioning markets have various mechanisms to aid its movement, and thus to solve the problems you would encounter while shopping in the bazaar in Marrakech. Usually we take these devices so much for granted that we do not notice them, although we do notice their absence when they cause a market malfunction.

In labor markets especially, search costs shape the market's performance. "When a great many people are unable to find work, unemployment results," Calvin Coolidge said. While belaboring the obvious was one of Coolidge's traits, this is a less trivial statement than it sounds. Job-seekers may be unable to find work not because there are no jobs to be had but because of search costs. Searching for a job is time-consuming and costly.

The scenario of your being overcharged in the Marrakech bazaar is a warning of how badly markets can malfunction if they lack mechanisms for transmitting information. There are solutions, though. Local people who regularly shop in the bazaar are in a different situation from tourists. The locals face transaction costs, just as tourists do, and they suffer from the ignorance about products and prices that Geertz noted. But there is a countervailing force to dissuade merchants from overcharging local customers: the merchants' desire for repeat business.

Unlike tourists, the regular bazaar shoppers establish relationships with particular merchants. Although they may check the current prices by bargaining cursorily with various merchants, in the end they usually return to bargain in earnest with their customary merchants. These are ties of convenience, not friendship. Buyer and seller remain adversaries. The shopper wants a low price and the merchant a high price. They bargain long and hard. But their interests are not completely opposed. The shopper values the assurance against being cheated that the relationship provides, and the merchant wants to leave the shopper satisfied enough to return tomorrow. The relationships economize on search costs and result in prices being lower for repeat customers.

Repeat-business relationships are only a partial solution to informational problems. A sophisticated market needs additional mechanisms for providing information.

＊　　＊　　＊　　＊

Most markets contain devices designed to overcome the frictions generated by search costs and thereby allow competitive forces to drive prices down. Services like *Consumer Reports* and the Yellow Pages lower search costs. Word of mouth is a handy source of shopping tips. Sellers intending to continue doing business over the long run might refrain from price-gouging in order to earn repeat business from their customers. Advertising and loss leaders may dislodge customers from rival stores. Brand names and trademarks can reduce search costs for consumers. Market intermediaries like wholesalers and trading companies reduce search costs for firms. There is a long list of market devices that aid the acquisition of information and mitigate the anticompetitive effects of the costs of search.

Search costs bring entrepreneurial opportunities. Even small search costs, as we have seen, can give rise to overpricing unless there is some additional force to counter their effects. Search being a wasteful activity, buyers might be willing to pay for a service that conducts the search for them. When there are costs of search, a mutually beneficial deal may be lost, because buyer and seller cannot locate each other. Intermediaries who serve as matchmakers—real-estate agents, for example—therefore provide a valuable service. There are gains to be made from rectifying the inefficiencies that arise from search costs.

Intermediaries like wholesalers and trading companies have found their market niche by serving to lower search costs. Imagine you work for a U.S. maker of high-fashion shoes that wants to outsource production to a lower-cost country. How do you go about finding local firms to contract with? You could spend a lot of time investigating the local firms, visiting their plants, checking the quality of their workmanship, and bargaining with them over prices. Or you could subcontract this search process to a specialist. In Taiwan, for instance, there are firms that operate as matchmakers between fashion houses in the United States and Europe and local Taiwanese shoe manufacturers. These trading companies act as a "hub of information regarding the managerial and financial conditions" of the Taiwanese manufacturers, according to geographer You-tien Hsing.[5] The trading companies gather information in the other direction as well: about the demands and reliability of the U.S. and European buyers. Employees of a trading company often stay in the factories to monitor quality while an order is being produced. If disputes later arise between the Western shoe company and the Taiwanese subcontractor, the trading company has the information it needs to judge which party is at fault, and so it can act as an honest broker. The trading companies earn profits by making markets work better.

Cutting out the middleman is a common refrain. But sometimes intermediaries are valuable. If information flowed freely, then the middlemen could be cut out; when information is not free, they serve a useful purpose.

"Information wants to be free. Information also wants to be expensive." This mantra of high technology applies as well to the low-tech world. It was coined by the computer guru Stewart Brand, who went on to explain, "Information wants to be free because it has become so cheap to distribute, copy, and recombine—too cheap to meter. It wants to be expensive because it can be immeasurably valuable to the recipient."[6]

Buyers are empowered by anything that makes it easier for them to acquire information. Any market innovation that lowers search costs, such as the advent of electronic commerce, makes markets more efficient. People waste less time and money on search. Better matches of buyer and seller are formed, and pricing becomes more competitive, to the buyers' advantage.

Sellers also by and large are helped when innovation lowers search costs. In the quest for information, resources are evaporated, and so improved market information is a win-win situation; sellers as well as buyers benefit when markets work more efficiently. There is an exception, though: sellers can be made worse off. Since search costs tend to lock buyers into sellers and can allow sellers to overcharge, a lowering of search costs can bring a disproportionate lowering of selling prices.

*　　*　　*　　*

Long-distance trucking has benefited from the improved matching that follows lower search costs. A truck that has delivered its load needs to find another load for its journey back to home base, rather than return empty. This used to mean the trucker or the dispatching office had to make a lot of telephone calls. Now, the internet makes available instant information on truck capacities and potential loads. Entrepreneurs have set up password-access web sites to provide the information (such as getloaded.com and datconexus.com), to which truckers and companies with goods to ship can subscribe for a monthly fee. Trucks now rarely have to return home with an empty trailer, and productivity gains of 20 percent or more have been reported. Trucker Richard Kirschman was one of the first to carry a laptop computer on board. (He powers his laptop using a lawnmower battery that he carries in a bowling bag.) Interviewed on National Public Radio, he spoke of a trucker he had met in a coffee shop in Dallas who had been stuck there for three days, unable to return to his home in New Jersey until he found a load of goods to take in that direction. Powering up his computer, Kirschman instantly found four different loads for his friend, who was soon on the road again.[7] The information flow brought by the internet has reinvented the trucking market.

Internet commerce, with its bits of information flying through fiber-optic cables at the speed of light, is about as far as we can get from the Middle Eastern bazaar—in style, at least. In essence, however, the two are similar. On the internet, just as in the bazaar, the methods of exchange are shaped by information and the costs of getting it. The bazaar, however, suffers from high transaction costs resulting from a lack of information-transmission devices. In electronic commerce, the situation is different. The internet's ease of communication has changed the balance of buyers' bargaining power with sellers. The internet has empowered consumers by giving them a lot of information.

Internet retailers like CDNow.com and Amazon.com offer low-search-cost purchasing. Their success in attracting customers rests on the fact that many buyers of compact discs and books find it more convenient to search in cyberspace than in physical space. At automobile sites like Autobytel.com and Carpoint.com, buyers can get bids from several different dealers from their own computer. Lowering buyers' search costs, the internet has shifted pricing in the favor of the buyers.

It can also help sellers. In some villages in rural India, the villagers have banded together and bought a computer. In Bagdi village in the state of Madhya Pradesh, farmers use the village computer to get printouts of the prices wheat, garlic, and other crops are fetching in nearby markets. This increases their bargaining power with the middlemen they trade with. "If the price he offers suits me, I'll sell it to him," said wheat grower Satya Narayan Khati. "Otherwise I'll take it to market myself." The improved information has made the pricing to farmers more competitive.[8]

While the internet has helped buyers by changing the balance of their bargaining power with sellers, there is another sense in which it has helped both sellers and buyers: by improving the efficiency of the market mechanism. Sellers have been helped by the expansion in the number of their potential customers, who need not be close by but can be anywhere in the world; vice versa, buyers have been helped by getting access to new sellers. Better matching means both sellers and buyers are better off.

Bill Gates, addressing the World Economic Forum in Melbourne, Australia, in 2000, spoke of the changes the internet has brought.[9] Markets, he said, are based on sellers finding the most appropriate buyer. In the old economy, this activity was loaded with overheads: the costs of promotion and of establishing a distribution network. The internet allows companies to bypass the middlemen and sell directly to consumers, bringing huge savings. To the extent that the transaction costs in the old economy were overhead, incurred regardless of scale, they were a handicap to small firms. Selling a modest volume of product often did not cover the overhead expenses. Now, with the internet in place, small companies can start up and survive. "As long as you are able to type in a few words that describe the type of product you might have, you can match demand and serve the demand even if it is only a few thousands units a year." We now have, Gates concluded, "friction-free capitalism."

Search has been automated. Shopping robots, or bots, explore hundreds of online merchants to find the best price for you. There are specialized comparison-shopping services for such items as books, compact discs, and computers. In addition, a large amount of wholesale price information is available online. Before, savvy car buyers went to some trouble to get hold of a book listing used-car prices. Now they can find it without charge on the internet. Comparison shopping is almost free, at least for the computer literate.

Those who take the trouble to comparison shop do a favor to everyone else. In the jargon of economics, they convey a positive externality.[10] A high-priced seller contemplating cutting the price of a product weighs the costs and benefits. The cost is lowered profits from customers who would have bought at the initial price. The benefit is increased sales to new customers. If there are enough price-sensitive shoppers, the seller is rewarded for cutting the price. Penny-pinching shoppers who search for the lowest price put pressure on higher-priced sellers to cut their prices, to the benefit of all buyers.

The internet's lowering of buyers' search costs has brought a perceptible lowering of prices, as economic theory predicts. A study of prices for new books and compact discs found that those sold on the internet are priced on average 8 to 15 percent lower than those sold through conventional retailers. People who buy cars online pay about 2 percent less than those who buy at an old-fashioned dealership, saving about $450 on an average car. The internet has reduced the price of a life insurance policy by 5 percent or more. The buyers' lower search costs, together with sellers' lower operational costs, translate into lower selling prices, as we would expect.

Despite the ease of comparison shopping on the internet, however, it has not eliminated the dispersion of prices. Spending a few minutes at PriceScan.com looking up a book of my own, *Games, Strategies, and Managers* (which despite its obscurity is listed by most online booksellers), I have learned that it is offered for $17.95 by Borders.com and Powell's Books, for $16.14 by Amazon.com and Barnes&Noble.com, and for as little as $12.71 by Buy.com, $12.57 by Kabang.com, and $11.49 by Alldirect.com. While shipping costs differ from seller to seller, the price inclusive of shipping costs has a similar dispersion. For delivery within a week, it ranges from $15.57 (from Kabang.com) to $20.10 (from Amazon.com).

More systematic studies find the same thing: the ready availability of price information has not driven prices of identical items into alignment. While prices tend to be lower on the internet than from conventional sellers, there is a significant dispersion of prices across internet sellers. With price dispersion measured by the difference between the highest and lowest prices charged for a particular item as a percentage of its average price, the typical dispersion, according to one study, was 37 percent for books and 25 percent for compact discs. For books, there is actually more price variation among internet retailers than among bricks-and-mortar retailers.[11]

Such a wide dispersion is a puzzle. New books and compacts discs are undifferentiated. A book is exactly the same book, wherever you buy it. If the internet has brought friction-free capitalism, it should have eliminated price dispersion, because every buyer would know where to go to get the best deal.

One possible explanation for the continued existence of price dispersion is laziness: shoppers do not bother to search for the lowest price. This seems a tenuous explanation, however, for most people would think it worthwhile to use a few seconds to save several dollars. It certainly cannot explain the continued existence of price dispersion on large-ticket items.

*   *   *   *

How can price dispersion persist when information costs are very low? It can't. Since price dispersion continues to exist, it must be that even internet markets are subject to frictions—there are still some transaction costs. These are not costs of locating sellers or learning their prices, for those costs are close to zero. The remaining transaction costs are more subtle. They come from difficulties of observing quality. The internet has not created perfectly frictionless markets. The need for buyers to be able to trust sellers has been heightened by the internet.

The hype notwithstanding, the internet in fact has not made information free. If shopping were merely a matter of finding the lowest price, the internet's comparison shopping devices would eventually force all retailers to match their lowest-priced competitors. But a book offered by one retailer may be distinguishable, in a shopper's perception, from the same book offered by another retailer, even though they are physically identical objects. The shopper is not buying simply a book, but a package of services of which the book itself is a part—the main part, to be sure, but just a part. In addition, the buyer is getting assurances of various kinds: that the book will be delivered as quickly as promised; that it will be delivered in good condition; that the retailer will allow it to be returned if it is not what was expected; that the retailer's employees will not fraudulently reuse the buyer's credit-card data. Buyers willingly pay a little more to reduce their uncertainty. Information costs include not only the costs of locating a seller but also the costs of getting assurance. The retailer's reputation can convey such assurance. A brand name is a device for providing information.

Beyond assurances of reliability, sellers offer a range of other services. If you have a relationship with your local bookstore, you may have built up trust in its proprietor's judgment, so that you would buy a book by an author you have never heard of merely on the bookstore's recommendation. Apparently homogeneous items often are not actually homogeneous: it matters where you buy them.

To further examine this point, let us leave the internet and go to a low-tech example. In India's cities, high-quality fresh milk used to be hard to find. To boost their profits, wholesalers and vendors would water it down. Buyers could judge the milk's freshness by smelling it, but they could not judge its butterfat content. As a result of the low quality, the sales of milk declined; per capita consumption fell 25 percent below what it had been twenty years earlier.

The economist George Akerlof created a thought experiment to show the logic of how markets malfunction when buyers cannot observe quality.[12] Imagine it costs a seller $1.00 to supply a quart of high-quality milk, and $.60 to supply a quart of watered down milk. A typical buyer would willingly pay up to $1.20 for good milk and $.80 for inferior milk. In either case mutual gains could be obtained from trade. If the buyer could recognize the milk's quality, both buyer and seller would benefit from a sale at a price somewhere between $.60 and $.80 for the low-quality milk and between $1.00 and $1.20 for the high-quality milk. If the buyer is unable to distinguish quality, however, both grades of milk would sell for the same price. Suppose all vendors look alike to our buyer, and he believes that 60 percent of them water down their milk. Then the most he would pay for a quart of milk is $.96, and probably less. (The arithmetic of this is that there is a 40 percent chance the milk is worth $1.20 to the buyer and a 60 percent chance it is worth $.80, so on average it is worth $1.20 × 0.4 + $.80 × 0.6, which equals $.96.) But this situation is not sustainable. It costs $1.00 to supply the good milk. An honest seller charging a price that covers her costs will not make a sale because of the buyer's well-grounded fear of being cheated. Honest sellers go out of business. The fraction of sellers watering their milk rises to 100 percent. Gresham's law rules in this marketplace: low-quality goods drive out high quality.

In India, as in many poor countries, this situation is common. The markets for many goods work unsatisfactorily, as Indian journalist Ashok Desai observes: "you get garlic mixed up, of all sizes and qualities, fresh and desiccated; you cannot get the large, uniform, clean garlic bulbs you get in Europe. Cotton comes ingeniously adulterated; edible oil is sometimes so dangerous that it kills people. These products never improve; their producers continue to produce the same indifferent products decade after decade."

India did solve the problem of adulterated milk (as described by economist Robert Klitgaard). India's National Dairy Development Board launched a campaign in the 1970s to improve the quality of milk. It provided inexpensive machines to measure butterfat content of the milk at each stage of the distribution chain, from farmer to wholesaler to vendor, and set up payment schemes under which the prices paid for the milk reflect its measured quality. At the final, consumer stage, brand names were created to give buyers trust in what they were getting. As a result the quality improved and consumption rose. Consumers and honest producers benefited.[13]

Solving the problem of quality assurance for milk did not just happen; it required a series of coordinated actions. Quality-assurance mechanisms cannot always be taken for granted. Pervasive in affluent countries, they are often missing in poor countries; their absence is one of the reasons markets work badly.

* * * *

Building channels for the flow of information, both to help buyers and sellers to get together and to allow buyers to verify the quality of what they are purchasing, is a major part of designing a market. "The secret of business," the shipping tycoon Aristotle Onassis remarked, "is to know something that nobody else knows." The secret of market design, conversely, is to enable information to flow.

Unevenly distributed information can make a market work inefficiently. Comparison shopping involves costs of time and effort, which may be small but are rarely zero. Deals that would be mutually beneficial fail to be made because it is too hard for people to find each other. The buyers' costs of search give the sellers price-setting power. Successful markets have devices like advertising that allow information to flow. Market intermediaries like wholesalers and trading companies reduce search costs for firms.

It is often difficult to judge the quality of what buyers are being offered. Buyers' fear of being taken advantage of can cause markets to function at a low level of activity. As I will discuss next, markets must develop mechanisms for signaling quality, like guarantees, brand names, and specialized brokers.

F I V E

⁙

Honesty Is the Best Policy

"**I**n a deal, you give and take. You compromise. Then you grab the cash and catch the next train out of town." This was the uncomplicated business philosophy of Irving (Swifty) Lazar, a flamboyant agent for Hollywood stars. For some, grabbing the cash typifies marketplace behavior. It is dog eat dog, the law of the jungle.

The reality is the reverse. Where people cannot be trusted, markets work badly. For the simplest of transactions, where a buyer pays cash for a recognizable item, trust is not needed. But most transactions are not as straightforward as that. In a well-run economy, business is based on the ability to make credible promises.

As a buyer, you depend on the seller whenever there is any uncertainty about the merchandise—which occurs with almost anything you buy. When you purchase food, you trust it will not make you sick. When you buy medication, you hope it will not bring side effects. You presume the car you buy will run reliably, and you expect the mechanic to repair it well. You hope your employees will not be lazy. Consulting a doctor or an accountant, you trust in their competence. Whenever the buyer cannot verify quality in advance, the seller must somehow be able to reassure the buyer. As a seller, on the other hand, you place faith in the buyer whenever you offer credit. If you let customers take your goods without paying for them, you trust that they will pay their bills.

"Honesty is the best policy—when there is money in it." With this quip

Mark Twain identified one of the keys to a well-designed market. Some people are innately honest; some are not. Well-designed markets have a variety of mechanisms, formal and informal, to ensure there is indeed money in being honest. Marketplace confidence rests on rules and customs that give even unscrupulous people reason to keep their word.

✳   ✳   ✳   ✳

The assurance that consumers want and will pay for may be over something as trifling as the crispness of a french fry. You might say, "Fries are fries." This would merely show that you do not have it in you to be a burger mogul. In the 1950s, Ray Kroc, the founder of McDonald's, was obsessed with them. "The french fry would almost become sacrosanct for me," he said later, "its preparation a ritual to be followed religiously."[1] He sent employees with hydrometers into farmers' fields, rejecting potatoes lacking the optimal water content. He devised a way of curing the potatoes to convert natural sugars into starch. He developed the "potato computer" to calibrate the cooking time for a batch of fries. Kroc found his firm's competitive edge in the uniformity of his fries—the reliably precise combination of starch and grease. In Minneapolis or Minsk, the brand name McDonald's promises you exactly what you will get.

Market mechanisms to provide quality assurance are many and varied. You buy batteries of a brand that you have already used and found to be long-lasting. You purchase a car from a manufacturer with a track record of building reliable cars, a record you can look up in *Consumer Reports*. You get a new muffler installed on your car at a repair shop that advertises a dependable warranty. You visit a doctor who is certified. You base a hiring decision on testimonials from previous employers. In choosing a lawyer, you rely on recommendations from friends. The marketplace has myriad ways of distinguishing high-quality producers from low-quality ones.

Reputation is a guarantee of quality. A well-known firm offers more security than a firm you have never heard of. Because any misbehavior could damage its valuable reputation, you can presume it will deliver on time and will not cheat you. The price dispersion that persists among internet retailers, for example, is a reflection of the consumer's need for assurance. Since they can charge more than their less established competitors, firms can earn a return on their good name.

Conveying information convincingly can be difficult. How can you persuade potential customers that your product is better than your competitors'? Suppose that you in fact do have a better product. Suppose also there is something you can do that your target customers observe. This action not only costs you something but also—and this is the key—would cost you more if you were insincere than if you were being truthful. Let us call that action a "signal." The customers, seeing you take the action, infer that you are indeed telling the truth.[2] When you signal, you are following the maxim that actions speak louder than words.

Advertisements can be signals. As Mark Twain remarked, "Advertisements contain the only truths to be relied on in a newspaper." A soft-drink maker mounts a campaign of lavish commercials featuring rock stars. All that the ads are saying, it may seem, is that a large sum has been squandered. But the profligacy is the point: it asserts the firm's confidence in its product. The firm expects that consumers, having tried it, will go on buying it, so over the long haul it will recoup its advertising expenses. The ads serve as credible communication because a maker of low-quality products could not earn a return on them. They are saying "try it, you'll like it" more believably than words alone could.

Signaling is one of nature's ways. On an East African savanna, a lion stalks a gazelle. Sensing the predator, the gazelle starts springing six feet in the air, over and over. Why does it jump in one place rather than fleeing while it can? What seems crazy behavior, biologists theorize, is actually rational. Jumping is the gazelle's way of communicating. It is saying to the lion, "I'm strong and healthy. It would be a waste of your energy, and mine, to chase me." It costs extra for a weak antelope do this—because of the risk that the lion will call the bluff and continue the chase—so it is a credible signal.

Why does the peacock have such an extravagant tail? It is heavy to carry around and it makes the bird vulnerable to predators. But it does have a reason for existence—as a means of communication. To female birds seeking a mate, a luxuriant tail is a signal that the male is healthy and will pass on good genes.[3]

Ostentation can be a credible boast of quality. Economic equivalents of the peacock's tail—an apparently wasteful display that actually has the purpose of lending credibility—are many and varied. Banks and insurance companies have head offices that are sumptuous beyond the needs of their dealings. The showy offices signal that the company is sound, distinguishing it from shakier companies that cannot afford them. As a signal that they expect to still be there for you long into the future, retailers locate themselves in high-rent districts like New York's Fifth Avenue when a less expensive address would serve. A venture capitalist agrees to back a start-up firm only if the entrepreneur puts up a substantial sum of her own money—not because the venture capitalist is short of cash, but as the entrepreneur's signal of sincerity.

A well-functioning market has an array of signaling mechanisms to communicate reliable information about quality. Signaling can overcome the problem of low-quality goods driving out high-quality ones, but it does not come for free. The peacock's tail is a burden; the bank's lavish headquarters and the soft-drink maker's expensive ads are a detriment to their bottom line.

*   *   *   *

How can a seller trust buyers to pay what they owe? A novel trick to get deadbeat customers to pay their bills was adopted by Paragon Cable, a New York cable-television company.4 Paragon did not sue delinquents, nor did it cut off their service. Instead, it delivered to their homes nothing but the C-Span programming, with its interminable political speeches, debates, and hearings. This was reportedly an effective bill-collection measure.

Concern for the future is the most basic incentive to induce people to keep their word. If you ask the seller of some item to let you have it on credit, will you get it? You might if what you are buying is some fruit from your neighborhood shop. You will not if it is a car. The difference, obviously, is the amount you can gain by reneging. If the fruit shop is convenient for your shopping, the value of continuing to shop there exceeds the few dollars from reneging. With a car, on the other hand, you gain thousands of dollars from cheating, and since you purchase infrequently, the seller cannot rely on your wish to do business again. Whether honesty is the best policy, then, depends on which is the larger: the future gains from ongoing business or the immediate gains from reneging.

Even where reneging has a higher payoff than the value of any ongoing business with this seller, you might still have an incentive to pay the bill if other sellers would also refuse to do business with you. The value of future business you lose on being blacklisted may deter you from cheating. Concern for your wider reputation provides a further incentive for honest dealing.

For reputational sanctions to exist, word must somehow get around. Gossip, therefore, can have real economic effects. Small groups usually are able to enforce standards of behavior. Floor traders in financial markets "as a group, police themselves," says a trader in sugar futures contracts. When anyone does something wrong, "they just tell the guy, 'You better not do this again. If you do . . . we'll just freeze you out.' "5

In a close-knit community like the floor traders or a traditional village, sanctions may be invoked spontaneously. In fluid societies where people come and go, reputation is harder to establish. An information channel is needed so others learn when a breach has occurred and who caused it. Credit bureaus, for example, serve as information repositories. For most consumers, the knowledge that they risk damaging their credit rating is sufficient incentive to ensure they pay their bills.

The market for fish in the United States used to suffer from the take-the-money-and-run syndrome. Wholesalers would send shipments of fish to out-of-state buyers only to have the checks bounce. The buyers could easily find other sellers and so could get away with reneging. Observing this, Neal Workman, an entrepreneur in Portland, Maine, formed a firm called GoFish to act as a debt-collection agency for the wholesalers. He soon realized that he could go beyond collecting debts because there was unused value in the information he was gathering. "You can only collect the bill once," he remarked. "You can sell the information about the guy that doesn't pay over and over and over."[6] GoFish began using the internet to provide subscribers with instant credit information about fish buyers. By this simple device, merely posting information, Workman reshaped the marketplace incentives. Buyers now had to pay their bills if they wanted to continue buying fish. This not only was profitable for GoFish but also improved the workings of the market overall.

In the New York wholesale diamond trade, dealers pass among themselves bags of diamonds worth millions of dollars, without written contracts. A handshake with the words *mazal u'brache*—"with luck and a blessing"—creates a binding agreement. The oral contracts work in part because the dealers are mostly Hassidic Jews, sharing a common outlook. With such large sums at stake, however, individual relationships would not provide a weighty sanction. The diamond marketplace is designed so that anyone who breaches a contract loses the future business not only of the person cheated but also of all the other diamond traders. The Diamond Dealers Club organizes the sanctioning. On joining, a new member agrees to submit all disputes to the club's arbitration. Members who breach contracts may be fined or excluded from trading for up to twenty days. Unpaid fines are posted for all to see. In the extreme, a member may be expelled from the club and thus from diamond dealing.[7] To last in the business, a diamond trader must be honest.

In Mexico, the footwear trade is regulated by the shoe manufacturers' trade association, which maintains a database on the retailers who buy from its members. If a retailer fails to pay a bill, it is recorded in the database for any member to look up. Knowing that such information will be available, a retailer is less likely to renege on a contract. This is an old device. In medieval Europe, merchant guilds provided the same contractual assurance for their members.[8]

Part of the service that online business-to-business exchanges offer is assurance. In the chemicals industry, for example, online exchanges allow buyers of industrial chemicals, from petrochemicals to plastics, to find suppliers anywhere in the world. Without trust, there would be no such market; buyers would buy the way they used to buy, from trading partners with whom they had built up long-standing relationships. "The average size of a transaction is in the $200,000 range," said John Beasley, head of ChemConnect, a chemicals exchange. "To complete a transaction online of that size, you must feel confident that the party is going to do what they say."[9] An exchange's competitive edge comes from its ability to assure its buyers that sellers will deliver quality goods on time, and to assure its sellers that buyers will pay their bills. Thus, most online exchanges screen the firms who use their services, and take action whenever a member reneges on a deal with another member.

"To live outside the law you must be honest," Bob Dylan sang in "Absolutely Sweet Marie." A well-designed market has a range of devices to keep track of reputations. Spreading the word about dishonest behavior is enough to keep most people honest most of the time.

*   *   *   *

In Vietnam, a lot of business is based solely on people's word. "We have no commercial law to settle disputes between enterprises," said Huynh Buu Son, a Ho Chi Minh City banker. "When businessmen sign contracts, they can't rely on legal texts, which allows them easily to cheat one another."

Beginning with the reforms of the mid-1980s, there was a resurgence of the private sector. By the early 1990s, small manufacturing businesses were booming. The Vietnam government's policies were not business-friendly, so entrepreneurs had to create the rules of the game for themselves. For Vietnam's private sector to be so dynamic, there must have existed some means of contractual assurance. Unable to use the courts, the entrepreneurs relied on their own devices.

Disputes were prevented partly by the threat of loss of future business. The sanction for nonpayment of a debt was to cut off further dealings with the debtor, though the entrepreneurs tried to prevent disputes from getting to this point. If a debt was not paid, one manager said, he "negotiates patiently." Getting money repaid, "is an art, which is very difficult to explain."

People in the same line of business would meet each other every day in teahouses and bars. An aluminum-goods producer said that when he meets fellow producers, they discuss the reliability of particular customers. Another, making steel products, said he meets other businesspeople every day to exchange information about customers. These regular meetings, he said, "create an ethic in doing business which helps the market work." If a customer cheated a manufacturer, the others would hear about it and might blacklist the debtor.

The entrepreneurs structured deals so as to limit their risks. When they saw a risk that the buyer might renege—when producing goods to order, for example, or selling to a customer in a distant city—they insisted on payment in advance. For long-distance transactions, the bus driver who delivered the product sometimes acted as the customer's representative, transferring the customer's money to the producer and in effect being a financial intermediary, a guarantor of payment.

A firm reduced the likelihood of disputes by choosing its partners well. The entrepreneurs carefully investigated trading partners. "The good customer is not one who pays a high price for your product," said one, "but one who is honest and implements his commitment with you." Many never had a dispute with a customer because of the effort they put into checking their customers' "financial capability and personality." Before beginning trading, one said, he investigated trading partners "carefully through friends, relations, other suppliers and customers." Nonmarket ties of family, clan, and friendship undergirded the market relationships.

That family ties matter in Asian business is not news. But while family networks sometimes helped to get a trading relationship started, they were not essential. About half of a sample of entrepreneurs said they had had no prior connections with the businesses that were to become long-standing trading partners. Each firm's own research acted in place of preexisting connections. Managers said they learned about a potential trading partners' reliability by directly visiting its factory or store. One said, "The best way to assure the quality and reliability of the supplier is to visit his site to investigate, measure, and test the quality of the materials." Another said, "The way to evaluate suppliers' reliability is to visit them frequently and test what they make."[10]

Trading relationships in Vietnam developed quite readily in response to the need for some contractual assurance. Self-help substituted for the missing legal system.

* * * *

Firms can do surprisingly well, then, without using the law of contract. Does this mean that the courts are unnecessary? Are informal relationships all that is needed to ensure that people live up to their obligations? Common sense says the answer must be no.

Some deals cannot work under informal contracting; they can be done only with the support of the law. "Where large sums of money are concerned, it is advisable to trust nobody," remarked Agatha Christie. The gain from taking the money and running may exceed any cost to one's reputation. For a transaction with a large upfront investment that yields a return only after a long delay, the law is needed.

Louis B. Mayer, the movie mogul, said, "An oral contract isn't worth the paper it is written on." He overstated things; as we have seen, oral contracts can work. But a movie star promised 5 percent of the gross would be well advised to get a watertight contract, for if the film turns out to be a blockbuster, the studio may try to wriggle out of the deal. For some transactions, there is no substitute for the law.

Where the law works smoothly, sellers and buyers need not fear getting shortchanged; they can sue for damages. But no legal system works perfectly. A contract does not necessarily provide unshakeable assurance. Contrary to the old saw, it is not always the case that a contract is a contract.

In some poor countries the law is almost unusable. Vietnam is extreme. In some other countries the courts exist but are so overloaded that it is often not worth the effort to use them to try to enforce a contract. In India there are 25 million contract-dispute cases pending. Civil cases usually take ten years or more to come to a decision. "We are a poor country, immersed in debt, and it takes money to get more courthouses, equipment and staff," according to Ram Jethmalani, an Indian cabinet minister. "I'm told we need five times as many judges, but I don't know where we'd put them."[11]

Even in countries with excellent legal systems, the law does not work frictionlessly. To go to the courts you have to pay lawyers' fees and be prepared for a lengthy process to an unpredictable end. Sometimes it is not worth it. If your trading partners know it would not pay you to sue, the law provides no basis for you to rely on them. The court may be unable to evaluate whether contractual commitments have been met. It may be impossible for an aggrieved party to provide legally acceptable proof that a contract has been breached. In complicated disputes involving high-technology production, for example, judging whether a product was made to specifications can hinge on arcane assessments. The law is useless if one cannot prove that a contract was breached. Contracting everywhere rests partly on relationships.

Essential as a good legal system is, it cannot generate the level of confidence that markets need. Informal means of contractual assurance are also needed.

We can see the interplay of formal and informal rule enforcement in sports. Compared with business, the issues in sports are relatively straightforward. The formal rules are clearly defined and easily implemented. The referee makes instant decisions, and there is no waiting for a court to judge a dispute. Even in sports, however, there is a place for informal mechanisms.

Rugby, for example, has potential for violence. The tackles are as fierce as in American football, but the players wear no protective equipment. A feature of the game is the ruck, in which players compete for the ball following a tackle. A sadistic player could aim a kick at a prone player's head or abdomen. The rules are of limited use in stopping brutality, for it would be easy to avoid detection by the referee. It is the possibility of self-enforcement that makes rugby relatively safe. The would-be perpetrator knows that he himself will soon be at the bottom of a ruck. This tends to be persuasive.

Baseball provides a similar test of self-enforcement. Fastball pitchers on occasion throw "bean balls" deliberately aimed at the batter's head. The pitcher claims innocence, of course: the ball just slipped from his fingers. (Though as an opposing batters said of the Yankees' Roger Clemens, notorious for his penchant for hitting batters with balls pitched inside, "Funny, he's not wild outside.") In an attempt to deter dangerous pitches, the league introduced the "warning" rule. After a bean ball is thrown, the umpire issues a warning; if another bean ball is thrown by either side, the second pitcher and his manager are ejected from the game. Old-timers' wisdom has it that the warning rule has actually made it more likely that pitchers will aim at batters. Before, managers like Leo Durocher would instantly order their pitchers to retaliate with bean balls of their own. Nowadays, a pitcher who throws a bean ball can get away with a warning, but his opponent cannot retaliate. Baseball's formal rule, arguably, is inhibiting a useful informal rule. The effect of the warning rule may be the opposite of what was intended. If retaliation were seen to be certain, there would probably be fewer "accidental" high, inside pitches.

In business, as in sports, the incentive to behave well rests on both formal and informal rules. The courts have blind spots and can be cumbersome. Market participants supplement the law of contract by developing their own self-enforcing mechanisms. Sometimes these mechanisms are quite deliberately designed, as I will discuss next.

※　　※　　※　　※

A crisis in U.S. industry followed the influx of imports in the 1980s and 1990s. When imports were less of a factor, firms in industries like the automobile industry, putting little competitive pressure on each other, had an easy life. When the imports brought new competition, their comfortable life was shattered and they suddenly had to scramble to become leaner and more efficient. They rediscovered the efficiencies that come from using the market. Some inputs, they found, could be procured more cheaply from outside firms than from in-house manufacturing facilities. Firms such as Xerox, Boeing, Motorola, Ford, and Chrysler changed the way they dealt with their suppliers. In setting the rules for their own market for inputs, they were effecting a kind of market design.

Some parts of the production chain have always been contracted out. Car makers, for example, have traditionally procured tires externally. Tire makers like Michelin built their competitive edge on years of innovation and reliable products. When the car makers started to think about other inputs they could outsource, though, they realized they needed a higher level of reliance.

In contracting out, the manufacturer places faith in its suppliers. A supplier that does not deliver on time or delivers substandard parts could harm the manufacturer, by slowing its assembly line or even bringing it to a halt. The courts may be too slow to remedy the problems caused by late deliveries. They may be unable to sanction substandard inputs if evaluating quality requires expert judgment. To ensure that suppliers reliably deliver quality goods, the manufacturer must put in self-enforcing mechanisms.

The suppliers also place faith in the manufacturer.[12] Imagine your firm makes car parts. A car maker is about to launch a new model and wants to subcontract the chassis. Since the chassis is unique to this model, to build it your firm must retool the factory. A little forethought will make you wary of making such a specific investment, for it will put you in a vulnerable position. Look ahead to after you have retooled. The price per chassis agreed at the outset covered your investment costs. Now the car maker, knowing your retooled machines are not usable for anything else, might demand the price be lowered. If the new price covers your operating costs (but not your retooling), it is in your interest to accept the new price rather than have the machinery sit idle. Fearing being held up in this way, you might not agree to the contract in the first place. (If the contract was watertight, such reneging would be ruled out, but contracts usually leave some opening for renegotiation, for it is impossible to anticipate all contingencies.) If all suppliers distrust the car maker, it will be unable to persuade them to make the specific investment, so the car maker will have to do it itself and produce the chassis in-house—even when an outside firm could have done the work more cheaply.

The switch to outsourcing more meant outsourcing some tasks involving specific investments. To achieve this, the manufacturers needed to make credible commitments to the suppliers. In some cases there was mutual hostility, from years of broken promises. The manufacturers had to overcome the suppliers' mistrust.

In order to contract out more work, the manufacturers reduced the number of suppliers they dealt with directly: Xerox cut them from six thousand to four hundred. This may sound backward, but it is part of switching from short-term contracting to long-term relationships. To maintain a relationship, as the Vietnamese managers attested, you must pay close attention to your suppliers, which you can do only with a limited number. The selected suppliers, usually the more established ones, were assured that they would keep their privileged status as long as they performed well. They took over the burden of managing the remaining suppliers, creating a supplier hierarchy.

Once the suppliers came to view a manufacturer as genuinely committed to outsourcing, the commitment became self-sustaining: the reliance on outsourcing in itself set the manufacturer's incentives right. The need to get still further specific investments made was enough to deter that manufacturer from acting myopically, for only if it was seen to be trustworthy would other suppliers make the investments.

On the suppliers' side, the incentives came from the prospect of further contracts. Before, a new contract went to whichever supplier bid the lowest. Now, the manufacturer's policy was to favor the incumbent supplier: if the supplier did a good job, it could count on the manufacturer renewing its contract.

A gushing 1994 article in *Fortune* magazine entitled "The New Golden Rule of Business" proclaimed the new kind of supplier relationship. "It's like a marriage," it reported a purchasing executive for a major corporation saying, and concluded, "U.S. companies are learning to cooperate in order to take on the real competition."

The newly cooperative relationships improved quality and lowered costs. Tom Stallkamp, a purchasing manager at Chrysler, speaking of the early 1990s, said, "For the first time in our history, we were cordially exchanging ideas with our suppliers on how to make our companies more productive." Manufacturers coached their suppliers in production and management techniques. They involved them early in the design of new models. Suppliers in turn shared their ideas on how to cut costs. They timed deliveries to suit the manufacturers' production schedules. Some manufacturers ceased inspecting goods as they arrived from the suppliers; instead they sent them directly into their production line, simply expecting the supplier to produce them defect-free.

The supplier-manufacturer transactions illustrate the relative roles of legal contracts and relationships. In a 1997 survey of purchasing executives, two-thirds agreed with the statement that "because U.S. companies have changed their methods of dealing with suppliers, the incidence of serious supplier disputes has declined dramatically." According to the survey, less than a fifth of serious disputes with suppliers were ending up in court. As a purchasing manager said, if an issue comes up, you telephone your counterpart "and deal with the problem. You don't read legalistic clauses at each other if you ever want to do business again."[13]

*　　*　　*　　*

"The freedom and extent of human commerce depend entirely on a fidelity with regard to promises," said David Hume in 1739. Two and a half centuries later, Kenneth Arrow said, "Virtually every commercial transaction has within itself an element of trust, certainly any transaction conducted over a period of time." As a result, "much of the economic backwardness in the world can be explained by a lack of mutual confidence."[14]

A well-designed market has a range of mechanisms to build mutual confidence. Contracting rests not only on the courts but also on informal devices based on reputation. Information must flow if reputational incentives are to work. Private sector organizations like trade associations, intermediary firms, and credit bureaus help with contracting, by spreading information about those who breach contracts and sometimes by organizing a collective blacklist of them. These informal devices complement the legal system in inducing people to keep their word.

SIX

⁙

To the Best Bidder

While Tokyo sleeps, the fish market at Tsukiji is buzzing. Starting in the early hours of each working day, seafood fetching around $25 million is auctioned. Tsukiji is not set up for tourists—you have to take care to avoid being run over by the miniature trucks carting fish to-and-fro—but if you can drag yourself out of bed that early, it is well worth seeing. Displayed for sale are some 450 different species. There are sea urchins, blowfish, live eels and shrimp, octopus, squid—all kinds of ocean and freshwater fish, fresh, frozen, dried, and smoked.

The tuna auctions are the highlight. The sleek silver tuna, three thousand or so of them, are laid out on pallets by the sellers, affiliates of the seven large fishery companies that supply Tsukiji with seafood. The wholesale buyers examine each tuna through its "window," a small cut in the tail, to assess its suitability for sashimi and sushi. Half an hour is allowed for this inspection, then the auctions begin. The auctioneers prod the bids upward, chanting in a peculiar fishmongers' form of Japanese. The buyers bid silently, using hand gestures. They instantly counter each other's bids, so it takes just seconds to sell a tuna worth up to $15,000. The auctions are over by 7:00 A.M. Having sold perhaps $10 million worth of tuna in an hour and a half, the auctioneers go off to restaurants across the street for a breakfast of sushi. Meanwhile, the buyers take the tuna to their own stalls in the outer rim of the marketplace, where they slice them up and sell the cuts to buyers from fish shops, supermarkets, and restaurants.[1]

Tsukiji facilitates Tokyo's wholesale fish trade. If the marketplace did not exist, the buyers and sellers would have to separately negotiate one-on-one deals, a cumbersome way to transact. For buyers, Tsukiji shows the range of goods available from the various fishery companies. For sellers, the auctions speedily reveal how much the buyers are willing to pay. The competitive market provides an efficient way of arranging trades.

*   *   *   *

Let us compare bargaining and competition in a little more detail. The value of fish fluctuates from day to day, depending on the vagaries of consumer demand and the size of the catch. With no objective basis for establishing value, negotiating a price could be frustrating. Imagine a buyer and a seller bargaining over the price of a tuna. The buyer has calculated that the most he should pay (that is, what he will earn reselling it in pieces) is $8,000. The seller has calculated that the least she should accept (her cost of supplying it plus a return on her effort) is $6,000. A trade would create a net gain of $2,000. The seller does not know the maximum the buyer will pay, and the buyer does not know the seller's minimum.

Suppose first that the buyer and seller are locked in together. They deal with each other or not at all. The price could be as low as the seller's cutoff of $6,000 or as high as the buyer's cutoff of $8,000. With any price in this range, both the buyer and the seller are better off than if they had no deal. There is no unique price the bargaining will necessarily reach. This indeterminacy leads each to try for a larger share of the pie.

The price that emerges from the haggling reflects their relative bargaining power. Threats, feints, and bluffs are sources of bargaining advantage. The buyer pretends he does not have much need for the tuna, and the seller acts as if her "rock-bottom price" is high. Each takes a calculated risk, for such intransigence could cause the negotiations to break down; they might bluff their way into positions from which they cannot retreat. Even if agreement is reached, it might be only after long drawn-out negotiations, with each testing the other's patience by holding out for a better deal. Both lose if there is a delay or impasse—but that can happen as an unintended consequence of hard bargaining.

Now let us change the story by supposing our buyer can buy from either of two sellers. One's cost of supplying the tuna is $6,000; the other's is $6,500. (To keep the story simple, assume the buyer wants a single tuna, and the sellers' tuna are identical.) Eschewing bargaining tricks, the buyer merely accepts offers from the two sellers, playing each off against the other. If one offers $7,500, he invites the other to undercut it. This seller willingly complies, offering, say, $7,400. The mutual undercutting continues until the offered price falls to $6,500, at which point the seller with the higher cost drops out of the competition.

There is no indeterminacy over the price with competition: it is equal to the higher of the two sellers' costs. Both buyer and seller are satisfied: the buyer's net return (value minus price) is $1,500 and the seller's net return (price minus cost) is $500. When competition exists, the tactics of bargaining yield little payoff. If one of the sellers tries to bargain hard, the buyer can turn to the other. The buyer, on the other hand, need not go to the trouble of haggling, since the competitive process is at work in his favor.

Competition is still more advantageous to the buyer when there are more sellers. If there are three, and the additional one's cost is $5,500, the price is driven down to $6,000. In general, the price under competition is the second-lowest cost, for that is where the competition stops. As the number of competitors increases, the gap between the lowest and second-lowest cost shrinks, so the price approaches the cost of the most efficient seller. More competition brings lower prices.[2]

Laboratory experiments have been used to compare bargaining with competition. In one such study, undergraduate students were asked to divide $10. In the bargaining version, the students were paired off. One made a proposal of how to divide the money, and the other could accept or reject the proposal. Acceptance meant the money was split between the two as proposed; rejection meant neither got anything. In the competitive version, a single seller received bids of up to $10 from up to nine buyers and accepted the highest one. The seller then was paid the sum bid and the successful bidder the remainder of the $10. In the bargaining experiments, the money usually was roughly evenly divided, though often with somewhat more than a half going to the proposer. Breakdown of the bargaining, with both bargainers receiving nothing, was surprisingly common: it occurred in one-fourth of the negotiations. In the competition experiments, the money was always successfully divided, and the bids were driven down to a few cents, meaning the seller got most of the money.[3]

Competition, then, has two effects. It changes the balance of bargaining power. The buyer does better facing two potential sellers than one, and still better facing ten. We did not need any fancy theory to tell us that, but there is also a less obvious effect. Competition lowers transaction costs, by doing away with the tough bargaining strategies that can delay—or defeat—an agreement. The competitive process ensures that the seller who makes the sale is the one with the lowest cost; competition thereby directs the buyer to the most efficient seller.

A seller unconstrained by competition can charge a markup above production cost. Competition between sellers drives the price down to the second-lowest production cost; when many sellers are competing, this production cost is close to that of the most efficient producer. Competition gets prices right, in the sense that the price paid measures the actual cost of supplying the item.

Over time, competition has further cost-lowering effects. It serves to discipline firms. A firm that has lower costs than its rivals is rewarded by extra sales. Another firm that persistently has higher costs either makes itself more efficient or goes out of business. The competitive process relentlessly drives costs down: it pressures firms to innovate so as to become more efficient, and its survival-of-the-fittest logic winnows out the inefficient firms. This works to the benefit of not only buyers but also the economy overall.

This is not to say that competition eliminates all transaction costs. In the Tsukiji market, for example, the three hundred or so buyers spend half an hour examining the tuna prior to bidding. All the buyers are evaluating exactly the same thing, the freshness and quality of the tuna. As an alternative, the auctioneers could develop a uniform grading scale and mark each tuna with its grade, economizing on the duplicative inspection. An absence of trust is presumably the reason why the auction house has not developed a grading scheme: the bidders will not risk thousands of dollars on the auctioneer's word.

Competition among buyers, as we will see next, similarly reveals information about how highly they value the goods.

*　　*　　*　　*

The art world uses competitive markets to measure value. An auction in Paris in the 1890s of works by Gauguin, Cézanne, and others helped establish postimpressionist art. "The critics perceived the auction as a confirmation of the art's importance," said art historian Michael FitzGerald, "that their own aesthetic evaluations could not confer." As Renoir earlier said, "There's only one indicator for telling the value of paintings, and that is the sale room."

There are two distinct types of art buyer, according to Hong Kong art dealer Maggie Fung. "One says 'I like it' and has to have it." The other says, "I am not sure I like it, I don't really understand it, but this guy is going to be famous."[4] In the first case (which economic theorists label "private values"), each bidder attaches a different, subjective value to the item for sale. They all know exactly how much it is worth to themselves, but not how highly the others value it. In the other case (which the theorists label "common value"), the buyers' valuations are objective: they are trying to assess the same thing, the painter's future marketability. The artwork is worth the same no matter who wins it, but at the time of bidding no one knows what this value is; each has an estimate that is subject to error. The competition works differently depending on which type of buyers are bidding.

Auction houses like Sotheby's and Christie's sell artworks using an open auction, in which the bidders raise their bids until only one bidder remains. Imagine you are bidding for a painting in such an auction, and that you know exactly how much you are prepared to pay for it (the private-values case). Your best strategy is to stay in the bidding until the price reaches your valuation, and then to drop out. If you ceased bidding earlier, you would risk seeing the painting sell for less than you value it; if you stayed in the bidding beyond that level, you would risk buying it and paying more than it is worth to you. If all of the bidders follow this strategy, then you end up being the winner only if you value the painting more than your rivals. The bidding stops at the price at which the second-last bidder drops out, so the price you pay is the second highest of the valuations.

The competitive process reveals information. After the auction, the seller knows which of the bidders values the item the most, and the price gives an estimate of its value. It is an underestimate, since the price is the second-highest valuation. But if the number of bidders is reasonably large, the bidding competition drives the price up close to the winner's valuation.

The logic of bidding is less straightforward when the item's value is common rather than private. There is an additional twist because the bidders have uncertain estimates of the common value. They risk falling into the trap of the "winner's curse": learning too late that the price has gone higher than the item is worth. If they are all knowledgeable, then the best estimate is something like the average of their valuations. The winning bid, of course, is higher than the average bid. The winner is likely to be the bidder whose estimate is the most optimistic, probably overoptimistic.

In *The Decline and Fall of the Roman Empire*, Edward Gibbon described a dramatic form of winner's curse. In the first century A.D., the entire Roman Empire was put up for sale. After mounting a coup against the emperor Pertinax, the army "proclaimed that the Roman world was to be disposed of to the best bidder by public auction." Two rich Romans bid against each other. "The unworthy negotiation was transacted by faithful emissaries, who passed alternately from one candidate to the other, and acquainted each of them with the offers of his rival."[5] The highest bidder, Didius, was declared emperor. He did not enjoy the perquisites of office for long, though, as he was assassinated shortly afterward. His head, mounted on a spear, was paraded through the streets of Rome.

In any auction, unwary bidders risk overestimating the value of winning (though rarely as badly as Didius). Bidders sometimes get caught up in the excitement of an auction and pay too much. But they need not be fooled. Experienced bidders avoid the winner's curse by bidding cautiously: they recognize they will win only if they have relatively high value estimates and bid accordingly lower. Laboratory experiments corroborate this: the subjects bid too high initially, but as they become more practiced, they tend to adjust and avoid overbidding. Alert winners are not cursed.[6]

In literary auctions, publishers bid for manuscripts by big-name authors. Hillary Clinton's account of her eight years in the White House fetched a reported $8 million in an open auction among eight publishers. The bidders were betting on the sales potential of her unwritten book, so this was a common-value situation. The size of the winning bid implies the winner, Simon and Schuster, anticipated that sales would exceed a million copies.

Literary auctions are susceptible to the winner's curse, some believe. "People are bidding furiously against each other," said John Sterling of Henry Holt, "doing crazy things, buying for too much money, and the next day suffering buyer's regret, asking themselves, 'Why did I buy that?' " This analysis is questionable. Suffering buyer's regret, auction after auction, would indicate a curious inability to learn from mistakes. An alternative analysis is that the publishers know exactly what they are doing, and the furious bidding is quite rational. Aware that their estimates of the book's value are highly uncertain, the publishers start by bidding warily. As the auction proceeds, they see how much the others are willing to pay, so they gain confidence in their own evaluations. As agent Elyse Cheney said, "you can gather steam, and lots of publishers get up their courage and spend." After winning the bidding for the Hillary Clinton book, David Rosenthal of Simon and Schuster said he was satisfied with the deal. "We would not have done it if there wasn't an excellent chance of its being very profitable."

Molly Friedrich, an agent, "adores auctions." As she said, "There's nothing more fun than having a good auction, knowing you auctioned a book well, with no dishonesty and everyone happy. You can settle into bed that night utterly validated as an agent." Despite such views, the traditional way of running these sales, with the bidders being told each others' bids and able to go on raising their bids as long as they choose, has begun to be supplanted by the "best-bid" method, which is the same as the sealed bidding used in government procurement: the author's agent invites a few publishers to submit a single bid, and the highest bidder immediately gets the book.

Some agents like the best-bid method because of its speed: it takes a few hours, whereas an auction can last a week or more as the price creeps up. "The best bid is becoming a more popular option than in the past," said Carolyn Reidy of Simon and Schuster, "because some of the agents are hoping to get the publisher's highest price right off the bat rather than have them bid a little more than someone else, slowly, which is not always to the agents' benefit." Those agents are mistaken. By using the best-bid method they are acting against their authors' interests, for it would usually yield a lower price than the traditional auction.[7]

With a single bid, the publishers do not in fact offer the highest price they would pay—because of the winner's curse. They fear finding, too late, that they have bid hundreds of thousands of dollars more than anyone else, which would indicate they had probably overestimated the book's sales potential. Anticipating the dismay of leaving money on the table, they underbid—as they should. With an open auction, by contrast, the winner knows there was another who was willing to pay almost as much. The price reached by the open auction, given experienced bidders, is a truer measure of the book's value than the overcautious price of the best-bid method.

The term *winner's curse* originated in the oil industry, where hundreds of millions of dollars are bid for drilling rights. At the time of bidding, the oil companies have geological estimates of the size of the oil deposit, but they are subject to error and the well may even be dry: this is a common-value situation. Industry lore used to have it that the bids would routinely go beyond the value of the oil in the tract. With millions of dollars at stake, however, there is reason to be skeptical that well-paid executives would repeatedly make the same blunder. The statistical evidence corroborates this skepticism: oil tracts won at auction on average earn a healthy return on their investment.[8]

The explosion of the price of sports broadcasting rights shows the power of competition. In 1964, Pete Rozelle, the commissioner of the National Football League, persuaded the team owners to allow the league to negotiate a joint television agreement on their behalf, rather than each team having its own local deal. The first national television contract, a two-year $28 million deal with CBS, was far higher than ever before. Where before the broadcasters played one team off against another, the league now obtained monopoly power from negotiating as a bloc. Huge further price increases followed.

New bidders, ESPN and Fox, broke up the cozy three-network setup and brought genuine bidding competition. By 1998, broadcasters were paying the league over $2 billion per year. English soccer saw a similar change. In the late 1980s, television rights for all of English soccer were negotiated for £2.5 million. Then, an upstart television provider, BSkyB, injected some bidding competition, to such an extent that in 1992, a single league, the Premier League, contracted with it for £45 million per year; in 2000 the bidding for a three-year deal rocketed to £537 million per year.[9]

These prices seem ludicrous to some. In the frenzy of the bidding, the critics say, the television executives bid far above real value. If that were true, we should question their competence (as should their shareholders). But this interpretation is unlikely to be correct. Rather, these prices show the rest of us what the television executives already knew—sports broadcasting is enormously lucrative. Before there was competition, that knowledge stayed with the broadcasters—who were content, no doubt, to keep it to themselves. The arrival of competition forced the insiders to reveal the value of the television rights, and to pass much of that value on to the sports leagues.

"I paid too much for it," the movie director Sam Goldwyn once remarked, "but it's worth it." When buyers are savvy, prices measure value. Each individual's estimate may be highly imperfect, but the final price is a good estimate of value. The competitive process serves to aggregate and reveal scattered information.[10]

*   *   *   *

The surest route to a competitive market is the arrival of new firms. If a monopoly exists, it charges high prices and earns abnormally high profits—higher than those prevailing in the rest of the economy. Such profits attract new firms into this line of activity, meaning the ertswhile monopolist now faces competition, and prices fall. Monopoly contains the seeds of its own destruction.

Barriers to the creation of new firms, however, can sometimes prevent competition from breaking out. In some industries, large firms have such an advantage as to stymie the market forces that normally generate competition. A firm holding patents is protected; an incumbent might lock up raw material supplies or product distribution channels. It is rare but not unknown for firms to have the benefit of persistent entry barriers. In such industries, monopoly and its high prices and low quality could prevail.

Governments have a checkered record over such entry barriers. Often the state itself is the culprit, preventing new firms from setting up. Entrepreneurs must apply for business licenses, to establish that their company's name is unique and provide proof of their start-up capital; then they must file with the tax and labor authorities. In Austria, setting up a new business takes an entrepreneur half a year and costs nearly $12,000 in official fees. In Mexico it takes over four months and costs about $2,500.[11] In Egypt and Bolivia the cost of working through the official licensing procedures adds up to more than twice the level of per capita income.

A large friction is built into the nation's markets by government restrictions of this magnitude. They reduce competition. Some licensing regulations are warranted in principle. Firms must be registered for tax purposes, and it may be necessary to verify that they will operate safely and not pollute the environment. Canada illustrates that it is possible to achieve those ends without damaging the economy: it takes just two days and less than $300 for an entrepreneur to get official approval. While the ostensible reason for regulating entrepreneurship is to protect consumers from unscrupulous firms or shoddy products, the real effect of onerous registration requirements is to reduce competition and increase the prices consumers pay. Incumbent firms usually have more resources at their disposal than their putative competitors, so they lobby for regulation that shelters them from competition.

It is not only the government, though, that erects barriers to new firms. In some industries natural impediments exist. Where there are economies of scale, so the unit cost of production falls as the volume of production rises, it is sometimes hard for an upstart competitor to get a foothold. The sheer size of the incumbents is a hurdle. In such industries there occasionally may be a role for state intervention to keep competition alive. Most successful market economies have antitrust laws and a regulatory authority to implement them. Laws against price-fixing safeguard buyers against conspiracies among firms to hike prices to monopoly levels. Laws governing mergers and takeovers ensure that no firm can buy its way into a dominant position and use its financial muscle to frighten off potential competitors.

The Microsoft Corporation was adjudged in April 2000 to have violated the U.S. antitrust laws (a decision that was affirmed on appeal in July 2001). It had built a monopoly in the operating-system market, preventing Netscape, Java, and others from becoming established as alternative platforms. Judge Thomas Penfield Jackson ruled that "Microsoft mounted a deliberate assault upon entrepreneurial efforts that, left to rise or fall on their own merits, could well have enabled the introduction of competition into the market" for operating systems.[12] He concluded that Microsoft had kept "an oppressive thumb on the scale of competitive fortune."

A 1980s equivalent of the Microsoft case was the court-ordered end to the

American Telephone &Telegraph Company's monopoly. In its early days the telephone industry was monopolized for a good reason: the high cost of setting up a network meant competition would have been wastefully duplicative. By the start of the 1980s, however, new technologies meant long-distance telephone services need not have only a single carrier. But AT&T was such a strong incumbent that market forces alone would not have brought any new competitors. Ending the telephone monopoly required government action. At the time it was controversial: "If it ain't broke, don't fix it," AT&T's supporters said. Hindsight shows the antitrust authorities were right to intervene, as the breakup of AT&T quickened innovation and lowered long-distance prices.

※　　※　　※　　※

Competition can be liberating. In *The Cherry Orchard*, Anton Chekhov conveys the thrill of winning. The estate of impoverished aristocrats (the cherry orchard of the title) was auctioned off. Lopakhin, a businessman of humble origins, described the bidding: "I bid forty. Him—forty-five. Me—fifty-five. So he's going up in fives, me in tens . . . Well that was that. I bid the mortgage plus ninety, and there it stayed. So now the cherry orchard is mine! Mine! Great God in heaven—the cherry orchard is mine! Tell me I'm drunk—I'm out of my mind—tell me it's all an illusion."[13] Lopakhin was excited because he had bought the estate where his father had been a serf. The competitive market signified changing times.

Competition sets prices right, inducing resources to flow to their highest-value uses. It disciplines those competing to operate efficiently. It generates information about demands and supplies. It brings lower transaction costs than the alternative of case-by-case bargaining does. Creating the conditions for active competition is one of the main tasks of market design.

SEVEN

⣿

Come Bid!

"Come bid . . . Come buy!" cries Sellem the auctioneer in the opera *The Rake's Progress*, as he works the crowd into a bidding frenzy.[1] Auctioning a marble bust, he chants,

> *—Fifteen—and a half—*
> *three-quarters—sixteen—seventeen—*
> *going at seventeen*
> *—going—going—*
> *gone!*

Every day, thousands of similar scenes recur at internet auction sites—except with a computer program acting as the auctioneer.

During the brief history of electronic auctions, from 1994, markets have been created in front of us as entrepreneurs have devised new ways of transacting. The public sector also has turned to using auctions to allocate publicly owned resources like the electromagnetic spectrum. These novel auctions raise some knotty design problems. Economic theory helps us understand how they work, and is being used in designing further new selling mechanisms.

*   *   *   *

Many transactions, such as in a supermarket or a department store, take place at prices fixed by the seller. An auction, by contrast, is interactive: the seller puts the pricing in the hands of the potential buyers and relies on the competition among them to get an acceptable price. Why are some items auctioned while others are sold by posted prices? The difference lies in the degree of uncertainty about the value of the item for sale. Posted prices are used for items that are traded frequently and therefore have a well-established market value. Auctions are used for unique items. How would you fix the price if you were selling Jane Austen's handwritten draft of *Pride and Prejudice*, say, or the costumes the Beatles wore on the album cover of *Sergeant Pepper's Lonely Hearts Club Band*? For goods that are standardized but whose value fluctuates, auctions are used at the primary point of sale to set a benchmark price. The bidding for pork-belly futures in the Chicago Mercantile Exchange serves to establish their current price, based on the traders' hunches about future supply and demand. In the Tsukiji auction, the fish catch varies in quantity and quality from day to day. In the Aalsmeer flower auction, the prices often rise or fall by 20 percent or more from week to week, reflecting the demand and supply vagaries of a perishable commodity. The essence of any auction, then, is that the bidders value the item for sale differently, but no one knows exactly how highly anyone else values it. The seller does not set a price because she does not know what price to set.

Auctions have a long, colorful, and sometimes disgraceful history. The ancient Greeks used them to sell slaves and wives. The growth of internet commerce has reinvigorated them. With their interactive price-setting, auctions are tailor-made for the internet, whose chief feature is its interactivity.

The founders of the online auctioneer eBay set a simple, effective design for their auctions. They did it their way. "We began, ran, and developed our site without the benefit of academic research," said cofounder Jeffrey Skoll. "It was all more 'wing and a prayer' really."[2] Let us imagine being charged with setting up eBay from scratch, and think about how we would go about systematically designing the auction mechanism.

In what form should the bids be accepted? Most auctions use an open auction, as is traditionally used to sell art and antiques, in which the bidders go on topping each others' bids until only one wants to continue. An alternative way of running the bidding is the Dutch auction, used to sell flowers at Aalsmeer, in which the price starts high and falls until a bidder claims the item. Another is the sealed-bid auction, in which there is a single round of sealed bids; the high bidder wins and pays his or her bid. Commercial real estate is sometimes sold this way. A variant is the second-price auction, in which there is a single round of bidding and the high bidder wins, but unlike first-price auctions, the price paid is the second-highest bid. Second-price auctions are used for selling stamps.

eBay chose open auctions. Economic theory endorses this decision: the open auction yields, on average, a price that is closer to the item's true value than do the other forms of auction.3 This is because bidders have more information in an open auction. If you win, the level of your winning bid reflects others' bids as well your own prior estimate of the item's value. Shrewd bidders who fear the winner's curse—the tendency for the high bidder to be the one who most overestimates the value of winning—bid cautiously to avoid overpaying. The information about others' bids revealed in an open auction makes you less worried about the winner's curse than when bids are sealed, and so you tend to bid higher. Most of the time, sellers get a better price with open auctions.

How can eBay economize on the bidders' time and attention? An ordinary open auction would require bidders to stay and watch it. Bidders with their own lives to lead may be unable to focus on it. eBay solves this problem by having the seller specify a time for the auction to end—usually seven days to the minute after it opens. Whoever has the highest bid at that time wins. Bidders whose time is scarce need log on to the auction only near the closing time.

Solving one problem, the fixed end time, brought a problem of its own, by creating a perverse incentive for bidders. Some wait until a few seconds before the end time, then submit a bid just above the current high bid, trying to leave the other bidders no time to respond. This practice is common enough to have a name, "sniping." (You can even get software to do this automatically for you from companies such as iSnipeit.com, which says its software "allows you to rest easy knowing that your competitors will have literally no time to react to your bid.") This practice works to the seller's disadvantage: it produces lower prices than an open-ended auction would, for the auction might close with some bidders left wanting to bid higher but unable to.

How can sniping be prevented? eBay's solution is to accept proxy bids. Bidders may confidentially tell eBay's automated bidding agent the maximum they are prepared to bid. If the current bid level is smaller than a proxy bid, eBay's computer automatically submits a bid on behalf of the proxy bidder, a small increment above the current high bid. The agent stays in the bidding up to the level of the proxy bid. Thus the proxy bidder could win, depending on the competition, at any price up to the level of the proxy bid. The price the proxy bidder pays is the second-highest bid plus a bid increment.

eBay's proxy bidding does not always succeed in eliminating sniping, however. Savvy bidders still often hold their bids to the last second, in the hope of preventing a bidding war. If they bid early, they may push others' bids up. If they bid late, no bidding competition may ever break out, and the price may stay low.

Amazon.com, eBay's main rival, made a different design choice. Its auctions have no fixed end time. If there are any last-minute bids, the scheduled end time is abandoned and the auction continues until ten minutes pass with no new bids. This feature addresses the problem of sniping: there is no point in trying to sneak a bid in just before the end, for that would automatically extend the auction. In this respect, Amazon's auction design is superior to eBay's, for it is less susceptible to gaming by wily bidders. One study, examining a sample of eBay and Amazon auctions, found that 37 percent of eBay's auctions had bids in the last minute, whereas only 1 percent of Amazon's auctions had them. With ten or twenty bidders competing, sniping is not an issue. If there are just two or three expert bidders, however, an Amazon auction would sometimes bring a higher price than an eBay auction.

Should reserve prices be used, setting a minimum price below which the item will not sell? eBay leaves this up to the seller. Theory says a reserve price is in the seller's interest when the bidding competition is weak. If set at the right level, it can drive the price up higher than the competition would.[4]

How can eBay protect its buyers from fraud or misrepresentation by sellers? Buyers cannot check the quality of the merchandise. A seller, perhaps knowingly, perhaps inadvertently, might represent a worthless painting as the work of a known artist. Shill bidding, under which an accomplice bids up the price in order to create a false idea of the item's value, is not unknown. Occasionally buyers have not received the goods for which they have sent off checks. eBay's clever solution to these problems is to allow regular sellers to establish a reputation for reliability and quality. After an auction eBay asks the buyers to rate the seller, and then posts the ratings and comments online for anyone to see. A seller is given a score that counts the number of favorable and negative comments received. This simple device works; eBay claims fraud affects less than 1 percent of its auctions. A reputation for honest dealing is valuable: bids go significantly higher when the seller has a high rating.[5]

Once eBay became large, however, it had to supplement the reputational mechanism by more formal methods of fraud prevention. Meg Whitman, eBay's chief executive officer, said, "We all had an intuition that as eBay's community of users became more like the size of New York City than the size of Los Gatos, we would have to deal with issues like fraud."[6] eBay hired a former U.S. prosecutor to track down thieves and con artists using the site. Also, firms arose to offer solutions to the problems of online trust. Appraisal companies such as eAppraisals.com offer buyers, for a fee, appraisals of the goods by experts in coins, stamps, antiques, and so on. Escrow companies such as Tradenable will hold a buyer's payment for a fee, until the buyer has received the item satisfactorily.

eBay has a competitive edge over rival auction sites, regardless of the design of its auctions, because of what is called a network externality. An auction site is more valuable to a seller if it already attracts more buyers. In turn, buyers go where the sellers already are, which makes the site still more attractive to sellers. Since eBay was there first, the network externality helps make its success self-perpetuating.

Myriad auction mechanisms can be found on the various online auction sites. Dutch auctions are used to sell containers on oceangoing cargo vessels. Sealed-bid auctions are used for selling vacation time-shares. A few sites allow package bidding. One wine auction site, for example, packages bottles into sets (usually different vintages from a particular vineyard). It then accepts not only bids on the individual bottles but also all-or-nothing bids on the package. If a bid for the package exceeds the total of the high bids for the individual bottles, the package bidder wins.

Hybrid pricing mechanisms—setting prices while allowing some auction-like elements of information generation—are used by online sellers of tickets for air travel and sporting events. Before the internet, fixing ticket prices in advance meant that when demand was unexpectedly low, seats went unfilled on planes and in stadiums. Internet sellers are able to offer deep discounts just before the flight or the game, earning revenue from seats that otherwise would have been empty. Without the instant two-way communication the internet provides, it would be hard to implement this pricing flexibility. The rapid flow of information about consumers' tastes that comes from online ticket sales works in the other direction as well, allowing sellers to set higher-than-normal prices for flights and games that turn out to be especially popular. Techniques known as "yield management" separate price-sensitive customers from price-insensitive customers, allowing the seller to charge a higher price to the latter. Customer-tailored pricing is not new: before the internet, airlines charged lower ticket prices to those who booked a week in advance or were willing to stay over Saturday night, and higher prices to those who wanted the flexibility of last-minute purchases. The internet, however, has brought more tailoring of prices to individual demands.

Buyers often care about more than just the price. Economist Paul Milgrom devised for Perfect Commerce an auction in which sellers compete in other dimensions as well as price.[7] If you are shopping for a photocopier, for example, you might have various requirements: speed, capacity, variable paper size, back-to-back copying, and so on. As well, you care about price, delivery date, and financing. You are flexible in your wishes: you are willing to give up something on one dimension in order to get better terms on another. You type in a wish list, indicating how important each of the different attributes is to you. Potential sellers similarly submit offers specified in all the dimensions. The auction program quickly identifies the seller whose bid best fits your wish list (which is not necessarily the lowest-priced offer). By matching buyers with the suppliers whose capabilities meet their individual needs, and helping them tailor a deal, the mechanism creates value that buyers and sellers share.

A year or so before the first internet auction sites began operating, a series of electronic auctions was already being run, with bids submitted from personal computers over a secure network and posted on the internet for all to see. Electronic commerce began not with eBay and its ilk but, as we will see next, in the public sector.

✻ ✻ ✻ ✻

The leaders of the U.S. telecommunications industry gathered in July 1994 in the ballroom of the Omni Shoreham Hotel in Washington, D.C., to bid in an unprecedented auction. The government was selling licenses to use the electromagnetic spectrum for paging services. (Each license represented a sliver of spectrum waveband over a region of the country.) Giant computer screens showed the current status of the bidding. Curtained booths took up one wall. Bidders had to provide proof of identity before being allowed to enter a booth to bid. Unseen by anyone else, they would key in their secret code and then their bids. After each round of bidding, the new bids were announced, to be greeted by some with cheers and by others with groans of disbelief.

Across from the ballroom was the "war room," from which the Federal Communications Commission (FCC) ran the auction. Security guards at the door permitted only approved people to enter. Computers in the war room registered each bid as it was made. The bid-increment committee (I was one of the three members) filled the role of auctioneer and implemented the rules. Tension ran high from fears that something would go wrong; no one had ever run an auction like this before.

As the bids rose tens of millions of dollars by the hour, the tension in the war room subsided somewhat, while in the ballroom it mounted. Wayne Perry of McCaw Cellular Communications said, "For once, the government is doing a great job of dragging money out of people." David Brock of Metrocall, a paging company, said, "It's a slugfest." The bidders were putting in twelve-hour days. "Every company would get on the phone at night to their headquarters and say, 'We need more money, we need more money,' " said Kathleen Abernathy of Airtouch Paging. "Back at headquarters, people were crunching the numbers."

The auction went on for a week, raising $617 million for ten licenses covering a tiny sliver of spectrum. Several more auctions were subsequently held, for larger chunks of spectrum to be used for mobile telephones, portable fax machines, and wireless computer networks. After the trial run in the Washington hotel, the FCC ran the auctions electronically. As of early 2001 they had fetched a total of $42 billion.

A new market was created with the spectrum auctions. Previously, the government had given the spectrum rights to telephone and broadcasting companies. Initially, licenses were assigned by administrative decision. Prospective license holders filed applications, and the FCC held comparative hearings to decide which applicant was the most worthy. This cumbersome method broke down under a backlog of unassigned licenses. Congress replaced it with lotteries, giving licenses to some lucky applicants. The lotteries succeeded in assigning licenses quickly, but the prospect of windfall gain attracted applicants in droves. There were nearly four hundred thousand applications for cellular licenses. In one not atypical case, some dentists won the right to run cellular-telephone service on Cape Cod; they immediately sold their license to a real telephone company, Southwestern Bell, for $41 million. The value of the licenses the government gave away during the 1980s, according to a Commerce Department estimate, was $46 billion.

Congress could not shrug off such figures, and in 1993 it passed legislation giving the FCC the authority to auction licenses. The FCC was to "design and test multiple alternative methodologies" for competitive bidding. The act specified a range of aims for the auction: achieving an "efficient and intensive use of the electromagnetic spectrum," promoting rapid deployment of new technologies, preventing monopolization of licenses, and ensuring that some licenses go to minority-owned and women-owned companies, small businesses, and rural telephone companies.

The spectrum auctions were large and complex. No one knew at the outset what the licenses were worth. Thousands of licenses were offered, varying in both geographic coverage and the amount of spectrum covered. The bidders included most U.S. telecommunications firms: long-distance, local, and cellular telephone companies and cable-television companies.

The telecommunications companies, seeking guidance on the principles of auctioning, discovered some theory of auctions in esoteric journals like *Econometrica* and the *Journal of Economic Theory*. They then hired the authors of some of those articles as consultants, and the FCC hired me.

Economic theory helped to answer key questions of auction design. Which of the basic forms of bidding should the government use: open bidding or sealed bids? Should the licenses be auctioned in sequence, or all at once in a large simultaneous auction? Should the government allow all-or-nothing bids on license packages, or only bids for individual licenses? How should the auction be structured to promote the interests of minority-owned and other designated firms? How should monopolization of licenses be prevented? Should the government demand royalty payments? Should reserve (or minimum) prices be imposed? How much should the bidders be informed about their competition? Faulty choices over issues such as these could have resulted in a mismatch of licenses to firms, or the government missing out on revenue it could have earned, or the auction in some way breaking down. As Vice President Al Gore said at the opening ceremony of one of the auctions, "They couldn't just go look it up in a book."[8]

The auction the theorists collectively proposed was novel. Given the complexity of the sale, we argued, it would induce more competitive bidding and a better match of licenses to firms than the time-tested alternatives. Despite initial hesitation—"I don't want the FCC to become a beta test site," said FCC official Robert Pepper—the FCC implemented the innovative auction.

＊　　＊　　＊　　＊

Any kind of bidding process would result in better matches of licenses to firms than would allocating the licenses at random, as the U.S. government had done before. But some kinds of auctions work better than others: this was why so much effort went into designing the spectrum auctions. The type of auction the FCC adopted came to be called a *simultaneous ascending auction*.[9] Multiple licenses are open for bidding at the same time and remain open as long as there is bidding on any of the licenses. Bidding occurs over rounds, with the results of each round announced before the start of the next one.

Many detailed rules are needed to support the broad principles of the simultaneous ascending auction. Months of work by FCC officials and the theorist-consultants went into ensuring the auction rules had no gaps that could be exploited by shrewd bidders: the rules cover more than 130 pages.

Among these details are the activity rules. Some bidders like to cautiously wait to see how others bid while not revealing their own intentions. If everyone bid in this way, the auction would take inordinately long to close. The activity rules drove the auction along. Each bidder specifies in advance how many licenses it hopes to win. A bidder is defined as "active" on a particular license if either it has the highest bid from the previous round or it submits a higher bid in the current round. The auction has three stages, each with an unspecified number of rounds. In the first stage a bidder must be active on licenses that add up to one-third of its prespecified total; in the second stage, two-thirds; and in the final stage, all of its prespecified total. If a bidder ever falls short of the required activity level, the number of licenses it is eligible to own shrinks proportionately. Other rules define the size of bid increments, the penalties for bid withdrawal, provisions for waivers from the activity rules, and so on. Bidding in this auction, said the *Wall Street Journal*, was "like playing a dozen hands of billion-dollar poker at once."

Why use a simultaneous ascending auction? Why not use the time-tested method, a sequential auction, in which the licenses are simply offered one after the other? Or why not use the quickest method, offering all the licenses simultaneously in a single round of sealed bids? The main reason is that the licenses are interdependent. For most of the licenses there is a close substitute: a twin license that covers the same region and the same amount of spectrum. Licenses are also complementary: a license may be more valuable if the holder also has the license for a contiguous region.

Some bidders needed to win multiple licenses. In defining the licenses, the FCC divided the United States geographically and the spectrum by waveband, making thousands of licenses. The FCC expected that some bidders would want to aggregate licenses, either geographically (a bidder might want, for example, not northern or southern California alone but both together in a package) or by waveband (putting together two or more licenses to make a larger piece of spectrum). The FCC did not know before the sale how the licenses should be packaged. Different firms wanted different packages. The auction mechanism had to be flexible enough to enable the bidders to construct their own license packages.

Both features of the auction—the *simultaneous* bids and the *ascending* bids—helped ensure that licenses went to the firms best able to use them. The ascending bids, with the bid levels rising as the bidders repeatedly countered their rivals' bids, let bidders see how much their rivals valued each license and which packages they sought. As closing approaches, each bidder knew whether it would likely put together its preferred package and roughly how much it would cost. With all licenses open for bidding simultaneously, a bidder had flexibility to seek whatever license package it wanted and to switch to a backup if its first-choice package became too expensive.

As well as aiding license packaging, the ascending auction allowed bidders to respond to each others' bids, diminishing the winner's curse (the tendency for unthinking bidders to bid the price up beyond actual value). However, with billions of dollars at stake (and, for that matter, having been advised by economists) the bidders probably anticipated the winner's curse by discounting their own value estimates. Seeing the level of the others' bids reduced their fear of the winner's curse and pushed up their bids.

The $42 billion raised over a series of auctions far exceeded any published predictions of the spectrum's value. Before auctioning began, the Office of Management and Budget had estimated that $10 billion would be raised. The industry responded skeptically to this estimate. BellSouth Chairman John Clendenin said, "There is no rational methodology on which that $10 billion was calculated." The government estimate, he asserted, "was sort of pulled out of thin air." MCI Chairman Bert Roberts said, "The government is smoking something to think they are going to get $10 billion for these licenses." To a cynic these responses might have looked disingenuous; after all it was in the industry's interest to talk down the spectrum's value. As it turned out, the government's estimate was actually too low. In terms of the money it raised and the information it revealed about the spectrum's true value, the auction was a success.

What is the government's role in spectrum allocation now that auctioning is used? It still has its regulatory function, parceling up the spectrum and coordinating its usage. Without a clear definition of property rights, the spectrum, like anything else, would not be used efficiently. What was turned over to the market was the decision—hard for a government official to make well—of who gets the right to use each piece of spectrum.

The main beneficiaries of the spectrum auctions were consumers, who got a speedy introduction of new telecommunication services at competitive prices, and taxpayers, through the revenue generated. "When government auctioneers need worldly advice, where can they turn?" the *Economist* asked, and answered, "To mathematical economists, of course." William Safire in the *New York Times* called it the "greatest auction in history."[10]

Spectrum auctions spread, as countries like Mexico, Canada, Italy, Brazil, and the Netherlands started to use them, becoming what the *Financial Times* called "the world's largest concerted transfer of money from the corporate sector to state coffers."[11] One of the U.S. auctions, which raised around $7 billion in 1995, entered the *Guinness Book of World Records* as the world's then-largest auction. In 2000, this record was wiped out: an auction of spectrum licenses in the United Kingdom yielded $34 billion, and then one in Germany went to $46 billion. In Spain, France, and elsewhere, though, spectrum continued to be allocated by what is called a "beauty contest," which means the licensees were simply selected by government officials according to some vague criteria—a process prone to favoritism.

Back in the United States, the auctions' success did not do away with the government's penchant for giving away what the public owns, as Congress voted to give spectrum for high-definition broadcasting to the television networks. The television industry holds far more sway over the politicians than the telecommunications industry, evidently, for the telephone companies pay billions for spectrum while the broadcasters get it for free. This is not unrelated—might we speculate?—to the networks' control over the news coverage of election campaigns. (A story still circulates in Washington—a folk tale, no doubt, but no less influential for that—of a television executive who telephoned the White House during the administration of Gerald Ford to lobby on some policy issue. If things did not go the networks' way, he warned, there would be many more broadcasts of clips of President Ford stumbling.)

Senator John McCain called the spectrum giveaway "one of the great rip-offs in American history." The FCC estimated the spectrum the broadcasters received for free was worth $70 billion. The broadcasters complained, meanwhile, about bureaucracy. "They cut the red tape lengthwise here in Washington," said Edward O. Fritts, president of the National Association of Broadcasters. "We have an FCC that is attempting to layer more regulation. We are proud of what we have accomplished, and would like to continue to do it unencumbered by red tape."[12] And, one might add, unencumbered by having to pay for their main input.

*   *   *   *

The simultaneous ascending auction has since found further applications. Stanford University used it, with the help of some economists on its faculty, to sell eight housing lots on university-owned land in 1996, grossing $3.6 million. (The proceeds went to replacing earthquake-damaged student housing.) The university did not have to prejudge the land values, for the market did the pricing. The simultaneous bidding ensured the plots (which were adjacent and the same size) fetched similar prices. The winning bidders felt good about it because the open bidding lessened their fears of overpaying. Carolyn Sargent, the university's housing director, said, "It was considered a huge success. Everyone thought it was fair, which was extremely important."

Economists have been designing other markets of late. Preston McAfee and I helped the Mexican government design an auction of the rights to mine some gold, silver, and phosphate deposits. The government expected that only a few firms would bid, so it wanted to use reserve prices. (The number of companies that actually submitted bids varied between three and six.) If there were no reserve price, with weak competition the bidding might have stopped far below the property's value. If the reserve price were too high, however, no one would have bothered to bid. Also, the government wanted the payments from the winning bidder not only up front but also in royalties on the value of the minerals extracted. Because the size of the deposits was unknown, the bidders would be taking on substantial risk. By shifting some of the risk from the firm to the government, royalties ensured that the firms did not bid low out of excessive caution. If set too high, however, royalties could reduce the winning bidder's incentives to extract the minerals, since much of the value would go to the government.[13] Using geological and financial data, we tried to mimic the procedure the companies would use to value a mine. Then we modeled how they would bid when faced with various combinations of reserve price and royalty, and used the results of these simulations to set the reserve prices and royalties. When the auctions were run in 1998, with the royalties set at 2, 2.5, or 3.5 percent (depending on the property), six properties fetched a total of U.S.$21 million.

In the labor market for newly graduated medical interns in the United States, interns compete with each other for jobs in hospitals, and hospitals compete with each other for interns. Once, the interns' market had no rules. Hospitals simply contacted any interns they judged to be promising and bargained with them directly. The contracting between interns and hospitals was chaotic; one observer called it a "helter-skelter process."[14] Each hospital tried to lock up the best interns before the opposition did. By trying to conclude a deal earlier than the others, they induced defensive responses in the rest. Hospitals were racing to sign up promising interns up to two years ahead of graduation, with little real information about their abilities. Students were applying for jobs years before they knew where their real skills and interests lay. Mismatches resulted.

The hospitals and the interns would have preferred that the transacting be done close to the graduation date, when more was known and so better matches were possible, but the free-for-all market drove them to contract early. A hospital and an intern reaching an early deal did not take account of the costs they were imposing on the other hospitals and interns. A hospital that decided to wait and see how candidates developed risked losing them to other hospitals.

The hospitals eventually designed some rules for the marketplace, with the help of economist Alvin Roth.[15] Now, each intern is given a list of hospitals and ranks them in order of preference. Similarly, each hospital ranks the interns. These rankings are loaded into a computer program, which computes the match of interns to hospitals, going as far as is feasible toward meeting the preferences of both the interns and the hospitals. The market's rules are subject to a reality check. Interns and hospitals are free to ignore the computer's matches and contract independently. But in practice few of its allocations are overturned by side deals.

As one student described it, the matching process is "the bane of most every fourth-year medical student's existence. In fact, it may qualify as the most stressful time in a physician's career." The tension builds "until the long awaited moment when their fate pops out to greet them on match day."[16] There is no way to design the market so as to quell the students' anxiety about the first job of their career. The matching market, however, has reduced the uncertainties. Without rules, the market for interns worked badly because of the externalities of signing early. With well-designed rules the market does what it is supposed to do: it identifies productive matches between interns and hospitals, each year efficiently matching over eighteen thousand fresh graduates with hospitals.

In yet another design exercise, a large manufacturing firm asked economist Charles Plott how to predict the sales of its products. The best source of information on future sales is the salespeople who meet the customers daily. How could the company harness their intuition, hunches, and beliefs? To take advantage of the market's ability to combine scattered information, Plott designed an electronic asset market. There are tradeable certificates saying something like "September, 1501–1600," meaning that if September sales turn out to be between 1501 and 1600 units, the bearer is paid one dollar. The certificates range over the possible sales totals. Some months ahead, the company gives each salesperson twenty certificates for each sales interval, and lets them trade among themselves. Anyone who predicts sales will be high buys the high-sales certificates, driving their price up, and sells the low-sales certificates, pushing their price down. The price of any given certificate, when the market settles down, reflects the salespeople's collective beliefs about the likelihood of the corresponding sales level. These prices predict sales, Plott reported, better than the company's standard forecasting techniques.[17]

*   *   *   *

In markets with any degree of complexity, competition does not just happen. The mechanisms that support competition are often designed by entrepreneurs—and sometimes by economists. A stringent test of an economic theory is to use it in designing a new way of doing business. In designing novel competitive mechanisms, economists are putting theory to quite practical use.

E I G H T

:::

When You Work for Yourself

$\mathbf{M}$ost of Vietnam's trucks were broken down in the early 1990s, according to Le Dang Doanh, head of the Central Institute for Economic Management, a Hanoi think tank. Imported from the Soviet Union, built using Soviet technology and production methods, they were notoriously unreliable. To make matters worse, the collapse of the Soviet Union had made spare parts unobtainable. Without trucks, the nation faced a transportation crisis. Out of desperation, the government granted each driver an ownership stake in his truck. "It's a miracle!" Le Doanh wryly observed. "Suddenly, all the trucks run."

What exactly is meant by ownership? The definition formulated by economists Oliver Hart and Oliver Williamson identifies two aspects.[1] The owner of an asset, such as a machine or a plot of land, has the right to any residual returns it generates. (*Residual* is used here to refer to anything beyond what the owner has committed to employees or creditors.) The owner thus keeps any extra earnings from the asset and so is motivated to utilize it productively. If the returns are unexpectedly high, it is the owner who gets the windfall. As well as residual income, the owner has residual control rights, that is, the ultimate power to decide how the asset is to be used.

Vietnam's trucks had been owned by the state. Or rather, it is perhaps more accurate and more consistent with our definition of ownership to say they were owned by no one. Residual control rights were fuzzy—it was unclear who had ultimate control over the trucks—and no one held the rights to any residual income they generated. Granting the drivers ownership meant that they were given residual control. Unshackled from the old bureaucratic rules and procedures, they could fix the trucks by whatever resourceful methods they improvised and could scavenge for spare parts. Since ownership also gave the drivers a share of the residual income, they were motivated to get the trucks running and to find new, lucrative uses for them.

The story of Vietnam's trucks exemplifies the proposition that the owner of an asset should, where feasible, be the person whose decisions most crucially affect its usage. Ownership is the strongest source of incentives. It is a spur to exerting effort, drawing up plans, taking risks. Owning a productive asset gives you the power to control how it is used, plus an assurance that the returns from it will be yours. Things that are owned in common often are not well kept. Ownership motivates you to learn about the asset's best uses, to maintain it and not run it down, and to match it with complementary assets so as to fully utilize it.

"Everyone has the right to own property alone as well as in association with others," says Article 17 of the Universal Declaration of Human Rights. "No one shall be deprived of his property." Beyond being a fundamental right, property is crucial to the marketplace. Secure property rights are the surest motivation for productive effort and risk-taking. Routine as it is, this proposition is of utmost importance.

*   *   *   *

The prophet Mohammed was an early proponent of property rights. When a famine in Medina brought sharp price increases, people implored him to lessen the hardship by fixing prices. He refused because, having once been a merchant himself, he believed the buyers' and sellers' free choices should not be overridden. "Allah is the only one who sets the prices and gives prosperity and poverty," he said. "I would not want to be complained about before Allah by someone whose property or livelihood has been violated."[2]

Only where there exists property can there be a market. Assurance against expropriation is needed if markets are to operate successfully. People will invest if they have some assurance that they will reap the returns on their investment. The defining feature of a market, noted earlier, is the participants' autonomy. People are free to make decisions to buy or to sell that reflect their own preferences, constrained by the rules of the marketplace and by the extent of what they own. The freedom of action that is the essence of markets calls for property rights so people control their own resources.

Ownership is not the only possible source of incentives, however. They can also be given to employees by means of a contract. Pay-for-performance schemes have some of the force of ownership. An executive offered bonuses for meeting targets, a salesperson on commission, and a worker earning piece rates all have a stake in their own output, much as if they were owners rather than employees. What is the difference between working for someone else under contract and working for yourself? Why is ownership the stronger motivator?

"Always anticipate the unexpected," Peter Sellers's Inspector Clouseau advised his manservant Kato in the film *A Shot in the Dark*. But of course we cannot anticipate everything. "It's useless to plan for the unexpected—by definition," as Alfred Hitchcock said. We can plan for unlikely events, but we cannot plan for events that are not merely unlikely but hard to envisage in advance. This puts a limit on what contracts can do.

Ownership matters precisely because the unexpected sometimes does occur. If every contingency could be anticipated at the time a contract is written, there would be no practical difference between being an owner and being an employee. As an employee, your pay-for-performance contract could be written to be watertight, giving you an unbreakable assurance that you will earn what your efforts generate. In fact, however, those writing a contract are unable to anticipate the entire range of things that could occur in the future. Contracts, therefore, are necessarily incomplete.

When something that is not written into the contract happens, the owner, as residual claimant, makes decisions unilaterally. If you are working under a contract and something unanticipated arises, your rights are unspecified. The rights conveyed by ownership, by contrast, stand even when the unexpected occurs. Unable to make provision for boundless contingencies, a contract is not as effective as ownership. With a contract we cannot anticipate the unexpected. With ownership, in a sense, we can. Ownership is society's way of handling the unexpected.

This explains why small firms tend to be the most dynamic and entrepreneurial. While large firms necessarily dominate industries where there are economies of scale, like the steel, automobile, and computer software industries, elsewhere small firms have an edge. Why? They are more flexible internally and less bound by bureaucratic rules and procedures. They are more nimble in responding to their environment, faster to adapt to changes in market circumstances.

But why are these advantages uniquely available to small firms and not to large firms? A large firm can divide itself into units responsible for their own costs and revenues, thereby heightening incentives. Many large firms have reorganized themselves in this way, trying to mimic the advantages of small, independent firms. What prevents a division of a large firm from operating as productively as a small firm? How can the whole be less than the sum of its parts?

When Microsoft was a young company, IBM had the opportunity to buy it out. If it had, would Microsoft, as a division of IBM, have grown to be the multibillion-dollar powerhouse we know today? Clearly it would not have. Why did it matter to Bill Gates that he was the owner-manager of the Microsoft Corporation rather than the hired manager of the Microsoft division of IBM? Why can't a firm create incentives for its employees that mimic ownership?

In fact it can, to some extent. Divisional managers are usually paid according to their divisions' performance. The terms of the contract shape the manager's actions. A contract offering the manager a sizeable fraction of the division's net returns would give strong incentives. Such a contract would provide most of the motivation that would otherwise come from ownership. In one vital respect, though, any employee's contract, no matter how potent its pay-for-performance terms are, falls short of ownership.

A divisional manager does not have residual control, so decisions can be overridden from above. The parent firm cannot credibly commit, via a contract that is necessarily incomplete, not to step in if something unanticipated arises. If the division turns out to be wildly more lucrative than anyone foresaw when the contract was written, the parent firm will probably find a way to harvest its profits. The firm's owners, and not the employees, hold the residual claims. For an employee, the upside returns are effectively capped, whereas for an owner they are unlimited. Had Bill Gates been a divisional manager within IBM, it is implausible, no matter what the fine print in his pay-for-performance contract might have said, that he would have been paid bonuses in the hundreds of millions of dollars.

Not being an owner—that is, lacking the rights to residual returns—puts a damper on the motivation to invest creatively and to take large risks. The market, unlike a firm, can commit to richly rewarding an entrepreneur in the event of an unanticipated blockbuster success. The location of ownership affects investment and performance. In situations that demand exceptional effort and where outcomes are highly responsive to such effort, decision-making cannot be effectively delegated; the owner needs to be directly involved.

*   *   *   *

For innovation, in particular, ownership matters greatly. The lone genius driven to invent—Thomas Alva Edison dreaming up the light bulb or Alexander Graham Bell the telephone—is legendary. But it is not obvious that this is the best way to organize research today. Should innovators own the rights to their ideas? Or is innovation more effectively achieved in a large organization?

Economies of scale arise in research. Large laboratories with seemingly limitless resources can afford to acquire the best people, the most advanced equipment, and armies of assistants. They pursue multiple lines of research, and what is learned in one often feeds into another. The pharmaceutical company GlaxoSmithKline, for example, spends $3.7 billion a year and employs fifteen thousand scientists in the search for new drugs, while Pfizer spends $5 billion a year and employs twelve thousand researchers.[3] A large firm ought to have an advantage in doing research, one might think, over a small firm concentrated on a single line of enquiry and operating on a shoestring. Are large or small firms the more effective at innovating? It depends.

The biotechnology industry shows the benefits both of being large and of being small. A new drug goes through three stages: two stages of research and then one of development. First is applied science: investigating whether a piece of pure scientific knowledge could lead to a workable medicine. Second is clinical testing on animal and then human subjects, to prove it works without dangerous side effects so that the government will license it. Third is the development of the drug into a manufacturable product, followed by a marketing effort directed at physicians, and then large-scale production. This final stage is usually done by one of the established drug companies. The big firms have obvious advantages in developing the product. The size of their manufacturing plants and marketing networks means they can outcompete smaller rivals. More interesting are the two earlier, research-focused stages.

A common pattern, especially when the drug is truly novel and not just a variation on a theme, is for the research to be carried out by a start-up firm. Sensing the potential in a new idea, an entrepreneurial scientist creates a company, persuades some venture capitalists to fund it, and spends a few years in intense scientific investigation. After the research stage is completed, at some point just before, during, or just after the clinical trials, one of the large drug manufacturers buys out the company.

How is it that start-up firms are more inventive than established drug companies? What if a major drug company hired the best and brightest biochemists and lavished them with resources? Would that not generate more innovation than if those same scientists worked separately in small, relatively impoverished start-ups of their own? Not necessarily. Ownership makes a difference.

Breakthroughs demand obsession. Success in solving a hard problem comes through thinking about it in the shower, while driving to work, during coffee breaks, over dinner, in front of the television. Isaac Newton, asked how he had arrived at his insights, answered, "By keeping the problem constantly before my mind." If Newton, possibly the greatest scientific genius of all time, had to keep problems constantly before his mind in order to solve them, then mere mortals need to be at least as focused. A large organization, necessarily bureaucratic, is at a disadvantage in trying to cultivate such fixation in its employees. Obsession with the problem at hand comes with ownership, broadly defined to include having not only a financial stake but also a personal stake in the success of the idea.

Entrepreneur-innovators who strike success sometimes become unimaginably rich. Employee-innovators typically receive little remuneration beyond their salary; when they are paid a bonus, it is usually a tiny sum relative to the value of their innovation. The market, granting the innovator the right to any residual returns, is a powerful inducement to innovative effort.[4] It is not only for high-tech innovation, though, that the incentives from ownership matter, as I will discuss next.

*   *   *   *

China's agriculture switched from collective to individual production in the late 1970s. This change gives us a reasonably clear-cut experiment in the force of property rights. Food production boomed with the farmers' new individual incentives. The marketization of agriculture lifted hundreds of millions of Chinese out of dire poverty. It was the biggest antipoverty program the world has ever seen.

A tiny beginning sparked this massive reform: a clandestine meeting of the householders in a small rural village. Desperation had hit the farmers of Xiaogang village in China's Anhui province by 1978. The commune on which they worked collectively was dysfunctional. Known as the granary of China, Anhui contains some of the nation's most fertile land. But Xiaogang's twenty families were not producing enough rice to feed themselves. They had been reduced to relying on begging in other regions. In years of unfavorable weather they starved.

Fearful of being arrested, the villagers met secretly and agreed to parcel out the communal land among themselves. They made a three-part resolution. First, as they were flouting government policy, the contracting of land to individual households was to be kept strictly secret; it was not to be divulged to any outsider. Second, they would continue to deliver the stipulated amount of rice taxes to the state. Third, if any of them were jailed, the others would raise their children until they were eighteen years old. They signed the pact with their thumbprints.

A rapid turnaround followed. The farmers of Xiaogang immediately became more productive. "Now is different from the past," one said. "We work for ourselves." Working their own plots of land, they could see a direct link between their effort and their rewards. Any of their output beyond what they owed the state they now retained to use for themselves or to sell. The amount of land planted in rice nearly doubled in one year, and the village began producing a rice surplus. As a farmer said, "You can't be lazy when you work for your family and yourself."

Word got out, despite their oath of secrecy. No one understood the inefficiencies of communal farming better than the farmers themselves. All over China, farmers were ready to change. With wildcat breakups of communes in other villages, the movement quickly proliferated. Individual farming spread "like a chicken pest," as a farmer put it. "When one village has it, the whole county will be infected."[5]

The grassroots reforms were initially resisted from the top. Foreseeing a loss of their power and perquisites, the local bureaucrats punished Xiaogang by cutting off its supplies of seeds, fertilizer, and pesticides. But the villagers were lucky: their uprising coincided with a change of mood in Beijing. A new breed of politicians saw an opportunity to exploit the agricultural changes as part of their drive, following the death of Mao Zedung, to oust the Maoists.

Provincial Communist Party officials visited the village and gave their blessings. Then a high-level Beijing official traveled to Xiaogang and neighboring villages to study the effects of individual farming. His report, which concluded that individual farming increased output and improved living standards, became influential when it was circulated among the national leaders. At a Communist Party conference in 1982, four years after the Xiaogang villagers' meeting, China's paramount leader Deng Xiaoping endorsed the reforms. In 1983 the central government formally proclaimed individual farming to be consistent with the socialist economy and therefore permissible. By 1984, just six years after Xiaogang started the movement, there were no communes left.

*   *   *   *

The communes had relied on appeals to work for the common good more than on individual incentives. Attempts had been made to create some personal incentives, but they were mostly ineffectual. Farmers worked in production teams. Each team member was assigned work points, which purported to measure how effectively he or she had worked, and pay depended on the number of work points accumulated. The link between individual effort and reward was weak, however, because it was impossible to track how hard each person worked and because there was an ideology of spreading the commune's earnings equally. In addition, since people belonged to a commune for life, the ultimate incentive—work or be fired—was absent. Adding to the lack of personal responsibility inherent in the collective was the commune officials' habit of taking grain for themselves in unpredictable quantities. Not only was commune members' pay unrelated to their own performance but, to make matters worse, it was cruelly inadequate. The state deliberately set the price of rice artificially low. The old Eastern European lament applied also in China: "We pretend to work, they pretend to pay us."

The upshot was that the farmers in the communes had little incentive to exert effort. It made little difference whether a farmer worked himself to exhaustion or dozed all day under a tree. Either way, the amount he took home to feed his family was much the same. "The enthusiasm of the farmers was frustrated," said Yan Junchang, a Xiaogang village leader. "No matter how hard I rang the bell or blew the whistle, I couldn't get anyone to go into the fields." The missing incentives translated into low output. Agricultural productivity was actually lower in 1978 than it had been in 1949, when the communists took over.

Some in the West used to see the communes in a romantic light. At a White House dinner party held in honor of Deng Xiaoping during his visit to the United States in 1979, just after the reforms had begun, he was seated next to Shirley MacLaine. The movie star took the opportunity to describe her trip to China in 1973, during the Cultural Revolution, that time of national paranoia when many who were out of favor with Mao Zedung's government were forcibly removed from the cities and compelled to work in communes. "Learn from the peasants," these displaced urbanites were ordered. Visiting a remote village, MacLaine met a white-bearded scholar, who told her that he felt much happier and more fulfilled on the commune, toiling in the fields from dawn to dusk growing tomatoes, than he used to feel working in a university. The scholar's affirmation had deeply moved her, MacLaine earnestly recounted. Deng, who had himself been forced to work for a time on a commune, patiently let her finish her tale. Then he dryly responded, "He lied."[6]

In the reformed system, each farmer has a long-term lease of a plot of land. The farmer must deliver an annual quota of produce to the state (which can be thought of as a rental payment for the use of the land) and may sell any above-quota output in markets. As a result, the farmer faces full market incentives, in the sense that any increased effort translates directly into increased income. Whereas in the commune system decisions were made by the collective leadership, in the new system farmers were free to decide what crops to grow and what animals to keep. Farmers experimented with new seed varieties and began to plant a diverse range of fruits and vegetables. As one farmer said, now "everyone uses his brain."

In addition, as the communes were being broken up, the government raised the price of rice. Between 1978 and 1980, the prices the farmers received rose about 30 percent. Food production grew by over 60 percent between 1978 and 1984. Farmers' incomes grew by 20 percent each year over this period. This growth was the direct result of the introduction of market incentives.

As agricultural output boomed, rural marketplaces developed rapidly. Farmers living near highways set up stalls to sell their fruit and vegetables. In the towns and cities produce markets were created. In his novel *Waiting*, Ha Jin depicts a rural town in the early 1980s: It was market day, so the sidewalks of Central Street were occupied by vendors. They were selling poultry, vegetables, fruits, eggs, live fish, piglets, clothes. Everywhere were wicker baskets, chick cages, oil jars, fish basins and pails. A bald man was blowing a brass whistle, a sample of his wares, and the noise split the air and hurt people's ears.[7]

The abundance of food on offer was in marked contrast to its absence just a few years earlier. The countryside was revitalized. The agricultural reforms led to a transformation of the rest of China's economy. The increase in productivity freed labor and capital to be moved into industrial production. Rural factories were set up at a rapid clip, creating employment for people who otherwise would have been underemployed as farmers. By 1989, a decade after individual farming started, almost one-fourth of the rural workforce was working in industry. The rural factories, along with the increases in food production, fueled China's sensational economic growth. National income per head of population grew at a rate of over 8 percent for more than twenty years, meaning that the average person's income quadrupled.

Most of China's farmers were crushingly poor at the start of the reforms. The number of rural poor, according to World Bank data, fell by 170 million in the brief period of the six years from 1978 to 1984. (This calculation defines the poverty line to be U.S.$0.70 per day in 1985 dollars, the income required for minimal nutrition of 2,100 calories per day.) Rural poverty was not eliminated. In 1995 about 180 million people, mostly in remote regions with barren soil and unreliable weather, were still earning less than a dollar a day.[8] But lifting hundreds of millions out of poverty is a stunning achievement.

It is a sad irony that it took markets to correct the shortcomings of collective agriculture. Chairman Mao Zedung's admirers in the West during the 1960s and 1970s liked to point to China's communes as a new and better way of organizing life. The communes were, supposedly, humane workplaces in which concern for one's neighbor replaced the rapacity of the market. Visitors to China would return home proclaiming the communes a triumph. Joan Robinson, a famous Cambridge University economist, asserted that as a result of "the appeal to the people to combat egoism and eschew privilege," China was economically successful. "Peasants are taught to feel that they are working for the nation, for the Revolution and for all the oppressed people of the world, but they are clearly and obviously doing good for themselves at the same time."[9] Robinson wrote her fulsome assessment of the communes in 1976, just two years before the Xiaogang peasants, who really did know what it was like to live on a commune, risked arrest to disagree.

A system based on exhortations to work for the common good may seem more admirable than one based on self-interest, but the romanticization of the communes trips up on the facts. The boom in food production following the reforms showed how badly the communes had been underperforming. In the communes, millions of peasants were on the verge of starvation. Under markets, prosaic as they may seem, the Chinese people have enough to eat.

✻   ✻   ✻   ✻

China's agricultural reform shows the force of property rights. The elementary lesson is that incentives have great force. There is an additional lesson, though, which is less conventional. The productivity gains were achieved without formal legal recognition of the farmers' ownership rights. China obtained the benefits of private property without actually having private property.

The reforms did not change the ownership of land, which remained essentially state-owned. Farmers were assigned individual plots but had no legal right to the land beyond that of a contract (the term of which initially was just three years, and later was lengthened to fifteen years). The farmers could not sell the land they farmed, nor did they have the right to use it for an indefinite period.

Some property insecurity came from the practice of land reallocation. Village leaders periodically reallocated land among the villagers. As people aged and young people formed new households, village leaders periodically redrew land boundaries. Also, village leaders on occasion reneged on their contracts, evicting villagers for their personal profit. In a typical such story, a Mr. Chen leased an orchard growing longans, a litchi-like fruit, in 1985 from the village of Zengcuo, in Fujian province. After Chen, working hard, produced a bumper crop, some villagers raided the orchard and stole all the longans. They claimed they were justified because Chen's rent payments were much lower than his earnings from the orchard. Since the orchard was collectively owned, they argued, all villagers were entitled to a share of the output. Far from punishing the raiders, the village government terminated its contract with Chen. It then leased the orchard to another farmer at more than double the rent.[10] A government constrained by laws does not behave in this way.

The government has taken the position that farmers have no claim to be compensated for any land taken, for all land belongs to the state and farmers are merely granted rights to use it temporarily. The insecurity of property has had perceptible effects. One study found that farmers apply less fertilizer and labor to plots that have a higher risk of reallocation. Another found that farmers are less likely to make long-term investments such as wells and drainage on land that is more at risk of confiscation.[11] What is noteworthy, though, is not that property insecurity has consequences. Rather, it is how small these consequences seem to be. Despite the absence of ownership, productivity is high. The farmers act as though their rights to the land are reasonably secure.

Cases of people being evicted from their land have been the exception, not the rule. Although the authorities are able to renege on contracts, they have refrained from doing so with sufficient predictability that the farmers are motivated to be productive. Because the contracts have been maintained in a reasonably credible way, the farmers work under their lease contracts almost as assiduously as if they owned the land. They willingly make long-term investments in "their" plots of land: investments in irrigation, drainage, terracing, and soil fertility, which pay off only over several years.

Lacking the institution of private ownership, China has an alternative mechanism, based on bureaucratic administration, which has allowed markets to work reasonably well. The absence of legally defined ownership, it seems, does not necessarily mean the absence of property rights—at least for the simple dealings of peasant agriculture.

One major part of the puzzle remains to be filled in. Just how have China's bureaucrats resisted the temptation to abuse their power over the farmers—or how has the hierarchy kept that temptation in check? The answer probably lies in the specifics of time and place (and therefore there is no implication that other countries could readily adopt the Chinese solution). The political situation in China through the 1980s and 1990s was stable but not impregnable. While the communist government faced no challenge, it had lost whatever legitimacy it might once have had, reform-era China being communist only in name. Its legitimacy as the government, and its ability to preempt any future political opposition, rested on its delivering economic growth. High officials in Deng Xiaoping's government understood enough about economics to recognize that growth requires markets and markets require assured property rights. The Communist Party had retained its highly disciplined organization and so was able to prevent self-seeking behavior by low-level officials. The state motivated local officials to maintain agricultural output growth by rewarding them with bonus payments and promotion, and by firing them if output targets were not met. Sanctions for extreme misconduct can be severe: officials found guilty of corruption may be executed. As a result of this party discipline, bureaucratic control provided a property rights platform that was ad hoc but secure enough that market forces could operate reasonably well.

The system was showing signs of strain by the 1990s as the farmers, unable to sell or rent out their land, were obliged to keep farming their small, increasingly uneconomical plots. Riots, sometimes violent, broke out, as peasants protested the high taxes and fees levied on them by local officials. One farmer said, "There are corrupt officials at every level—township, county, and city—and they have been collaborating to get more for themselves."[12] What is noteworthy, though, is not so much that officials abused their power but that the abuse for the most part was contained.

Conventional wisdom says that markets cannot exist without private ownership underpinned by the legal system. The conventional view underestimates how robust markets are. The support markets rely on can come in nonstandard ways. While markets usually require more reliable property rights assurance than bureaucratic discretion is able to provide, there are exceptions, like China. Property rights are not synonymous with legally defined ownership. A little property rights assurance can go a long way. But China is atypical; most bureaucracies cannot provide the assurance investors need. They cannot bind themselves against changing the rules, so investors fear expropriation and are deterred from investing. A commitment to respect property would require that the government feel secure enough that it sees a stake in the economy's long-term growth. China met these conditions for a time, but most authoritarian governments do not.

Formal ownership rights are needed. But it is not easy to assign them from scratch. Institutions are needed to define and maintain property rights. In Western Europe and North America, these institutions have been built up gradually over the centuries. As Thomas Jefferson said, "Stable ownership is the gift of social law, and is given late in the progress of society."

Even with land, an asset for which it is easier than most to define rights, the institution of private property is subtle. Property rights do not just appear by magic. They require action by the state, and they can be difficult to set up. The state has to build a range of institutions. Procedures for assigning initial ownership must be set up. Public registration is needed so that land titles are accurately recorded and easily verified. Property boundaries must be physically demarcated. Credit markets, escrow services, and the like are needed so people who have little savings can buy land based on their future earnings. Laws governing land ownership have to be written. Judges and lawyers must be trained to adjudicate disputes.[13] The Japanese government, for example, began a drive to formalize farmers' landownership in the late nineteenth century and did not complete it until the middle of the twentieth century.

*   *   *   *

Ownership, then, is society's way of handling the unexpected. For high-tech entrepreneurs as much as for Vietnamese truck drivers, ownership brings the freedom to look for creative solutions as well as rewards for implementing them. Holding the rights to both residual control and residual income, the owner is enabled and motivated to use the asset to its best advantage. Ownership serves to motivate effort and risk-taking when returns have an unpredictably large upside.

Private ownership is not synonymous with property rights. Ownership is the surest way of securing property rights, but not the only way. In the right circumstances, nonstandard means of achieving property security, like bureaucratic administration, can be effective. For simple transactions, a little bit of property rights assurance is sometimes enough to get markets working.

Defining property rights and building mechanisms to maintain and enforce them, then, are key elements in designing a market. But property rights do not solve all problems. Not everything should be owned. Next I will ask: where should ownership end? Ownership has costs as well as benefits, so property rights sometimes should be circumscribed.

NINE

⁘

The Embarrassment of
a Patent

A Scotswoman named Mary Blair opened a sandwich bar in the English village of Fenny Stratford and, in a flippant allusion to her nationality, called it McMunchies. She promptly received a stern letter from McDonald's, the hamburger chain, informing her that "Mc" was their property. "McDonald's Restaurants Ltd. is the registered user of the 'Mc' prefix as a registered trademark." They gave Blair a week to remove her sign or be sued. "I can't hope to fight a company with the finances of McDonald's," she said.

The burger behemoth fiercely guards its property rights to its name. McSmile, a restaurant in Vilnius, Lithuania, was unsmilingly subjected to legal action by McDonald's, as was McBagel, a bakery in New York, McCoffee, an espresso bar in Half Moon Bay, California, and McAllan's, a sausage stand in Silkeborg, Denmark. McDonald's ever-vigilant lawyers do not stop at food service businesses. They have hounded a Swiss internet medical services firm called McWellness, a Canadian hotel chain called McSleep, and an Austrian hairdressing salon called McHair.[1] (Perhaps on the cover of this book, to be on the safe side, the author's name should have been listed as "Millan.")

"How can they own 'Mc'?" Mary Blair asked. "It means they own half the names in Scotland." The history and traditions of Scotland notwithstanding—"Mc" simply means "son of" in Gaelic—McDonald's insists it does.

Pierre-Joseph Proudhon asserted, "Property is theft." Of all the slogans that have moved people to political action over the centuries, this is one of the silliest. It does at least point out, though, that private ownership is not unambiguously a good thing. This is especially the case with names and ideas.

Without intellectual property protections, a modern economy could not function. A firm that has invested in building up its brand name deserves to have it protected against interlopers. Authors and composers should own the rights to what they create. For inventors to be able earn a return on the effort they put in, society must recognize their property rights to their ideas, or there would be little incentive for innovation.

Via trademarks, copyrights, and patents, the law recognizes intellectual property, as it should. But such safeguards risk becoming too heavy-handed. The mechanisms designed to sustain intellectual property have an unavoid-able downside: they restrict usage. The costs of assigning ownership in ideas sometimes outweigh the benefits.

New ideas drive the economy. Technological advance is a prime source of long-term economic growth, as economic theory and statistical studies confirm.[2] A functioning marketplace in ideas is essential to a nation's economic health. For it to work well, intellectual property must be protected neither too much nor too little.

* * * *

If a marketplace in ideas is to exist at all, its rules must be specifically designed, for an idea is a peculiar kind of commodity. When you use it, it is still there for others to use. When you pass it on to someone else, you still have possession of it. You do not forget how something works upon explain-ing it. The peculiar character of an idea is that, as Thomas Jefferson said, "the moment it is divulged, it forces itself into the possession of everyone, and the receiver cannot dispossess himself of it." Moreover, "no one possesses the less, because every other possesses the whole of it." Like the air we breathe, ideas are "incapable of confinement or exclusive appropriation."

To rephrase Jefferson in the jargon of economics, knowledge is a public good: anyone can use it, and it does not disappear once it is used. This puts inventors in a predicament. They find it difficult to earn a return because users can benefit from their ideas without paying for them. For a market in ideas to be able to function, there need to be special kinds of property rights. Intellectual property laws must recognize that ideas can be widely transmit-ted; all that property rights in ideas can do is to control how the ideas are put to use.

If property rights in ideas did not exist, innovators would be unable to cover their costs of invention, and little would be done. Innovators need to be able to capture a portion of the value they create. Society's solution to the problem that ideas are inherently nonexclusive is to write laws that make them exclusive, giving the ideas' owners the right to extract a fee from those who make use of them. The government designs and administers the rules governing intellectual property: patents protect inventions; copyrights cover creative works; trademarks cover brand names.

Innovators are driven by a range of motivations, to be sure, of which pecuniary reward is just one: there is intellectual curiosity, personal pride, professional prestige. Money is not the only motivator, but it is a forceful one. George Washington, asking Congress to pass copyright legislation, argued that copyright would increase the nation's stock of knowledge, and knowledge is "the surest basis of public happiness." Abraham Lincoln said, "The patent system added the fuel of interest to the fire of genius."

A patent may be granted on any new and useful process, machine, manufacture, composition of matter, or design for an article of manufacture. Laws of nature like $E = mc^2$ are not patentable. To be eligible, the invention must be new, useful, and nonobvious. A patent enables the patent holder to exclude anyone else from making use of the patented invention for twenty years. The enforcement of patent rights is after the fact, via the patent holder bringing suit against alleged violations. The possible defenses against a charge of patent violation are fourfold: the patent should not have been awarded, since it was not novel or nonobvious; the patent application misrepresented the prior art; the invention was patented earlier or had already been in public use; and the patent was extended beyond its proper scope.

Copyright is another form of intellectual property. It applies to any "original work of authorship" that is "fixed in any tangible medium of expression" (*original* meaning it was not copied, and *authorship* entailing "a modicum of intellectual activity"). It thus applies to literary works, musical works, pictures, computer programs, and so on. Copyright grants to the holder the exclusive right to reproduce the work in question, to distribute copies, to display it publicly, and to prepare derivative works. It extends for the life of the creator plus seventy years. There is no application process; it automatically applies to a work of authorship. If there is a dispute over ownership, the copyright owner must prove that the work in fact did originate with the claiming author.[3]

Copyright protection is not absolute. The doctrine of "fair use" holds that people may use, without payment, a certain amount of copyrighted material for scholarly or creative purposes. Thus a professor may use excerpts of a film to make a point in class, and a novelist may quote from another novelist. The law recognizes, in other words, that some leakage of copyright is desirable.

Trademark protection is yet another form of intellectual property. Trademarks exist to enable firms to identify their products. By registering a trademark, a firm obtains a legal claim to the name. Other firms then are unable to pass their goods off as the trademark holder's. Trademark rights do not prevent others from selling the same goods under a clearly different trademark. Proving an infringement of trademark requires proving that the alleged infringer is likely to confuse consumers.

The holder of a patent or a copyright has the right to demand from users royalties or other forms of payment based on intensity of use. Thus new pharmaceuticals, for example, as we saw, are priced far above their cost of production, the premium being a reward to the patent holder. The prospect of earning a patent-induced premium spurs innovative efforts. Patents promote creativity.

Patents, nevertheless, do have a drawback. A patent is a legally sanctioned restraint of trade. Once an idea is already in existence, it is wasteful to restrict its use. Some potential social value is left unrealized when the owner of the idea is permitted to charge a monopoly price for an item embodying it (because, with the price set higher than the cost of producing additional units, some consumers who value it at more than the production cost do not get to enjoy it). Granting the monopoly rights to the idea does succeed in rewarding its creator, but only at the cost of making the idea unduly inaccessible. A patent is, literally, a license to overcharge.

This is what Thomas Jefferson had in mind when he wrote of "the embarrassment of an exclusive patent." In a perfect world, he said, "ideas should freely spread from one to another." Echoing Jefferson, the U.S. Supreme Court said in the late nineteenth century that a patent puts "a heavy tax upon the industry of the country. It embarrasses the honest pursuit of business."

✻   ✻   ✻   ✻

Intellectual property represents a compromise, then, between encouraging new ideas and allowing the full use of existing ideas.[4] Ideally, innovators would be rewarded without impeding the productive usage of their ideas. It is hard to find a way to do this, however. Most countries seek an approximate balance of the benefits and the costs of patents by putting a fixed end date on the property right. After the patent expires, no one owns the idea and anyone can freely use it. The vast amount of technological innovation that occurs in North America, Western Europe, and Japan shows that patent laws by and large get things roughly right. They succeed in stimulating research and development. But they are also a restraint on trade.

Heated debates rage around intellectual property. Not only are vast sums of money at stake but, as we saw with the AIDS drug patents, it can be literally a matter of life or death. Should McDonald's own "Mc"? That is one such intellectual property question; others are less trivial. Should poor countries be released from patent obligations so their sick can have access to drugs against AIDS and other diseases? Should computer software, as a matter of course, be free? Should patents be granted for new methods of doing business? Should music lovers be allowed to freely swap recorded music over the internet, or are the record companies and musicians entitled to claim remuneration?

Debates such as these never seem to end. There is a reason for this. Whatever course of action is chosen, it has some shortcomings. "Weakening intellectual property means less innovation," say those who favor stronger protections. They are right. "Strengthening intellectual property, by excluding some users, shrinks the total value of the ideas," say those who favor weaker protections. They are right, too.

Unconditional assertions about intellectual property are rarely valid. The trick is to find the right balance. To the legal criterion for judging a patent award—the invention should be new, useful, and nonobvious—economists add a further criterion: the benefits from awarding the patent should outweigh the costs.

To evaluate any given policy on intellectual property means getting our hands dirty. We cannot do it properly by armchair theorizing. To weigh the costs and benefits, we need quantitative estimates. By how much would innovative activities be cut if intellectual property protections were weakened? By how much would usage of ideas shrink if they were strengthened? Hard as it is to quantify these hypotheticals, for a rational evaluation we must try.

We should ask, Would the innovation have been developed in the absence of intellectual-property protection? If the answer is yes, then the benefits of the protection are nonexistent, and so by the cost-benefit criterion it is unwarranted.

Such a situation arose in 1998, when Congress extended the term of copyright from fifty years after an author's death to seventy, so it will be an extra twenty years before books enter the public domain. Book buyers are harmed by this. A book's price is higher than if it were free of copyright because the publisher continues to owe royalties to the author's heirs and does not compete with others printing the same book. For books still under copyright, like *The Grapes of Wrath* and *For Whom the Bell Tolls*, the list price of the American paperback edition is $12 and up. Books out of copyright, like *Tom Sawyer* and *Pride and Prejudice*, have a list price of around $5 in mass-market editions and around $8 in higher-quality paperback editions. A college student wanting the cheapest available edition pays over twice as much for a copyrighted book. Against this drawback of the longer copyright, there is no countervailing benefit. Authors are hardly likely to find motivation in the prospect of earnings that will arrive fifty years after their death. Also, the legislators applied the extension retrospectively to existing copyrights. This is impossible to fathom. Authors do not need incentives to write books they have already written.

✳   ✳   ✳   ✳

As the information economy has grown, so have debates about whether information should be owned. To some, intellectual property is a relic of an earlier age. They see a struggle for cyberspace, as copyrights and patents fence off what should be free. A headline in the satirical magazine *The Onion* put their worries in a nutshell: "Microsoft Patents Ones, Zeroes."

Tim Berners-Lee, the inventor of the world wide web (which he did not patent), has called for software developers to fight the patent system. He and other computer engineers believe software should be nonproprietary, so people could give it to each other and build on each other's work, as indeed happened in the early days of computers. John Perry Barlow, founder of the Electronic Frontier Foundation, a group fighting against intellectual property in cyberspace, said, "Copyright is not about creation, which will happen anyway: it is about distribution." This is the key question: if software were free, would creation happen anyway?

Some programs are written with no expectation of a patent. The Linux open-source software is an example; Linux developed as it did because users, unhindered by patents, shared their ideas and built on each others'. Writing code is not the same, though, as writing poetry. Some programmers want to change the world; many just want to make a living. The writing of much of the software we use every day was driven by the profit motive. If software were free, less of it would be produced.

The evidence on the effects of the patenting of software is inconclusive. There are examples of patented software that probably would not have been written were it not for the prospect of patents. Following the various court rulings in the early 1980s allowing the patenting (rather than just copyright-ing) of software, research-and-development spending by software-related firms increased steadily but unspectacularly. Patenting brought no sharp increase in software production, nor did it lead to a sharp decrease.[5]

The growth of electronic commerce, sparking the invention of novel ways of trading, brought demands for yet another extension of patent protec-tions, culminating in a 1998 U.S. federal court ruling that business methods could be patented. The court found that an invention should not be excluded from a patent simply because it was an abstract idea; it could be patented if it produced a useful, tangible result. This ruling made it possible, in particular, to patent a novel market design.

A flood of patent applications followed. In the rush, some applicants received patents for business methods that, being easy to devise or similar to existing practices, hardly merited the description "new and nonobvious." Priceline.com received one for the so-called reverse auction, in which a buyer names a price which a seller then may accept. Amazon.com received a patent for a one-click internet buying system. DoubleClick received one for a method of delivering and targeting advertising over networks. CyberGold received one for incentives to reward consumers for paying attention to inter-net ads. Some of the more questionable patents for business methods have been challenged in court, on the grounds that the business method was already common practice before it was patented. A "wave of absurdly obvious patents on business methods," remarked the *New Scientist* in 2000, "has engulfed the United States."

Business method patents have their place, all the same, even if they have often been awarded for innovations that do not deserve to be patented. Some market designs really are new and nonobvious. In the category of "Trading, Matching, or Bidding," for example, the U.S. Patent Office, as of early 2001, listed more than two hundred patents.[6] Years' worth of effort can go into inventing a complex auction form for business-to-business transactions: thinking through the logic of bidder responses so as to choose the most effec-tive design; ensuring there are no gaps in the rules for the bidders to exploit; and writing software that handles extensive computations and is easy for the bidders to use. The ability to patent is socially beneficial for business meth-ods like these auctions that require a major development effort and would not be created without a return.

To judge the worth of business method patents, we need to quantify the costs and benefits. A search of the literature (using Google's patent-pending search engine) fails to come up with any such research. Despite many glitches in implementation, though, the patenting of business methods and software probably can foster useful innovation.

Next, let us look at a case where, by contrast, the courts have installed intellectual property safeguards that are arguably too restrictive.

*   *   *   *

In music, intellectual property attracts even more controversy than in business methods or software. Law professor Pamela Samuelson, for example, believes in free copying. The entertainment industry thinks it "should control every single copy, wherever and whenever it's played, and have a pay-for-use system so that no one can ever share anything again," she said. "I think that's a fascist world. I wouldn't want to live in it."[7] The issue came to a head in 2000 when a consortium of the five largest record companies mounted a legal battle against Napster, the free music service, charging it with copyright infringement.

Napster enabled its members to swap copies of recorded music via the internet. Members installed music files in their computers, usually copying them from commercial compact disks. Other members, locating the songs they wanted via a Napster server, downloaded the files into their own computers. With Napster's membership in the millions, music files flew through cyberspace.

A federal court ruled against Napster and ordered it to remove the copyrighted songs from its service. Was the clampdown on Napster justified? Some of the debate was about what the framers of the Constitution had in mind when they introduced copyright. The sanctity of property also entered the debate, with Napster opponents maintaining that downloading a music file was equivalent to shoplifting. A more fruitful analysis would focus not on semantics and history, but simply on costs and benefits.

Shutting down Napster meant depriving fans of their enjoyment of the music, when transmitting it to them was essentially free. Not shutting it down meant a possible reduction in creative activity, if record companies, songwriters, and musicians were not fully remunerated. (To complete the cost-benefit calculation, there is a third effect: a possible reduction in record-industry profits. But this nets out at zero in the overall societal costs and benefits, for it is exactly matched by more money in the pockets of the music fans.)

If Napster had carried on, would it have caused a significant falloff in creative activity? An earlier case of free music copying offers a comparison. The Grateful Dead allowed fans to tape its rock concerts and circulate the bootleg tapes, provided they did not sell them. "I think it's okay," said Jerry Garcia, the band's leader, in 1975. "If people like it they can certainly keep doing it. I don't have any desire to control people as to what they're doing and what they have." Despite the bootlegs—or because of them—the Grateful Dead earned more from their concert tours than most other rock bands. John Perry Barlow, who was a lyricist for the Dead before he became an internet activist, said permitting the copying "was the smartest thing we could have done. We raised the sales of our records considerably because of it."[8]

The court heard expert testimony on Napster's effect on compact disc sales. On Napster's side were consumer surveys suggesting that Napster actually promoted purchases. Members who used Napster to sample the music before buying it tended to buy more, not fewer, compact discs. On the record companies' side was a study finding that the turnover of music stores near colleges had declined when Napster was operating. This sales decline was interpreted as a consequence of Napster (though instead it might have come from the students switching to buying their compact discs from online stores). The presiding judge, Marilyn Hall Patel, found that none of the studies were "without flaw," but ruled that the record companies had "shown a meaningful likelihood" that Napster reduced their sales.

If Napster-based copying was reducing the total stock of recorded music, though, it was not by much. The record industry's cries of doom are unsupported. In 2000, at the height of the Napster boom, the revenue from compact disc sales was higher than ever.[9] It is likely, therefore, that Napster's net effect was positive; the benefits to its members probably were larger than any harm it caused the record industry. If so, the cost-benefit criterion calls for a looser interpretation of copyright than what prevailed in the courts.

To reinforce the point that weaker protection of intellectual property sometimes works better than stronger protection, let us turn now to the story of the Homebrew Club and Silicon Valley.

*   *   *   *

In June 1975, a computer enthusiast stole a copy of Basic, the first commercial software produced by the fledgling company Microsoft (or Micro Soft, as it was then called). The program, which consisted of a roll of paper tape punched with a series of holes, had been written by Microsoft founders Paul G. Allen and William H. Gates. While the details are murky, by one account the tape was taken during a demonstration of the new software at a hotel in Palo Alto, California, the Rickeys Hyatt House. According to computer pioneer Steve Dompier, "Somebody, I don't think anyone figured out who, borrowed one of their paper tapes lying on the floor."

Fifty copies of the "borrowed" program were made and distributed for free at the next meeting of the Homebrew Club, a group of Bay Area computer buffs who used the club for swapping ideas on building and programming computers. Any club member who took one of the tapes was supposed to come to the next meeting with two tapes to give away. The pirated copies proliferated.

This infuriated the twenty-year-old Bill Gates, and he sent an open letter to all the major computer publications complaining about it. The computer enthusiasts' attitude, Gates wrote sarcastically, was that "hardware must be paid for, but software is something to share. Who cares if the people who worked on it get paid?" He concluded, "The thing you do is theft."

Soon after the purloining of the Microsoft program, Silicon Valley saw a burst of new companies, many of them founded by Homebrew Club members. "Bill Gates owes his fortune to us," said Dan Sokol, the club member who made the fifty copies of the stolen tape. "If we hadn't copied the tape, there would never have been an explosion of people using his software."[10]

The confrontation between the Homebrew Club and Microsoft epitomizes the two conflicting forces that were to shape Silicon Valley and the entire computer industry. On one side were the interests of individual companies. As Bill Gates said, companies producing software require some protection of their property rights so they can earn a return on their effort. On the other side were the interests of the industry as a whole. As Dan Sokol implied, an industry undergoing rapid technological advances needs ideas to circulate freely so that current best practice is immediately diffused.

A balance is needed between spreading innovations and rewarding innovators. Getting the balancing act right is difficult, but through a fortuitous confluence of circumstances, Silicon Valley did it by evolving a novel structure for the labor market for computer engineers.

Why Silicon Valley? What made it such a fertile marketplace of ideas? Most industry experts in the 1970s would have predicted that the center of the computer industry would not be Silicon Valley but Route 128 near Boston, Massachusetts. Route 128 was already home to a thriving computer industry. Its firms were the most dynamic in the world. Close to Massachusetts Institute of Technology, it could tap many of the best brains in computer science. But it faded from the scene as Silicon Valley charged ahead. What was the difference?

Silicon Valley's success traces back to a variety of factors. The proximity to and help from Stanford University's engineering school got Silicon Valley started, and Stanford continued to supply it with a flow of highly trained engineers and managers. The lifestyle in California attracted educated young people to stay or move there. The propensity of the leading Silicon Valley firms to subcontract most manufacturing tasks made for flexibility. The ready availability of venture capital made it easy to start new firms, though this is as much a symptom of Silicon Valley's success as a cause of it. Luck also undoubtedly played a role.

The main reason for Silicon Valley's success, argued Annalee Saxenian in *Regional Advantage*, her influential book on what makes Silicon Valley tick, is its culture of mobility and sharing. The labor market for engineers operated differently in Silicon Valley than in Route 128. Unencumbered by tradition, Silicon Valley developed a culture of open relationships between employees of competing firms. Ideas were freely exchanged. Engineers changed jobs often, and no one disapproved if they took what they learned in the old firm to the new one. Massachusetts was more hidebound. Loyalty to the company and long-term employment were valued. Ideas were tightly held within firms.

The job-hopping in Silicon Valley is frenetic. Engineers average a short eleven months in any one job (compared with the three years' job tenure of the average American). "The mobility among people strikes me as radically different from the world I came from out East," remarked a Silicon Valley manager. "There is far more mobility and far less real risk in people's careers."

The job mobility has two consequences, one direct and one indirect. Engineers moving to new jobs take with them what they learned in their old jobs. New ideas are in this way spread through the industry. "Here in Silicon Valley there's far greater loyalty to one's craft than to one's company," said a manager. "If you are a circuit designer, it's important for you to do excellent work. If you can't do it in one firm you'll move on to another one." Also, when engineers from different firms meet casually in the valley's coffee shops and restaurants, they help each other out, bouncing around ideas on how to solve each other's current technical problems. Their incentive to brainstorm with engineers from rival companies is that it might eventually forward their own careers. Each wants to prove how smart he or she is, so that when the other company has a job vacancy—which could be in the near future—his or her name will come up. "The network in Silicon Valley transcends company loyalties," said another manager. "I have senior engineers who are constantly on the phone and sharing information with our competitors."[11] Thus, both the job-hopping and the prospect of job-hopping cause ideas to flow across firms. The Silicon Valley computer technologists followed the maxim Seneca had promulgated two thousand years earlier: "The best ideas are common property."

Why did the Silicon Valley labor market develop a culture of sharing while in Route 128 there was a culture of concealment? The explanation, argued legal scholar Ronald Gilson, lies in differences in laws. The law sometimes protects firms' investments in ideas by prohibiting employees from using in a new job what they learned in an earlier job. A postemployment covenant not to compete stipulates that within a specified period, typically one or two years, a former employee may not go to work for a competing firm. Massachusetts law enforces such covenants, whereas Californian law prohibits them. An employee of a Route 128 firm would risk being sued upon switching to a rival firm. A Silicon Valley employee has no such fear. The job-hopping that has driven Silicon Valley's success arguably traces back to California's weaker protections for intellectual property.

A covenant not to compete, like a patent, is a legal restraint on trade. Massachusetts law, by enforcing it, encourages a firm to innovate by granting it property rights in its employees' innovations, at the cost of preventing employees from seeking better jobs and inhibiting the usage of existing ideas. Not enforcing it, as in California, has the opposite effect. The spreading of ideas through job-hopping is not in the interest of the firm that does the innovating, for it dilutes the firm's returns. But the industry as a whole advances, on the strength of every firm's ideas. Ideas are used more extensively than if they remained inside a single firm. The post employment covenant lies at the root of the differences between Silicon Valley and Route 128. A subtle aspect of market design, in other words, was a crucial element of Silicon Valley's success.

In general, weak intellectual property protection may or may not be a good thing. As Bill Gates said of the stolen program, the disadvantage is that the lessened rewards to the innovating firm could mean no one bothers to innovate. Here the special nature of the computer software industry comes into the story. The life cycle of a new idea in computing is very short. It may be enough that the innovating firm can count on having the idea to itself for perhaps a few weeks. Given the rapid pace of change, a brief period of exclusive use may give the firm enough of a competitive edge that it pays to innovate. Silicon Valley's mores probably would not work so well for other industries. Even in the computer industry, they may not even work well at different stages of development. Ideas flowed freely when the industry was new, but as it matured, the Silicon Valley firms began invoking the law to guard their rights to their ideas. How freely proprietary ideas should be permitted to circulate depends on the specifics of the situation.

If California had stricter intellectual property laws, Silicon Valley's growth might have been stunted. Property rights matter for how well a market works. While leaving intellectual property completely unprotected would mean there would be little incentive to innovate, it is possible, on the other hand, to extend intellectual property rights too far. There are limits to what should be owned.

*   *   *   *

For all that intellectual property protections can be too heavy-handed, in some lines of activity the need for them is undeniable. In the pharmaceutical industry, with the development of a new drug costing hundreds of millions of dollars, secure intellectual property is essential. As we saw with the AIDS drugs, though, the downside of patents can be cruel.

Patents are not the only way of defining property in ideas. An alternative to patents is a buyout mechanism. The government would buy the rights to an innovation and then put the patent in the public domain and let anyone freely use it. The innovator would receive a lump-sum payment, and this would motivate innovation in place of the monopoly profits from a patent. Patented drugs would no longer be overpriced. With the technology freely available to all, the market would be competitive and the price would be driven down to manufacturing cost.

An early precedent for a buyout is the prize the British Parliament offered in the eighteenth century for a method of determining longitude, as chronicled by Dava Sobel in her absorbing book *Longitude*. Untold lives had been lost in shipwrecks caused by navigation errors, so the prize offered was a rich £20,000. A host of inventors submitted ideas, most of them hare-brained. The problem of measuring longitude accurately was solved by a humble clockmaker, John Harrison, with his invention of the chronometer. Its design was made available "for the use of the public" and it came to be mass-produced and universally used aboard ships, making sea journeys far less hazardous.

Could a buyout mechanism be as successful in generating innovation in pharmaceuticals as it was in begetting the chronometer? With the design of the market, as always, the devil is in the details. Two difficulties must be resolved.

The promise to pay must be credible. Following the invention of the chronometer, according to Dava Sobel, the British government balked at paying Harrison the £20,000 prize, raising spurious objections. Harrison struggled the rest of his life for acknowledgment, receiving the full money he was due only after forty years. Buying out a newly developed drug would mean paying many millions of dollars to an already highly profitable pharmaceutical company. A government about to make such a lavish payment is likely to be subject to political pressure from those who see it as a misuse of the taxpayers' funds. The critics could argue that the money would be better spent on the sick than giving it to a drug company. Such pressure might be hard to resist. If the companies anticipate that the government might renege, they will be reluctant to invest up front the millions needed for the research. Without some credible form of commitment, some way of assuring that the promised payments will be made, the buyout mechanism would fail.

The other difficulty is in how to set the buyout price. To generate the ideal amount of research effort, the price should equal the social value of the new drug. The difficulty is, as usual, one of information. The value of an innovation is impossible to assess in advance. Governments—and everyone else—lack the knowledge to set the buyout price optimally. If it is set too low, it will not succeed in generating any new drugs. If it is set too high, on the other hand, the taxpayers' money will be misspent. In the case of the prize for the measurement of longitude, for instance, the flurry of activity set off by the announcement of the prize and John Harrison's own actions suggest, with the benefit of hindsight, that a more modest prize might have worked as well.[12]

A research tournament is an alternative way of generating innovation. This offers a cash prize, as with the buyout mechanism, but is awarded differently. The prize is paid on a specified date and is not delayed until whenever the innovation is successfully completed. It goes to the company progressing the furthest toward developing a drug with the prespecified characteristics, even if the drug is not yet finalized. The U.S. Department of Defense, for comparison, uses research tournaments. In 1991 it ran a fly-off of prototypes for a new tactical fighter aircraft between Lockheed's YF-22 and Northrop's YF-23. The prize, won by the Lockheed plane, was a production contract worth an estimated $90 billion. Similarly, some U.S. electrical utilities sponsored a 1993 contest for the most energy-saving refrigerator; Whirlpool won the $30 million prize.

A research tournament has both an upside and a downside, as does any kind of incentive for innovation, so how well it works depends on the specifics.[13] A difficulty is, once again, setting the prize at the right level. Another is that the government must somehow judge which company's research is the furthest advanced. An advantage is that it is not hard to commit in a credible way to paying the prize, since the government is unconditionally obliged to pay someone a certain sum at a certain date. If the firms were concerned that the government might renege on a patent buyout, a tournament might be more successful in generating research.

Neither the patent buyout nor the research tournament is a perfect way of motivating innovation; but neither is the conventional patent system. It is an open question whether they, or still other alternatives or supplements to the patent system, can succeed in getting new drugs developed and existing drugs affordably distributed. Creative new designs are still needed for the marketplace for ideas.

✳ ✳ ✳ ✳

The Marx Brothers found themselves in a contretemps over intellectual property while making the film *A Night in Casablanca*. Five years before, the Warner Brothers studio had made *Casablanca* with Humphrey Bogart and Ingrid Bergman. Warner Brothers sent a letter to the Marx Brothers threatening to sue them over their film's title.

"I had no idea that the city of Casablanca belonged exclusively to Warner Brothers," Groucho Marx wrote in reply. "What about 'Warner Brothers'? Do you own that too? You probably have the right to use the name Warner, but what about Brothers? Professionally, we were brothers long before you were." And so on for three pages. The Warner Brothers lawyers wrote back asking for a plot outline. After another surrealistic response, they earnestly requested additional plot details. The correspondence came to a halt after the lawyers were flummoxed by a third missive full of Grouchoisms.

Echoing Warner Brothers, the *St. Petersburg Times* of Florida wrote to the *St. Petersburg Times* of Russia in 2000 demanding that it give up its internet address, www.sptimes.ru, since it infringed on the Florida newspaper's rights. The Russian paper retorted that St. Petersburg, Russia was founded long before St. Petersburg, Florida, so the Florida newspaper should change its city's name. They heard no more from Florida.[14]

Farcical as these squabbles are, they illustrate, once again, that property rights should have limits. Groucho Marx made the case, in his inimitable style, that some things just should not be privately owned. From the point of view of society at large, nothing would be gained from assigning property rights to the name "Casablanca" or "St. Petersburg", and something would be lost.

Which brings us back to McDonald's. Their claim to own "Mc" is actually not as frivolous as the claims of the *St. Petersburg Times* and Warner Brothers. Everyone, not just McDonald's, has a stake in the institution of trademarks. Brand names are one of the market's ways of providing credible information. Driving through an unfamiliar neighborhood, you might stop at a McDonald's, rather than a no-name restaurant, because the golden arches tell you exactly what you will get. The name "McDonald's" is an assurance of cleanliness and value for money. McDonald's has invested heavily in building its brand and is justified in defending it.

When one Ronald Goldspink opened a cafe in Withernsea, United Kingdom, and called it MacRonald's, he was sued, and probably appropriately, for he was free-riding on the McDonald's brand. Where is the line to be drawn? After McDonald's objected to her calling her shop McMunchies, Mary Blair said, "This is a small corner shop. We sell cold sandwiches, cold meats, and the odd sausage roll. How can anyone in their right minds confuse us with McDonald's?" That is exactly the right question. Is a given restaurant, by calling itself Mc-something, doing identifiable harm to the McDonald's name? Sometimes it will be, other times it won't be.

Common sense says there are limits. McDonald's prevailed in its suit against the internet health services firm McWellness. Persuading the court to order McWellness to change its name, the burger company's lawyers argued, "McDonald's will likely expand the use of its 'Mc' formative marks to include the same services on which the McWellness mark is intended to be used."[15] Since the company might enter the health-care business at some unspecified future time, in other words, it was entitled to trademark protection for investments not yet made. Such an argument could sway no one but a lawyer.

To sum up, in the design of the marketplace in ideas, property rights play the crucial role. Rights to intellectual property must be defined, for without them there would be limited incentives to innovate. They also must be constrained. A balance must be found between motivating new ideas and allowing the full use of existing ones.

Intellectual property elicits fervent opinions: some say it is an oxymoron; others say the current rules are immutable. Neither view is correct. Because intellectual property involves mutually incompatible aims—rewarding the innovator versus allowing full usage of the ideas—there is no universally ideal degree of intellectual property protection. Whether it should be strong or weak varies with the circumstances.

TEN

::::

No Man Is an Island

Iharm others merely by driving my car. Contributing to traffic congestion, I add a little to the other drivers' lateness, not to speak of their blood pressure. My car's presence on the road, even if I drive carefully, slightly increases others' chances of being in an accident. My car's exhaust fumes pollute the air others breathe.

Economists call such unintended side effects "externalities," meaning any costs (or benefits) external to a transaction or activity. An action brings an externality if it affects, without compensation, others than the decision-maker. Externalities can arise in any market. Since they cause the market to underperform if they are left uncorrected, they may need to be addressed in the market design.

The various externalities from driving are limited by mechanisms that induce drivers to take account of their effects on others: the rules of the road help rein in careless drivers, as does the ability to sue them; regulations on engine emissions put a cap on pollution; and gasoline taxes raise the cost of driving.

One major externality, though, mostly goes uncorrected: congestion. Americans lost an estimated 4.5 million hours while stuck in traffic in 1999. In Los Angeles, Atlanta, and Seattle, the average driver spent more than an hour per week in traffic jams. By driving on a crowded freeway, instead of car-pooling or postponing my trip, I add a little time to everyone else's journey. The delay I cause any one driver is small, but summed over all the drivers affected by my presence, the extra commuting time I cause may well exceed any inconvenience I would have suffered had I not driven. My decision to drive does not take into account the full social costs of my actions.

The U.S. Federal Highway Administration estimated that in 2000 the negative spillovers from driving—the costs of congestion, pollution, and accidents—totaled $446 billion. Some of these social costs were covered by drivers: fuel and vehicle taxes and insurance premiums came to $108 billion.[1] The remainder is the externality from driving. It averages about ten cents per mile driven.

*　*　*　*

While self-directed decision-making is what powers markets, it can also be counterproductive. "No man is an island, entire of itself," said John Donne in 1624, anticipating the concept of externality. An externality can cause a market to malfunction. With a negative externality like pollution, the decision-maker is not accountable for the full costs of the activity, since others bear some of the costs. Too much of the polluting activity therefore takes place. Externalities are not only negative; they also can be positive, as when one firm's research and development spills over and benefits other firms. With a positive externality, there is too little of the activity, since some who benefit do not pay their share. For the market to reach its full potential, its rules must encompass the externality by somehow inducing decision-makers to take account of their effects on others.

Communities sometimes solve externality problems for themselves. If few enough people are affected, they can arrange an amicable solution. In a small country town, off the beaten track, locals drive considerately out of neighborliness. The self-help solution works in some circumstances but not others. For many externalities a bottom-up solution falls short. Urban road congestion is unlikely to be solved by everyone voluntarily driving less. Solving it requires some broad-based decision-making. Sometimes the only workable solutions are top-down ones.

Externalities can be addressed by government-set rules that require people to behave in ways that mitigate their effects on others. Speed limits and other safety-based rules of the road curb driving externalities, as does the law against driving while drunk. The pollution consequences of driving, similarly, are addressed by controls. In Los Angeles, the freeway metropolis, vehicle exhaust fumes used to be a major source of the city's suffocating air pollution. Laws prohibiting leaded gasoline and limiting cars' emissions addressed the problem.

For large and very damaging externalities (the Los Angeles smog caused health problems), outlawing the activity may be the only solution. It is a blunt approach, though, and the cure may be worse than the problem. A more finely tuned remedy is a tax. Putting a price on the externality, a tax induces the decision-makers to take it into account.

A tax on gasoline, by raising the price of driving, helps contain pollution and congestion (although the externalities driving is estimated to cause are larger by far than the U.S. gasoline tax). A tax on alcohol helps contain the externalities from drunk driving. Increasing the alcohol tax, the data show, significantly reduces highway fatalities.[2]

"If you drive a car I'll tax the street," goes a line in the Beatles song "Taxman." Even congestion can be taxed. In 1963, William Vickrey, who later won the Nobel Prize in economics for his work on auctions, proposed a plan for pricing urban car travel in Washington, D.C. Roadside receptors would scan each car that passed, sending the data to a central computer, which would calculate the congestion charge and bill the driver.[3] The fee would be larger when the congestion was greater, and zero when there was none.

Futuristic as the proposal seemed at the time, technology has caught up with Vickrey's imagination. Singapore has put Vickrey's idea into practice, charging drivers for the use of certain roads at peak times. Every car contains a dashboard unit into which the driver inserts a prepaid card. Whenever the car passes a toll station (mounted on an archway above the road) a fee is electronically extracted from the card. The fee varies with the type of vehicle and the time of day. If a car has no card, an infrared photograph is taken of the license plate and the driver is automatically fined. The intention was "to get people to plan their trips better," said transport-authority official Zainal Abidan. "If they don't really need to use these roads, they won't."[4] Traffic in the central business district during peak times fell 13 percent.

Once it is properly priced, the externality from congestion disappears. But this requires more than just the metering technology. It also requires setting the fees correctly. The point is not to raise revenue for the government; it is to make people pay the true cost of their driving. The fee should be just enough to deter those who would value the rush-hour trip less than the congestion costs they would cause others. It is hard to set the fee at just the right level, for this entails estimating the other drivers' losses from the congestion. This difficulty arises with any externality-correcting tax, as the first proponent of such taxes, A. C. Pigou, recognized: the practical difficulty of determining the right taxes is "extraordinarily great. The data necessary for scientific decision are almost wholly lacking."[5] Taxes will not resolve an externality if they are set at the wrong level, and they may even make matters worse.

Given that the price is set right, taxing the externality can make almost everyone better off. You pay a congestion tax one way or the other: if not in cash, it is in the time wasted and the frustration of sitting in traffic jams. Taxing road use would reduce congestion. For those who continue to drive at rush hour, the speedier trip is worth the fee.

Taxation and regulation are top-down externality solutions. Another solution is partly bottom-up, partly top-down. This is to define property rights (top-down) and then let people resolve their externalities by bargaining within a framework defined by the law (bottom-up). Any externality can be viewed as resulting from the incompleteness of property rights. If the air were private property, the owner could charge polluters for the "use" of it, and then there would be no externality. No one can own the air, of course, but in some other cases broadening property rights can be an effective solution.

Given clearly defined property rights, individuals may negotiate a mutually beneficial solution to an externality, as Nobel laureate Ronald Coase pointed out. Imagine a cattle rancher who harms his neighbor, a corn grower, by not maintaining the fence, so the cattle wander into the cornfield and damage the crop. Suppose that fixing the fence would create value (since the repair cost is smaller than the cattle's damage). If the corn grower has recourse to the courts, then the cattle rancher would fix the fence under the threat of being sued. Alternatively, depending on how the law assigns responsibility, the corn grower would pay for the fence to be fixed. Either way, an outcome that is better for both would be reached. Since correcting an externality results in extra value being created, the market participants themselves have an incentive to address it, and sometimes, given well-defined property rights, they can.

Similarly, the threat of being sued turns the cost of careless driving back on you. If you cause an accident through your own recklessness, those you harm can demand compensation, and chances are the courts will require you to pay it. Civil law creates an incentive for safe driving.

Free decision-making in the shadow of the law will not solve all externalities: air pollution is one example. Many drivers contribute to the pollution, so those harmed by it cannot identify who to sue. Since I cannot be sued, the courts provide me with no incentive to limit the harm I do. Taxes or regulation are the only workable solutions when the source of the damage cannot be pinned down.

Externalities are ubiquitous, so every one of them cannot and should not be taken into account, but where they are sizeable, they must be addressed if the market is to work as it should. Which externality solution is the best varies with the circumstances. The checkered history of ocean fishing, which I will turn to next, is a case study in externalities. Just about every possible solution has been tried—usually with a notable lack of success.

✻   ✻   ✻   ✻

In *Cannery Row* John Steinbeck portrayed the lives of workers in the pilchard canneries of Monterey, California, in the 1930s and 1940s. In the less well-known *Sweet Thursday* he returned to the Monterey of the early 1950s. By then the canneries had closed. The industry had collapsed, following the disappearance of the fish. There had been a natural decline in the fish population resulting from a drop in ocean temperatures. But in part the demise of the fishery, to Steinbeck's dismay, was man-made. "The canneries themselves fought the war by getting the limit taken off fish and catching them all. It was done for patriotic reasons, but that didn't bring the fish back. As with the oysters in *Alice*, 'They'd eaten every one.' . . . Cannery Row was sad when all the pilchards were caught and canned and eaten."[6]

Fisheries today are in a state of crisis. The management of marine ecosystems "has failed to achieve a principal goal, sustainability," according to marine biologists Louis W. Botsford, Juan Carlos Castilla, and Charles H. Peterson, writing in the journal *Science*. "Almost a half of the individual fish stocks are fully exploited, and another 22 percent are overexploited." As a result, "the global marine fish catch is approaching its upper limit." A subsequent study in *Science* by nineteen of the world's leading marine biologists concluded that the overfishing had been going on for many centuries, leaving many fish populations disastrously vulnerable, and concluded, "Even seemingly gloomy estimates of the global percentage of fish stocks that are overfished are almost certainly far too low."[7] In the United States alone, species such as red snapper, New England cod, Chesapeake Bay blue crab, swordfish, Atlantic billfish, winter flounder, shrimp, tuna, and shark suffer from overfishing. What causes the chronic overfishing?

Governments are part of the problem. Countries such as Spain and Taiwan subsidize their fishing fleets, in the name of preserving employment, resulting in an overcapacity that creates pressures to overfish. As a result of the U.S. and Canadian governments' subsidizing ever-larger boats, the Georges Bank fishery off New England, once highly productive, was fished out. Doling out subsidies is a way to avoid inducing the industry to adjust to new realities. It hastens the depletion of fish stocks. United Nations Food and

Agriculture Organization (FAO) statistician Christopher Newton said, "The history of fishing is to postpone problems until you run out of fish." So heavy is the subsidization that, according to the FAO, $90 billion is spent each year around the world to catch $70 billion worth of fish.[8]

The main reason for overfishing is not the subsidies, however, but an externality. Overfishing occurs primarily because the fishers respond to the incentives they face.

Fish swim freely, so fishing is different from farming. The open ocean and its contents cannot be parceled out as land is. Property rights are hard to monitor and enforce. No one owns the fish before they are caught. With ill-specified property rights, the market works badly. Biology sets a maximum extraction rate. If too many fish are caught, too few are left in the ocean to reproduce at a rate that maintains their population at a sustainable level. Free-market incentives, however, lead to overfishing.

"Right now, my only incentive is to go out and kill as many fish as I can," said John Sorlien, a Rhode Island lobsterman. "I have no incentive to conserve the fishery, because any fish I leave is just going to be picked by the next guy." His logic is watertight. The fish will be caught and will not reproduce, even if he behaves responsibly and refrains from catching them. He cannot by himself ensure the fish stocks are maintained. His choice is to catch either a large number today and few tomorrow, or a smaller number today but no extra tomorrow. Responsible behavior goes punished. There is a race to fish. The logic of the situation traps each fisher into taking as many fish as he can. There is an externality, in that others bear the costs of one's own overfishing.

The fishing industry takes 80 to 84 million tons of fish each year from the world's oceans. According to the World Wildlife Fund, fishing at a rate that would allow the fish to regenerate would mean catching just 60 million tons per year. Jim Leape of the wildlife fund said, "The oceans can no longer absorb the abuses we have piled on them."[9] How can overfishing be prevented? The various solutions that have been tried cover the full range of externality remedies.

If the ocean were controlled by a single owner who expected to continue to own it in the future, the problem would be solved. The single owner would recognize that his self-interest lay in conservation. A single-owner fisher benefits tomorrow from leaving fish in the ocean today.

The idyllic palm-fringed coral atolls of the Marshall Islands dot the Pacific Ocean five hours' flight west of Hawaii. Their population and landmass are tiny: sixty thousand people live on a total area of seventy square miles. But because there are more than twelve hundred widely scattered islands and because all the ocean within two hundred miles of land is in their territorial zone, the Marshall Islands government controls a vast swathe of open ocean. The ocean is their main resource. Remote and unassuming as they are, the Marshall Islands are perhaps unique in the world in their fishery management. The government has implemented the single-owner solution to the overfishing problem. It made an exclusive agreement with a U.S. private company, Ocean Farming Inc., under which it alone may fish the Marshalls' eight hundred thousand square miles of ocean. In exchange, Ocean Farming pays the government a royalty of 7 percent of the value of the fish it harvests.[10]

Ceding control of the oceans to a single fishing company, however, is not usually practical or politically desirable. The Marshall Islands had no domestic commercial fishing industry, so there was little opposition to contracting out the entire ocean. (Local island fishers are permitted under the contract to continue small-scale fishing for their own needs.) Most fisheries around the world support many independent fishing boats, whose owners and crews would mobilize political opposition against a monopolization of the fishery. For this and other reasons, single-owner solution is usually not an option. A variety of other solutions to the problem of overfishing have been tried, both formal and informal, with varying degrees of success.

Communities of fishers sometimes devise informal solutions: collective mechanisms to counter overfishing. In the Bahia region of northern Brazil, fishers work within an intricate code of conduct governing both the total amount of fish that can be taken and how much each of them may take. The members of the community sanction those who violate the code, refusing to speak with them in social situations or sabotaging their boats and nets. In Tonga, fishers obey social norms requiring them to share their fish. Anyone who catches more than his family can eat must give it away according to rules that favor the needy and the elderly. The local fishing communities of Japan also manage their resources in a sustainable way. Because they have specific geographic boundaries and the same families engage in fishing from generation to generation, all understand the code of conduct and social sanctions effectively support it. In the U.S. state of Maine, some communities regulate lobster fishing in local waters, determining who may fish when and where. They back their conservation measures with force. Anyone who flouts the community's rules risks having his traps cut free or even having his boat sunk.[11]

Informal solutions work only within tight-knit fishing communities.

With large, anonymous groups of fishers that outsiders can enter, social sanctions hold little sway and so government intervention is usually needed to prevent overfishing.

Regulating fisheries, governments have imposed controls on the number or size of boats. They have specified that fishing can take place only within a certain season. Each of these is a blunt form of control, and each leads to predictable distortions. Regulatory controls on inputs induce the fishers to compensate by overusing whatever inputs are unregulated.[12] Restrictions on the number of boats have brought bigger boats with extra equipment and crew. Restrictions on the length of the vessels have induced companies to build wider, heavier boats. Restrictions on the number of crew have resulted in investment in high-tech fishing gear; adding electronic devices for locating fish increases a vessel's catch dramatically. Restrictions on equipment, on the other hand, have meant extra crew being hired. A short fishing season induces firms to invest in high-capacity boats so they can catch as much as possible in the time allowed; the investments sit idle for the rest of the year. A short season also means that for much of the year the fish must be delivered frozen to the customer, providing less value than if it were fresh.

Recognizing these distortions from regulation, some governments have switched to a new, more market-based method of conservation. Rather than controlling inputs, the regulators assign to each fishing vessel a quota, defining how much it is allowed to catch. Quotas directly address the basic issue—that overfishing is a consequence of the fact that no one owns the fish—by establishing property rights. By eliminating the externality each fisher's decision imposes on the others, quotas eliminate the race to fish.

Quotas mean the fish are able to reproduce, making future fishing easier. Rick Garvey, a biologist who monitors quota compliance for the Australian government, said, "Fishing may be the only economic activity in which you can make more money by doing less work."[13]

The countries that have gone furthest in establishing fishery property rights—including New Zealand, Canada, and Iceland—allow quotas to be bought and sold like any private property. A new entrant or an incumbent wanting to expand needs to buy quotas. This means the quotas end up with the most efficient producers. Unlike under regulation, the fishers have reason to invest in productivity-improving skills and equipment.

Quota holders have a large stake in preserving the fishery in order to maintain the value of their quotas. In New Zealand, the fishers have formed associations to fund research aimed at conserving the stocks of scallops, snapper, and orange roughy.

Halibut fishing off British Columbia, Canada, was in a state of crisis in the 1980s.[14] Catches had plummeted. The regulators successively reduced the length of the fishing season in a vain attempt to prevent overfishing, to such an extent that by 1990 fishing was allowed for just six days of the year. The exceedingly short season meant that fishing was intense. Fights would break out among the fishers for the best areas. Safety was compromised as boats stayed out even in dangerous weather. After the regulators introduced individual quotas in 1991, the economic efficiency of the halibut industry improved significantly. The need for the short season disappeared, so fish were caught when needed and marketed fresh. The number of active boats fell. Fishing became a more profitable and less acrimonious activity. Conservation was achieved.

✻ ✻ ✻ ✻

The fishery illustrates the force of property rights. Overfishing occurs because no one owns the fish before they are caught. Creating property rights, by means of quotas, removes the incentive to overfish. But it is an imperfect solution, for the monitoring of the property rights is expensive and leaky.

Workable property rights in fish are not created by the stroke of a pen. Quotas do not eliminate the need for regulatory supervision. The regulator must devise rules on who initially receives the quotas. Dividing up the rights to the catch is inevitably a source of contention among the fishers. Ongoing and extensive government monitoring is needed to check that the catches do not exceed the quotas. This is intrusive and costly, for activities at sea are harder to monitor than most land-based activities. Official inspectors check catches upon landing, and there are stiff fines for exceeding quotas. In the British Columbia halibut fishery, every single fish is tagged with the vessel's code as it is landed on the dock so it can be traced through to final use. Some regulators require vessels to carry on-board observers or video cameras. Some countries, such as Australia, use military aircraft to patrol their waters, checking for boats that should not be there. Even the most sweeping solution to the problem of overfishing, granting monopoly rights as in the Marshall Islands, does not eliminate the need for oversight from the government, for it must be able to monitor the fishing company's catches to be sure it is receiving its due royalties. Property rights in ocean fishing come only if the government expends sizeable bureaucratic, investigative, and enforcement resources.

No system of monitoring, moreover, is infallible. New Zealand goes to greater lengths than most countries to prevent out-of-quota fishing. It insists on full documentation, with paperwork recording each step of the fishes' journey from point of landing to final consumption or export. Fishers may not sell fish to anyone other than a licensed fish receiver. Catch reports, licensed-fish-receiver receipts, cold-storage records, and export invoices are all collated and checked for discrepancies. Overfishing and misreporting are criminal offenses. Fishery officers police the illicit trade in fish with a zeal that recalls Elliott Ness's crusade against alcohol sales in the prohibition-era United States. In a typical incident, a man was arrested for selling a sackful of unauthorized crayfish (or rock lobster) at a pub. Even so, the poaching persists. An estimated 450 tons of crayfish are sold on the black market each year.[15] This is one-seventh the size of the legal catch. It is almost impossible to perfectly enforce property rights in fish.

Quotas are still harder to implement if more than one country is involved. Many fish swim between jurisdictions. Swordfish, for example, migrate widely, back and forth between equatorial areas to cooler waters, so conserving their stocks requires international cooperation. More than thirty countries harvest swordfish, and genuine conservation requires that they all agree on the limits and on how cutbacks are to be shared. Where large sums of money are involved, international agreements are hard to come by, and negotiations often fail.

International confrontations over fishing periodically hit the headlines. A Russian gunboat once rammed a Japanese fishing boat in the Bering Sea. South African officials once detained a Spanish trawler for using illegal twenty-kilometer-long nets. Icelandic and Norwegian fishing boats have exchanged gunfire in the North Sea. Factory fishing in the South Pacific by Japanese and Taiwanese boats has led to regular disputes with various island states, sometimes with boats being seized. Declining fish stocks sparked a tuna war in the Bay of Biscay between Spain and the United Kingdom, a turbot war in the North Atlantic between Canada and Spain, and a cod war in the North Sea between the United Kingdom and Iceland.

Some international accords have been negotiated. The United States and Canada operate an agreement on sharing Pacific salmon. Japan, Australia, and New Zealand have an agreement that defines country-level quotas on the southern bluefin tuna. In both cases the negotiations were concluded only after animosity had undermined relationships between the contending countries.

Compliance with international quotas is still more uncertain than with domestic quotas, because enforcement is more problematic. In 1999, five years after the bluefin tuna agreement was signed, Australia and New Zealand complained to an international maritime tribunal that Japan had overfished in violation of the agreement. "Japan is putting in jeopardy a very important, highly migratory stock that is already in a seriously depleted state," said Tim Caughley, a New Zealand government lawyer. Japan's officials defended its fishing as "experimental." The sixteen hundred tons of above-quota tuna that Japanese boats had caught in one year were "essential" to its research efforts to assess the bluefin tuna population. (The "experimentally" caught tuna ended up being auctioned in Japan's fish markets for use as sashimi, fetching up to $100 per kilogram.) The tribunal ruled against Japan. "It is regrettable that Japan's views were not fully understood," said Foreign Minister Masahiko Komura after the ruling. The "experimental" fishing beyond quota continued.[16]

The fishery, in summary, is impervious to perfect management. In a fixed and stable community of fishers, codes of behavior backed by social sanctions can confine fishing to a sustainable rate. But in most fisheries new fishers can enter, so there is no such stable community, and an absence of government oversight brings disastrous overfishing. Government regulation of fishing, on the other hand, causes distortions and in any case usually fails to avert the overfishing. The best feasible solution is catch quotas. By creating property rights, quotas directly tackle the externality of the fishers' decisions on how many fish to take. While this is the most market-oriented of the solutions, it can be implemented only with extensive government monitoring.

Let us turn to another market encumbered by an externality that is resistant to solution: the labor market for sports stars.

*   *   *   *

A noisy demonstration took place in Kansas City in May 1999 over a curious kind of injustice. "Share the wealth," the protesters' placards demanded. What had aroused their anger was not world hunger or globalization or the environment or civil rights—it was a perceived inequity in baseball. The demonstration took place at a game between the Kansas City Royals and the New York Yankees, as some five thousand fans stormed out of the stadium. Some of them wore Yankees caps with dollar bills stuck to them, to symbolize that money rules baseball.

Odd as the incident was, the protesters had a point. The baseball players' labor market is skewed. The Yankees splurge on players. Lavish spending translates into on-field success. That success can be bought is illustrated by the Florida Marlins. Spending freely, the newly founded club won the 1997

World Series. The next year it cut its payroll to less than one-fifth of what it had been by trading away its best players, becoming the worst team of the year. Between 1996 and 2000, the only other club to win the World Series was the Yankees, the club with the league's largest salary bill. Of the 189 postseason games played from 1995 and 2000, just three were won by teams in the bottom half of the salary distribution. The gap between the payroll for the lowest team and that for the highest in 1989 was $30 million; by 1999 it had grown to $160 million. The sportscaster Bob Costas said pay disparities are the root of baseball's ills, threatening to create a "monopoly on sustained success."[17]

"There is no way we can be competitive," complained one of the Kansas City protesters, a Royals fan. "They are more of a circus act than a baseball team. You go out there for the carnival atmosphere. You don't go there to watch a competitive game." Or you don't go at all. The lack of competitive balance in the league harms all the teams, not just the poorer ones, as some fans will not pay to watch predictably one-sided games, and television ratings will fall. Fans like their own team to be somewhat better than the opposition, but not too much better. A team that wins with absolute inevitability is almost as boring as one that perpetually loses.

The data on attendance at baseball games confirm that competitive balance matters. A close competition is not the only thing. Fans like to watch the skills of outstanding players like Derek Jeter: the data show that the quality of both the home team and the visiting team significantly affect attendance. But if the quality of each separate team is held constant, attendance is higher when a close contest is expected (as measured either by the betting odds or the difference between the two teams' recent win percentages). Statistical studies of other sports, like American football, Australian-rules football, international cricket, and English soccer, also conclude that more fans show up at games that are expected to be close.[18]

The history of professional sports in the United States shows the value of an even competition. The league structure evolved slowly. The first professional teams in baseball and basketball were "barnstormers," like basketball's Harlem Globetrotters: they played exhibition games intermittently against each other and against amateur teams. Initially, therefore, the teams were autonomous. After about twenty years, however, they relinquished their independence and formed themselves into leagues (baseball in 1871, basketball in 1937). The formation of the leagues was a response to consumer demands. The barnstormers, winning easily against much weaker opponents, offered a spectacular exhibition of their players' skills. But it soon became clear that fans preferred, and were more likely to attend, organized championships. Exhibitions of skill were not enough: fans wanted intense play and the tension of winning and losing serious games. Professional sports attracted large numbers of paying spectators only after the leagues were formed and rules were put in place to provide reasonably balanced competition.[19]

Healthy sporting competition requires a reasonably even distribution of player talent, then, so that there is a competitive balance among the teams. Every team in the league has a stake in keeping the competition somewhat even. Nevertheless, the teams in large-population regions tend to bid away the best players.

An externality generates the imbalances in baseball. A strong team acquiring extra stars increases its share of the pie by raising its chances of winning, but it shrinks the total size of the pie by unbalancing the on-field competition. A lopsided player trade affects not just the two teams directly involved, but also, via its effects on competitive balance, the entire league. But since each team bears only a fraction of the harm its trading causes the league, individual teams have inadequate incentives to promote competitive balance. When the New York Yankees acquired the slugger Jose Canseco in 2000 on a salary of $3 million a year plus bonuses, for example, the *New York Times* commented, "they don't really want him or need him; they just wanted to make sure he wasn't going to play anywhere else."[20] Because the benefits of an even sporting competition are shared by all the teams, a team might bid for a star regardless of the effects on the league.

Now imagine a weak team that lacks the player talent to reach the playoffs, and is unlikely in the foreseeable future to acquire significantly better players. The club may be tempted to profit by trading away any star players it has, for its hard-core fans would continue to pay to attend games even if it dropped from, say, twelfth in the league to eighteenth. Profitable as this is for the individual team, it harms the collective interest of all of the teams by making the competition still more uneven.

Spectators and teams value an overall sporting competitive balance. But rich teams are tempted to bid for all the best players and weak teams are tempted to sell off their best players. Competitive balance is unlikely to be achieved, therefore, without some limits on player movements. A completely free market for players' services would not work well. To take account of the competitive-balance externality, a degree of coordination is needed—some rules to govern the players' labor market.

⁂   ⁂   ⁂   ⁂

Here is the catch. It is the league that sets the rules on the movement of players among teams, and the league's motives are mixed. Achieving competitive balance is one of its goals, but not the only one. The league consists of the teams' owners, who have a stake in holding down the players' salaries. Anything that restricts competition among the clubs for players is in the club owners' mutual interest. "In no other labor markets," noted economists Sherwin Rosen and Allen Sanderson, "are employers collectively allowed to impose restrictions on payments to workers."[21]

Over the years, sports leagues have introduced numerous policies in the name of competitive balance. In many of these instances competitive balance has merely been a subterfuge for holding down the players' pay. The policies adopted by the major U.S. professional sports leagues—the reserve clause, the rookie draft, salary caps, and revenue sharing—have often failed to achieve competitive balance. But they have succeeded in keeping the players' incomes down.

A form of involuntary servitude called the reserve clause, introduced by baseball in 1880, bound the player to a club for his entire playing career. The club could sell the player to another club, which then received the remaining career-long rights to him. The reserve clause did not induce balanced competition, because rich teams still bought any players they wanted (the data show no increase in the unevenness of baseball teams after it was abolished). Its only effect was to limit the players' salaries, which eventually led, in 1976, to the courts ruling it illegal.

The rookie draft in American football operates by reverse order of finish: the team doing worst in the competition gets the first choice of rookies. By restricting the market for rookies, this limits rookies' salaries. Like the reserve clause, it seems to have had little effect on competitive balance. Rich clubs buy the best players, regardless of where they are drafted initially.

A salary cap—a specified limit on team spending on salaries—is another policy intended to achieve balanced competition. This is used by the National Basketball Association and the National Football League. A share of gross league revenues is designated to go to the players (48 percent in basketball and 63 percent in football). That sum is then divided by the number of teams in the league, to give the maximum payroll per team. Though the salary cap is generally viewed as having had some success, it is not hard to evade, and it has not equalized spending on salaries in basketball. In 1997–1998, the Chicago Bulls and the New York Knicks had payrolls 2.5 times larger than those of the Los Angeles Clippers and the Milwaukee Bucks.[22] This variation occurred because of exemptions: for example, a team may match outside offers made to its players. The true gap, however, is probably much larger than published salaries indicate, because of creative accounting, deferred payments, and unreported payments. "We have spent substantial hundreds of thousands of dollars of the owners' money," said NBA commissioner David Stern, "to make sure that the agreement is lived up to by the owners themselves."[23]

The salary cap means that small-market teams can, and do, win the basketball championship. But it also transfers earnings from the players to the owners. Capping the players' salaries is a blunt instrument for competitive balance.

Revenue sharing among teams is one of the more effective competitive balance policies. Redistribution occurs via ticket and television revenues. National television revenues are shared equally among the teams in the major U.S. sports, but local television revenues are not shared. In basketball and ice hockey, gate revenues are not shared with the visiting team, though as noted, basketball has league-wide sharing of revenues with players. In the American League of baseball, the visiting team gets 20 percent of gate revenues and the home team 80 percent; in the National League, the corresponding numbers are 5 and 95 percent. In baseball, the richer teams pay a tax (which went as high as $17 million per team in 2000), while the poorer teams receive payments (of up to $23 million per team in 2000). Football does the most revenue sharing of the major U.S. sports. The ticket receipts are divided 60/40 between home team and visitor. There is no local televising of games, and national broadcast revenues are shared equally among the teams. Together with salary caps, revenue sharing has allowed the Green Bay Packers, for example, who play in the smallest city of all football teams, to be competitive; revenue sharing accounts for nearly two-thirds of Green Bay's receipts. The downside is that the teams that draw in large numbers of spectators by playing attractively are called upon to subsidize the teams no one wants to watch.

In U.S. sports, then, the reserve clause and the rookie draft have redistributed money between players and clubs but have done little to balance the competition. Salary caps are often evaded, and only limited revenue redistribution has been achieved. While these methods are potentially effective, neither fully addresses the problem of competitive balance. Salary caps put the burden on the players rather than the clubs, and revenue sharing penalizes success. The problem of competitive balance has been solved, at best, partially.

Outside the United States, two further policies toward even competition are used. One is to split the teams into higher and lower divisions, each with its own separate competition. The competition within each division is more even than it would be if all teams competed with each other. At the end of each season, the worst teams are relegated to a lower division, and the best teams in the lower divisions are promoted, thus providing additional incentives to perform. The divisional structure has the advantage of punishing failure, not success.

The other policy is transfer fees. The club acquiring a player pays a fee to his current club. The fee is negotiated, and if the offered fee is too low, the current club can block the trade. Transfer fees can mount up: in European soccer in the late 1990s, fees of $20 million or more were not uncommon. To acquire the player Luis Figo in 2000, Real Madrid paid Barcelona a transfer fee of $56 million. Transfer fees seem to have been no more successful than the other policies in generating competitive balance. In English soccer, for example, the same handful of clubs dominate its Premier League year in and year out. According to Viviane Reding, a European Union commissioner, transfer fees had failed to prevent "the widening of the gap between the economically powerful and the economically less powerful clubs."[24]

Sports leagues, then, need to address the externality from each team's personnel decisions. But the market designers are the owners, who are not neutral. A possible solution might be to bring the players into the league's rule-setting process, though this is unlikely to occur unless the players' union is powerful. A good design for a sports labor market is yet to be implemented. In market design, it matters what the interests of the designer are.

*　　*　　*　　*

Sometimes a market spontaneously arises to take care of an externality. Beekeepers provide a benefit to fruit growers, as the bees pollinate the fruit trees. If this were not rewarded, too few bees would be housed near the orchards. In the state of Washington, growers pay beekeepers to place hives among their trees. The beekeepers move with the seasons: in the early spring they put their hives in the cherry orchards in the south of the state, then in the late spring they truck them northward to the apple orchards. The fruit growers pay the beekeepers pollination fees.[25] The would-be externality is addressed by contract.

Some externalities are not resolved as easily as that though, pollution being one example. An infamous case occurred in Minamata Bay, Japan. The Chisso Corporation, a chemical producer, dumped tons of industrial waste containing mercury into the bay between 1932 and 1968. The local people contracted mercury poisoning from eating seafood. Brain damage and paralysis followed. "I saw patients screaming and scratching the walls in agony," said Eiko Sugimoto, a survivor of the disaster.[26] Hundreds died and thousands fell ill. Children were born with physical defects. Even after researchers had proven that mercury was the cause of the illness, the company continued its dumping for another ten years. It stopped only when the production method it was using was superseded by a cheaper one. Some of the side effects of market activity cannot be left to the market.

Some externalities can be corrected by defining and enforcing property rights. In other cases the harmful activity can be taxed. In extreme cases the only solution is to ban it. In a well-designed market, the rules are set so that transactions bring few uncompensated side effects. As the ocean fisheries and sports leagues illustrate, however, such a design can be hard to set right.

We have now addressed all of the basic features of market design. A workable platform for markets has five elements: information flows smoothly; people can be trusted to live up to their promises; competition is fostered, property rights are protected but not overprotected; and side effects on third parties are curtailed. For the remainder of the book I will look at how these five elements of market design get to be implemented—or fail to be.

ELEVEN

⠿

A Conspiracy against the Public

Mobutu Sese Seko, as president of Zaire (which after his death reverted to calling itself the Democratic Republic of Congo), stole billions of dollars from the nation's mineral trade. Mobutu built for himself a dozen mansions around the country. One had floors of Italian marble and faucets of solid gold, a discotheque, a nuclear shelter, a fifteen-thousand-bottle wine cellar, musical fountains in the garden, and a private zoo stocked with rare animals. While Mobutu guzzled pink champagne, elementary state functions went neglected. In a nation rich in deposits of copper, cobalt, uranium, gold, and diamonds, people barely scraped together a living as the economy crumbled.[1]

An intrinsic tension exists between state and market. On occasion it becomes unhinged. The government has an essential role to play in designing markets. But intervention in markets has a downside, for governments cannot necessarily be relied on to act as they should. Governments sometimes hamper markets. Mobutu is an extreme example, but regrettably politicians and bureaucrats who expropriate from their citizens are not rare. Government officials sometimes obstruct markets and profit from them by extorting bribes. They also on occasion help favored market participants to conspire against the public.

*   *   *   *

In Russia, business operates under state harassment. While many bureaucrats are honest, others routinely squeeze bribes from firms. "The whole situation is so corrupt, everywhere you go people forget about the interests of the industry," says a Moscow entrepreneur. "They simply mind their own interests. Everyone wants to grab a buck." Bribes are paid when registering a business, arranging a lease of a state-owned building, obtaining a loan from a state bank, bringing imported goods through customs, getting an export license, reporting income to the tax authorities, undergoing a fire or safety inspection, and having a telephone line installed. Corruption is one of Russia's most prevalent crimes; each year prosecutors uncover around three thousand cases of bribery of government officials—and this is just the tip of the iceberg. The amount taken in bribes, by one estimate, exceeds the sum of government expenditures on education, science, and health care. Corruption adds perhaps 5 to 15 percent to the price of goods and services.[2] "If you are in the government and you don't take a bribe now, people don't look at you as honest," said Russian political analyst Sergei Markov. "They look at you as stupid."

Firms must pay off not only corrupt officials but also criminal gangs. Payments for "protection" are rife. Officials are sometimes indistinguishable from criminals. A Moscow prosecutor complained, "The main way the *mafiya* penetrates into the economy is through the bureaucrats. They are our main enemy. The *mafiosi* are only the second enemy."[3]

One of the most elementary propositions in economics is that people will not invest if they cannot keep the fruits of their investment. Russia's economic performance fell behind that of many of the eastern European reforming countries through the 1990s. One of the major reasons for this lag was the insecurity of property rights. In a survey of small manufacturing firms in five transition countries—Poland, Romania, Slovakia, Ukraine, and Russia—the managers were asked about their exposure to corruption. In Russia and Ukraine, almost all said bribes were paid for business registration and fire, sanitary, and tax inspections; in Poland, Romania, and Slovakia, 20 to 40 percent reported bribes. A firm's willingness to reinvest from its retained earnings is clearly related in the data to its susceptibility to corruption.[4] The firms most at risk of extortion invested nearly 40 percent less than those least at risk.

The economic growth data confirm this: more corruption means less investment and less growth. Measuring countries' corruption levels in a way that allows comparisons is not easy. Indexes of corruption levels in various countries have been constructed based on questionnaires given to foreign business consultants. Such indexes are necessarily subjective and inexact, but they give us a sense of how much corruption discourages investment and lowers growth. When economist Paul Mauro ran a statistical analysis across seventy countries, using these corruption indexes and national income and investment data, he found that where the index of corruption is higher, the rate of investment is significantly lower. Measuring corruption on a scale of 0 to 10, with 10 meaning the country is perfectly free of corruption and 0 meaning most corrupt, the data show that a two-point improvement in the corruption index pushes investment up by four percentage points, which in turn boosts economic growth by over half a percentage point.

India's corruption index is 3.3, and Italy's is 7.3. The statistical results say that if India were to reduce its corruption level to that of Italy, its annual growth rate would be 1 percent higher than it currently is: it would grow at a rate of 6 percent, instead of the 5 percent rate it averaged through the 1990s. Compounded over a few years, this would bring a marked improvement in Indians' standard of living. If Italy reduced its corruption to the level of the United States, 9.3, its growth rate would be half a percent higher.[5]

The general tendency for corruption to derail markets and impoverish a country is hardly surprising. Interestingly, though, there are a few exceptions. Indonesia under President Suharto had fast growth for thirty years despite widespread corruption.

In the late 1960s Indonesia had been one of the world's poorest countries. The average Indonesian had a lower income than did people in countries like Bangladesh, Nigeria, and Ghana. Under Suharto, the macroeconomy was stabilized: budgets were balanced and inflation was kept in check. Agricultural reforms encouraged food production, and oil exports brought foreign earnings. The sustained growth that followed meant that by the 1990s Indonesia became a middle-income country. Per capita income in 1992 was three times its 1960 level. The benefits of this growth were widespread. The proportion of the population below the poverty line fell from 60 percent in 1970 to 11 percent in 1996. In 1997, just a year before Suharto's fall from power, the United Nations honored him for his success in reducing poverty.

Meanwhile, Suharto's family and cronies became immensely wealthy, allegedly siphoning billions of dollars into offshore bank accounts. Suharto's government was like "a monarchy, with a king whose authority has never been questioned, and whose children believe their wealth is God-given," according to a Western ambassador. Estimates of the Suharto family fortune range from $15 billion to $45 billion.

The Suharto family influence reached far and wide. They held significant shares in over twelve hundred companies, according to one estimate:

banks, airlines, hotels, shipping companies, telecommunications companies, shopping malls, television and radio stations, and newspapers. They monopolized the production of paper, plywood, and cement and had stakes in timber companies, flour mills, fertilizer factories, toll roads, power stations, and petrochemical plants. Family members' firms received lavish subsidies and tax breaks and won government contracts without competitive bidding. Foreign firms seeking business in Indonesia usually had to take on a member of the Suharto clan as a partner or agent. Major U.S. companies like Hughes Electronics and Lucent Technologies had joint ventures with the Suharto children. Jusuf Wanandi, a Jakarta-based policy analyst, noted Suharto's "abuse of power in all the things he has done—in forming monopolies, in manipulating state contracts, in using state enterprises for his own purposes."[6]

Markets flourished regardless, and with them economic growth. Indonesia's rapid growth came from healthy investment, higher than that in most of the developing world. (Private sector investment was 17 percent of gross domestic product over 1980–1996. While this was lower than that in some other Asian countries such as Korea and Malaysia, it was higher than that in South Asia, Latin America, and sub-Saharan Africa.[7]) Despite the corruption, both locals and foreigners viewed Indonesia as a secure place to invest.

Indonesia and Russia had comparable levels of total corruption; in fact, in the data Indonesia looks even worse than Russia. According to the watchdog organization Transparency International, Indonesia had the dubious distinction of being the world's third most corrupt country in 1999, while Russia came in seventeenth place.[8] How then did markets operate in Indonesia under extensive corruption, while in Russia markets were stifled?

* * * *

The differing effects of corruption in Indonesia and Russia are explained by a theory of Andrei Shleifer and Robert Vishny.[9] If the fire inspector, the tax evaluator, the customs official, the state-bank loan officer, and the business-license registrar each have the power to damage a firm, they can all extort profits from it. Under free-for-all extortion, each knows that any money left with the firm will probably be taken by some other bureaucrat, so each takes as much as possible. With everyone separately putting his hand in the till, however, the firms are discouraged from investing. Thus, there will be little left to take bribes from next year. The bribe-takers' unrestrained greed deters productive activity, with the result that the total bribes are lower than they could be.

Imagine now a different situation, in which the bureaucrats are tightly disciplined—no less corrupt, but farsighted enough to realize that over the long run they will receive more if their greed is held in check. Limiting the amount they extort enables the firms to invest and grow, ultimately generating a bigger surplus for the bribe takers to exploit later.

This theory fits Russia, where uncontrolled corruption has deterred investment. Before the fall of communism, the Soviet Union apparently maintained discipline over extortion. After the end of communism, self-defeating competitive corruption broke out. "The Communist Party robbed the whole country," according to Mark Masarsky, president of a Russian small-business association. "But they took bribes in accordance with their rank in the hierarchy. Now everyone takes bribes as though it is his last day at work."[10]

In Indonesia, the corruption was rigidly controlled from above and so did not deter investment. President Suharto kept a tight rein on the bureaucrats and controlled the legislature. Most politicians were beholden to him. He personally appointed and promoted all senior bureaucrats, judges, and military officers. Suharto had a variety of channels to monitor bureaucrats. A soldier himself before he became president in a 1967 coup, he turned the army into a tool for his political ends. He installed military officers in the bureaucracy. Large firms bought protection by employing former military officers, who could report troublesome bureaucrats. Petty corruption among low-level clerks in government offices was rampant. But this was small change. Suharto periodically fired officials whenever their bribe-taking became too blatant. A dramatic demonstration of his power came in 1985 when he abolished the entire customs bureau because of its corruption. Suharto's purpose was not to eliminate corruption but to monopolize it.[11]

Suharto's ubiquitous controls ensured that any large-scale surpluses flowed to his family. The discipline over the bureaucrats got markets working. Once businesspeople were assured they would not be expropriated, they invested and the economy boomed. Those at the top prospered immensely, as bribes rose commensurately with profits.

The design of a market matters, therefore, even with illicit activities like corruption. Markets work better, obviously, without corruption than with it. But given that corruption exists, whether functioning markets can coexist with it depends on the rules governing the corruption. Markets worked in Indonesia because the state was able to control freelance corruption and thus limit the investment-deterring effects that corruption usually has. Given that corruption exists, it does less harm to markets if it is monopolized than if it is free for all.

Indonesia's system relied on the power of one man, and fell with him. Suharto resigned in 1998 after riots in which over a thousand people died. The end came partly because of the external shock of the 1997 Asian financial crisis, which was beyond the ability of Indonesia's stunted political, legal, and regulatory institutions to cushion, and partly because of the people's disgust at the Suharto government's cronyism. Demonstrating students chanted "KKN," for *korupsi, kolusi, nepotisme*. In the students' opinion, corruption, collusion, and nepotism were the causes of the crisis. The economy plummeted, contracting in 1997–1998 by more than 16 percent.

Built as it was on ad hoc foundations, Indonesia's market economy could not prosper indefinitely. Reliable political and economic institutions are needed to support property rights so markets can deliver economic growth. Corruption deters business by undermining property rights. What is noteworthy about Indonesia, however, is how long it was able to function without the normal institutional mechanisms for assuring property rights. For thirty years its economy boomed, despite its ad hoc foundations. The crisis cost about three years' worth of growth. Devastating as it was, Indonesians were nevertheless far better off after the crisis settled down than they had been before the growth spurt.

Corruption occurs not only at the level of government officials but also sometimes among market participants, as I will discuss next.

*　　*　　*　　*

In a smoky restaurant in Nagoya, Japan, twenty or so midlevel executives of local construction firms are seated on floor cushions around a low-slung table, eating sashimi and drinking sake. Kimono-clad young women kneel to pour their drinks, light their cigarettes, and dutifully laugh at their jokes. The executives banter boisterously, as old friends. They bargain hard nevertheless. They are here to discuss a road-building project the Nagoya city government is about to put up for competitive bidding. Their agenda is to decide which of their companies will get the contract.

Dango is the name given in Japan to a negotiation among bidders to decide which firm will get the job. The designated firm submits a high bid and its "rivals" bid still higher, maintaining the illusion of competition. For the firms this is a congenial way to do business. Under *dango* each firm knows that it will eventually "win" a contract, without having to go to the trouble of competing, and *dango* spares the firms the discomfort of low prices.

A conspiracy to raise prices is an archetypal bottom-up mechanism. The conspiracy must neutralize the incentives for both member and nonmember firms to act in ways that could destabilize the collusion. Three difficulties must be overcome. First, the conspirators need a way to divide the spoils. Squabbling over how to share the profits could cause the breakdown of the conspiracy. Second, an agreement is worthless without some way of enforcing it. Since contracts to fix prices are not enforced by the law, any collusive agreement must be designed to be self-enforcing. Third, collusion contains the seeds of its own destruction. The high profits earned in a successfully colluding industry attract new firms into the industry. The competition from these new entrants then tends to destroy the collusive arrangements. The success of *dango* in the face of these formidable obstacles is an impressive achievement, a tribute to the ingenuity of the conspirators. How does *dango* work?

It takes at least two to *dango*. The firms form an association, ostensibly with innocuous goals such as promoting safety in construction works. One company is nominated to organize the *dango* group and to set out the *dango* rules. Each participating company notifies the *dango* organizer of which public projects it is interested in. The *dango* organizer sends fax messages to every company stating the time and location of the *dango* conference. Part of the organizer's job is to keep track of which companies have been assigned contracts and to ensure the work is spread evenly. He must also mediate any quarrel over contract assignments.

Dango is a sociable process. The conspirators hold their meetings in restaurants, tea rooms, and golf clubs, thus bringing to life Adam Smith's dictum, "Merchants of the same trade seldom meet together, even for merriment or diversion, but the conversation ends in a conspiracy against the public, or in some contrivance to raise prices." According to tax agency data, the Japanese construction industry each year spends $5 billion or more on entertainment.[12] That is a lot of merriment and diversion.

Not all is fun, however, as a Tokyo journalist points out. "The *dango* organizers have their hands more than full, not only adjusting bids between firms; they must also maintain relations with the various power holders and the *yakuza* [gangsters]. Their evenings are filled with incessant eating and drinking bouts, often to the point of getting physically weak, even ill. . . . It's not an easy job, by a long shot." One sympathizes.

* * * *

The job of the *dango* organizers is essentially that of designing a market of their own. They set informal rules that determine who wins the government contracts.

During the negotiations over the division of the spoils, the conspirators must agree which firm is going to win the particular contract, what price it should bid, and how the other firms are to be compensated.

How is the designated winner chosen? The firms collectively want the firm with the lowest cost for a particular project to be the designated winner, for this ensures that the profits to be divided among the conspirators are maximized. But the negotiations are complicated by the fact that production costs are private information to the firm, and each seeks to gain bargaining advantage from this private information. The group must develop negotiating procedures that are not susceptible to manipulation by members.

The *dango* firms devise procedures for choosing the winner. In some cases winning is simply allocated by turn. From the participants' point of view, this is not the ideal way to collude, for it is unlikely to select the lowest-cost firm. In other cases, formal *dango* rules evolve. The contract goes to the company located closest to the delivery point, for example, or the company that is making the strongest efforts to receive this particular order. When there are successive contracts for the same job, later contracts go to the company that received the initial contract. An alternative rule for allocating the winner works by giving points to each bidder based on both the number of times the firm has participated in bidding and the size of the firm's bid when it won a contract in the past. These rules can be interpreted as attempts to ensure that the winner is likely to be the lowest-cost bidder, and therefore to maximize the total shared profits. They do not always work to everyone's satisfaction: periodically, a *dango* is exposed when a member, dissatisfied with his share of the spoils, leaks details to the press.

How do the conspirators agree on how high the winner should bid? Here the government makes the decision easy. In advance of the bidding it sets a ceiling price. The optimal collusive bid is at or close to this ceiling. Often the ceiling price is leaked to the bidders, typically via former Ministry of Construction officials now employed by the bidding firms. In many *dango* cases, according to a Japanese newspaper, "local government officials effectively have helped hide the abuse by setting estimates that include generous profit margins for the contractors."

How are the losers compensated? During the *dango* negotiations, cash and gifts are exchanged. Upon winning the bidding as planned, the designated firm pays money to the other bidders. These bribes are euphemistically called "cooperation money" or "compensation money." A *dango* among kitchen equipment suppliers against the Matsuyama City government, for example, yielded $35,000 total profit on a winning bid of $114,000. The profits were shared equally: the winning firm paid each of the six other *dango* participants $5,000 each and kept $5,000 profit for itself.

Because collusion is illegal, there is some need for secrecy. Within a construction company, only a few managers are involved in *dango* relationships. By the account of an executive of a construction firm, organizing *dango* resembles a John le Carré operation: "No one, not even inside the company, can easily find out who the *dango* organizers are. This is because *dango* is not the kind of activity to be done openly. If the press learns of a *dango* arrangement, the reporters' investigations must be quickly localized and handled at the level of the *dango* specialists. The system is designed to allow for deniability at the top levels, and so structural arrangements are made for the company's upper management not to have a hand in it."

In the bidding for a contract, any firm other than the designated winner has an incentive to depart from the collusive agreement and bid a little less than the designated winner's agreed bid, thus winning the contract and earning a large profit. What is the *dango* enforcement mechanism? The ongoing nature of the firms' interaction makes it possible for agreements to be self-enforcing. Firms do not deviate because they know that they will suffer retaliation in future bidding contests; the cost of deviating now is the loss of future profits. Ongoing relationships are found in most industries in any country, however, so this retaliation capability is clearly not enough in itself to generate collusion. Gangsters, allegedly, are sometimes an additional and more immediate means of *dango* enforcement. The government helps by requiring that all bids be made known to all bidders after the bids are opened. This helps keep the *dango* together, for each bidding firm is aware that if it does not bid as specified, all the others will learn of its deviation immediately.

How are new entrants excluded? Once again, government policy facilitates the conspiracy. In the most common tendering system, only officially qualified firms are invited to bid. This policy has a public safety rationale: it is designed to ensure that the selected firm is capable of doing work of acceptable quality. But it makes it difficult for new firms to enter the industry. Conveniently for the conspirators, the government solves one of the trickiest problems in running a cartel.

The government officials who restrict the entry of new competing firms are probably not corrupt; they may be honest but motivated by simple bureaucratic caution. The officials know that if something goes wrong—say, the bridge that is to be built falls down later in an earthquake—then they will suffer blame if they award the contract to an outsider firm, even if they have thoroughly checked the firm's competency.

For a firm to be put on the list of qualified bidders, only work it has done in Japan is taken into account. This procedure prevents entry into the market by foreign firms, for they do not have a history of work in Japan. The logic is a classic catch-22: you cannot win a contract unless you bid, but you are not allowed to bid unless you have won a contract.

* * * *

The main victim of *dango* is the Japanese taxpayer. The price of construction projects is inflated by an estimated 15 to 30 percent. The Japanese government spends lavishly on public works, awarding over $100 billion worth of construction contracts annually for roads, bridges, tunnels, and airports. The unduly high prices attributable to *dango* mean that many billions of dollars of taxpayers' money are wasted.

A new Tokyo subway line by 1999 had run up a massive $10 billion construction bill, 50 percent more than projected in 1989. The cost overruns caused Shintaro Ishihara, Tokyo's governor, to assert that the project was ridden with *dango*. He retracted his claim just slightly after being criticized by the municipal bureaucrats charged with overseeing the construction. "I don't know that *dango* is involved," he said. "I don't think so, but it's very strange, isn't it, very mysterious that such discrepancies in cost would arise, considering there were so many smart people here working on the bidding."[13]

Why does *dango* persist, and why is the construction industry so hard to reform? Reported profit data provide no evidence that the firms involved benefit greatly. Doubtless some of the profits from *dango* make their way into the pockets of the firms' owners and are hidden by creative accounting, but most do not. The firms must try so hard to earn the monopoly profits that they end up with little net gain. Firms use up resources in competing for monopoly profits. Much of the excess profits that *dango*'s high prices generate are bid away in the competition for political favor; they end up in the hands of the politicians.

The construction industry is the largest single source of political contributions in Japan. The political funding process is so murky that no one knows how large the construction industry's contributions are; they probably come to billions of dollars. According to a Japanese newspaper report, the large construction companies distribute money to politicians according to how influential the individual politician is in the awarding of public contracts: twice a year each politician is assigned a letter grade that determines how large a contribution he receives. Tokyo prosecutors in 1993 arrested Shin Kanemaru, the deputy prime minister, on charges of income tax evasion.

They found in his office safe over $50 million worth of cash, bonds, and gold bars—donations that had come mainly from the construction industry— intended not for his personal use, according to Mr. Kanemaru, but to realize his "cherished dream of political reform."

Dango is not merely a transfer from taxpayers to firms to politicians. The price-fixing causes real losses in economic efficiency. Three effects work to cause production costs to be inefficiently high under *dango*.

First, competitive bidding allocates the job to the firm best able to do it. The bids reveal relative production costs; the low bidder is the right firm for the job. Despite the efforts *dango* organizers make, negotiations will usually be less effective than bidding as a means of selecting the low-cost firm.

Second, firms that sidestep the discipline of competition tend to produce inefficiently. They fail to search for cost-reducing innovations; they pay inflated wages and salaries and spend money on lavish perquisites for the executives. Productivity in the Japanese construction industry is lower than in the U.S. and German construction industries. This low productivity might be attributable to *dango*. A caveat is needed here, however. Japan's construction industry has a dual structure. Some of the larger firms are highly sophisticated technologically, as is evidenced by the conspicuous success in international competition of firms like Kumagai-Gumi. Small construction contracts, especially those offered by local governments, are reserved for small firms, on the grounds that they could not win contracts in open competition with the more efficient large firms.

Third, if the colluding firms cannot completely deter entry by inefficient newcomers, industry costs will be higher than they would be under competition. If competition were introduced into the Japanese construction industry, there would probably be a shakeout, forcing thousands of the smallest firms into either bankruptcy or takeover by the more efficient firms. The *dango* organizers reserve certain projects for small firms, to ensure that all firms receive contracts at some time. The government is currently covering unnecessarily high average production costs.

The word *dango* is unique to Japan but the practice, of course, is not. Collusion in public construction bidding occurs in Europe; the Organisation for Economic Cooperation and Development has noted that "such practices are the direct cause of unduly high prices in bids and are incompatible with the sound management of procurement policy." The U.S. construction industry does not refrain from conspiratorial bidding: it has its own equivalent of *dango*. A majority of the criminal cases the Department of Justice files under the antitrust laws are against bid-rigging by construction firms, mainly relatively small road-building companies and electrical contractors doing work for local governments.

*   *   *   *

Governments sometimes conspire to undermine markets. Corruption cuts into productivity because firms that fear they will be at the mercy of bribe-takers are reluctant to invest. Price-fixing also cuts into productivity by preventing the price system from doing its job of allocating resources. Constructive government actions are needed, as I will argue next, to help the market system work as it is supposed to. But there is a risk that government intervention will be perverted in counterproductive directions.

T W E L V E

::::

Grassroots Effort

A Warsaw museum, mounting a retrospective exhibition in 2000 on everyday life under communism, entitled it "Gray in Color." If you visited a communist country like Poland in the 1980s, you would have been struck by its drabness. Reflecting on life under central planning, Czech Republic President Vaclav Havel said that people nowadays "often forget what it looked like here before the fall of communism. How gray life was, how gray streets were, how the sign for a fruit shop was the same all over the country."[1]

How did so many countries come to be centrally planned? The road to hell, as the saying goes, is paved with good intentions. Albert Einstein wrote an article in 1949 called "Why Socialism?"[2] His answer: the market economy brings crisis, instability, and impoverishment. "The economic anarchy of capitalist society as it exists today is, in my opinion, the real source of the evil." The only way to eliminate this evil, he concluded, was by establishing socialism, with the means of production "owned by society itself." He advocated a planned economy, which "adjusts production to the needs of the community, would distribute the work to be done among all those able to work and would guarantee a livelihood to every man, woman, and child."

At the time, Einstein's position was widely shared. Forty years later, though, those living in the planned economies of the Soviet bloc dramatically dissented and threw out the planners. Since the fall of communism, few argue that central planning can work. With the benefit of hindsight, we see that planning delivered the opposite of what Einstein hoped for. The planners were unable to adjust production "to the needs of the community." In the Soviet Union, basic necessities were scarce. Shops had bare shelves and surly staff. When a shop did have something in stock, it was shoddily made, and you had to queue for it. The planners were likewise unable to "guarantee a livelihood to every man, woman and child." The attempt by China's planners to engineer a massive shift of resources from agriculture to industry, in the grotesquely misnamed Great Leap Forward of 1959 to 1961, caused the worst famine in world history, with an estimated 30 million deaths.[3]

How could a genius like Einstein, whose very name connotes supreme intelligence, a man of indubitably good intentions, espouse ideas that we see nowadays to be utterly wrongheaded? That central planning would fail was not self-evident in Einstein's time. Nor was it self-evident that the market system could work any better.

How much of the economy should be left to markets? The pitfalls of central planning are fundamentally problems of information. The planners cannot mobilize the knowledge they need for their decision-making. An economy cannot, therefore, be successfully controlled from the top. How is a system of markets able to function with no one in charge? The answer—which on first hearing strikes many as surprising, even implausible, but is nevertheless true—is that markets gather information dispersed among millions, and prices steer the economy.

What is the role of the state in the economy? An honest answer cannot be unequivocal. Two propositions identify the strengths of markets as well as their limits. First, their vigor comes from their decentralized nature: they empower people to find creative solutions to problems. This is opposite to the state, which is intrinsically centralized. So resilient are markets that sometimes they operate without the support of the state and even in the face of state harassment. It does not follow, however, that the state should stay away. The second proposition is that for the elaborate exchanges occurring in modern economies, the state is indispensable, providing goods and services that markets would undersupply and acting in the background as market rule-setter and referee. These two propositions are not equal. There are limits to decentralization, but the primary point is that decentralized—that is, market-based—decision-making is essential for economic success.

*   *   *   *

Communist planning is dead, but an autopsy can be informative. The failures of central planning teach us about the workings of its opposite, the market system. Communism negated all the tenets of markets. Whereas markets are inherently decentralized, the communists tried to centralize everything. Private ownership was outlawed. Firms were owned by the state. Rather than competing with other firms to sell their products, firms merely delivered them to the state. Prices did not rise and fall to balance supply and demand. Instead, planners set prices, at levels little related to production costs, and tried to dictate the movement of goods. Entrepreneurship was banned, and bureaucrats determined investment. In the place of financial markets, state banks allocated finance. In the absence of a rules-based commercial legal system, bureaucrats enforced agreements and resolved disputes case by case.

The upshot of the denial of markets was an economy that, despite using ruthlessly authoritarian methods of control, was woefully inefficient. For firms, planning meant following the orders of distant bureaucrats. The managers were less concerned with how best to produce things than with how to work around the plan's rigidities. The result was low productivity. The incentives the planners offered producers were necessarily blunt. Rewards were based on measured output. Glass was measured by the number of square meters produced. Cutting corners to ensure they met their quotas, the glass factories made glass in plates so thin that they often broke before being installed. Steel output was measured by the ton. The fastest way to make a ton of steel plates was to make them thick, so the steel factories made them so thick they were often unusable. The productivity of car manufacturers was measured by the number of cars produced. Not surprisingly, the cars did not run well. Output per worker in the Soviet Union and Eastern Europe in the 1970s, it has been estimated, was over a third below that in Western Europe and the United States. This computation adjusts for cross-country differences in capital, so it says that the planned economy made workers one-third less productive than they could have been. The productivity of China's peasants under planning was about a half what it became after the communes were abolished.[4] The result of controlling the economy from the center was waste.

Why did economy-wide planning fail? Part of the answer is obvious, part of it less so. The power to run the economy was concentrated in a few hands. Stalin's bureaucrats, it would seem uncontroversial to suggest, did not reliably have the best interests of the people foremost in their minds. Power corrupts, and the planners had absolute power over the economy. As Edmund Wilson put it in *To the Finland Station*, his sympathetic history of socialist thought, "Lenin's aims were of course humanitarian, democratic and anti-bureaucratic; but the logic of the situation was too strong for Lenin's aims."

The Communist Party "turned into a tyrannical machine." Wilson concluded that the state's taking over of the means of production can "never guarantee the happiness of anybody but the dictators themselves."[5]

To pin the blame on the planners, however, is to overlook the deeper reasons for planning's failures. Imagine yourself as a central planner. Your task is to design the entire economy. You want to do the best for your country: to ensure, as far as possible, that everyone's needs are met. How do you go about doing that?

It is hopelessly difficult. To manage the nation's production of something as simple as pencils, you must somehow figure out how many pencils are going to be needed over the coming year; split the order among the various pencil factories; coordinate the activities of the retailers and the pencil makers; align the production schedule of the pencil manufacturer with the schedules of the suppliers of the graphite, wood, and rubber; and set appropriate prices for the pencils and the inputs.

The task of calculating the optimal allocation of the economy's resources is so immense as to be impossible to carry out even today, with the biggest and fastest modern computers. This was not foreseen when communist planning began. In 1916, just before the Russian revolution, Lenin wrote that "the bookkeeping and control" necessary for running a socialist economy were "extraordinarily simple operations of watching, recording and issuing receipts, within the reach of anyone who can read and write and knows the first four arithmetical rules." He also said, more pithily, that any cook could be taught to administer a planned economy. The fallacy of planning is encapsulated in his quip. An economy could not be efficiently directed by a cook—or an Einstein. The Soviet Union's plan had to coordinate hundreds of millions of people and hundreds of thousands of firms. It was and still is computationally infeasible.[6]

There are some twenty thousand different job categories in the United States, as listed in the *Dictionary of Occupational Titles*.[7] A central plan could not begin to cope with such diversity. Among the more obscure jobs held by someone somewhere are barrel scraper, bologna lancer, cereal popper, dukey rider, egg smeller, napper, puddler, puffer, scratcher, and wall attendant. In response to this kind of complexity, all the planners could do was to snuff it out.

This is not the end of the problems you face as our imaginary central planner. It is not only the billions of flows of goods and services from firm to firm and from firm to consumer. Even if you could map the multifaceted spider's web that is the economy, your attempts to devise a central plan would founder on a still deeper barrier. You would not know enough about the detailed workings of the economy to be able to plan it.

Knowledge is dispersed through any economy. To decide how much steel, say, could be produced and how its production should be allocated among the various steel producers, you as the planner would need to understand what it takes to manufacture each ton of steel. But this information would have to be extracted from the producers, and there is an incentive barrier to their revealing it. If a firm reported its production costs to be low or its capacity high, you would order it to produce a large quantity. This fact would not escape the attention of the firm's managers. To get easier targets, firms under planning, as a matter of course, hoard their knowledge.

The planning process involved "an enormous amount of falsification in all branches of production and in their accounting systems," reported a 1950s Soviet manager who had defected to the West; "everywhere there is evasion, false figures, untrue reports."[8] In their reports to the ministries that supervised them, managers misrepresented their firms' costs and capacities. They exaggerated their needs of labor, materials, and equipment; failed to report improvements in techniques; concealed the productivity of new machines; understated the number of engineers on hand; and overstated the time needed for a task. Similar misrepresentation occurred at all levels of the hierarchy. Inside the firm, production-floor supervisors padded their reports to middle managers, as did middle managers to top managers. The misreporting did not even end at the level of the firm. The bureaucrats in direct charge of the firm understated its capacity to the central planning commission. The result was a cumulative divergence between actual and reported capacities. The entire Soviet economy ran according to a plan built on biased information.

This informational shortfall was no mere glitch in the Soviet system. It is inherent in central control. Much information arises at ground level. Knowledge relevant to the running of an economy consists of not only scientific and engineering knowledge but also more mundane facts, often about things that are transitory and seemingly trivial. Knowledge of local conditions and of special circumstances is sometimes valuable, and people acquire it as a by-product of their day-to-day tasks. Those who hold crucial information might try to use it to their own advantage, recognizing that what they report to the planners will be used in ways that ultimately come back to affect them. Often this results, as with the Soviet managers, in their keeping their knowledge to themselves.

Apart from whether people choose to pass their knowledge on to the center, it may not even be feasible to pass it on. The anthropologist James Scott has revived the ancient Greek word *mētis* to invoke local knowledge, commonsense, cunning, practical skills, know-how. *Mētis* consists of a "wide array of practical skills and acquired intelligence in responding to a constantly changing natural and human environment."[9] A ship is more likely to survive a raging storm if it is in the charge of a veteran captain, who has *mētis*, than a physicist who is expert in fluid mechanics and structural stability but lacks seagoing experience. A great chef may write a cookbook, as Scott points out, but it would contain only a fraction of the chef's knowledge, and an amateur would be unable to match the chef's cooking by slavishly following the recipes. Many skills arising from repetition and practice are intuitive and not reducible to written rules. Much of what occurs in any economy involves *mētis*. What cannot be written down cannot be incorporated in a plan.

"How can you be expected to govern a country that has 246 kinds of cheese?" asked Charles de Gaulle, voicing the frustrations of being France's president. De Gaulle might have been able to govern the country, but he would not have been able to plan the entire French economy.

*   *   *   *

If we reject economy-wide planning as unworkable, we are forced to conclude that markets must play a significant role. How do we know, though, that markets are up to the task? In such a complex system as a modern economy, how can competitive markets, with no one in overall charge, avert anarchic chaos?

Trades occur in elaborate chains. Starting as raw materials, goods work their way through many firms, each of which adds value, until finally the finished items reach the consumers. Even something as everyday as getting milk from the cow to the dairy factory to the supermarket and then to you is a thorny logistical problem, requiring that many people be coordinated. How can the market solve it?

"It is not from the benevolence of the butcher, the brewer, or the baker, that we expect our dinner," Adam Smith noted, "but from their regard to their own interest. We address ourselves, not to their humanity but to their self-love, and never talk to them of our necessities but of their advantage." Guided by prices, people make their choices. Goods get produced and delivered to the people who want and can pay for them. Self-interest is harnessed to the greater good. Intending only his own gain, a producer or a buyer is "led by an invisible hand," Smith famously concluded, "to promote an end which was no part of his intention."[10] The metaphor of the invisible hand Smith formulated in 1776 is the classic account of what drives a market economy.

It was nearly two centuries before Adam Smith's insight was taken beyond the metaphor of the invisible hand and given a rigorous theoretical foundation. Are competitive markets able to harmonize the actions of millions? Léon Walras took the first big step toward answering this question in the late nineteenth century, formulating a mathematical model of an economy in which, for each good or service in the economy, there was an equation representing the balance of supply and demand. Walras left unanswered the key question of whether it was possible for supply to equal demand simultaneously in every market. This stayed unresolved until 1954, when Kenneth Arrow and Gerard Debreu, in a densely mathematical article that was to earn them Nobel Prizes, "confirmed the internal logical consistency of Smith's and Walras's model of the market economy" (to quote the Nobel committee).[11] One of the supreme achievements of economics, the Arrow-Debreu theory identifies certain precise conditions under which individuals' separate decisions add up to a consistent overall outcome. Prices steer the economy, by rising or falling to restore balance whenever there is a shortage or a glut. The economy can be coherently directed by the market's invisible hand.

In a market economy, the calculations and decisions over the running of the economy are broken down into smaller pieces than under a plan. Given well-functioning markets, prices act as a self-correcting mechanism. If more is demanded of some item than is being produced, potential buyers, willing to pay more than the going price to avoid missing out, push the price upward. The higher price induces producers to increase their output. If there are unfilled jobs for barrel scrapers, the employers raise the offered wage, people change their jobs in response, and the vacancies get filled. With a price system, unlike under central planning, no central authority needs to know when there is an imbalance of supply and demand.

Evidence that price movements can guide an economy to a stable outcome comes from experimental economics, in research done by Vernon Smith and others.[12] An economy is simulated in the laboratory, with experimental subjects, usually undergraduate students, being put in the role of consumers and firms (and to get them to take their decision-making seriously, they are offered cash payments based on the outcomes of their decisions). Provided the experimental market's rules are well designed, prices quickly settle down at their theoretical equilibrium levels (that is, where supply equals demand), even though no one in the economy knows enough to be able to figure out what those prices should be. As Vernon Smith said,

"People are born traders." The rules governing trading induce the experimental economy to "compute" the outcome that equates demand with supply.

What is sometimes called the wisdom of the market results from the dispersion of decision-making. Markets make fewer big mistakes than planners. This is not because businesspeople are necessarily smarter than bureaucrats. The folklore of the computer industry, for example, relates a host of wrong predictions from those best placed to know. In 1954, John von Neumann, the mathematical genius who helped invent the computer, said, "I think there is a world market for maybe five computers." In 1977, Ken Olson, president of Digital Equipment Corp., said, "There is no reason anyone would want a computer in their home." In 1981, Bill Gates, founder of Microsoft, is reported to have said, "640K ought to be enough for anybody." Businesspeople are as prone to forecasting error as anyone else. In a market economy, though, many such forecasts, some right, some wrong, are being acted on simultaneously. Monopolizing economic decision-making in a planning agency, by contrast, means restricting the number of paths that get explored. A market economy works not because forecasts are usually correct but because the consequences of incorrect forecasts are held in check. With a market economy the nation spreads its bets.

*   *   *   *

Since it is impossible to plan the entire economy effectively, markets must be allowed to operate. It does not follow, however, that markets should encompass the whole of the economy. The story of the internet shows us the advantages of decentralized systems like markets—as well as the limits of decentralization.

The internet works like a market economy. Just as a market economy is a system that connects firms to other firms and to consumers, the internet is a system that connects computer networks to other computer networks. They share the same chief characteristic: a decentralized structure and a resulting freewheeling nature. The "strongest feature" of the internet, according to John Quarterman, the manager of an internet firm, is that "no single entity is in control, and its pieces run themselves, cooperating to form the network of networks that is the internet." The world wide web, according to its inventor, Tim Berners-Lee, took off "by the grassroots effort of thousands."[13]

The internet has no central planning bureau, no equivalent of Gosplan, the Soviet Union's planning agency. Instead of a strong central authority, many people control small parts of it. The multiple networks that combine to form the internet are operated by thousands of service providers and hundreds of telecommunication companies.

The internet was designed from the start to have a modular structure, so that parts of the network could be changed without disrupting the rest of it. This paid off: it made the internet adaptable and participatory. Users' needs drove its development. It is constantly being upgraded. Its open structure allowed it to develop not by plan but by evolution. Its inventors did not foresee what it would become. Initially devised as a tool for the military and scientists, it was transformed into a surrogate for the postal service, the library, and the shopping mall.

Imagine what the internet would be like today if it were centrally controlled. Picture Microsoft or IBM, say—or, for that matter, the U.S. Postal Service—as the internet's Gosplan-equivalent. Central control would have stunted the internet. Diversity would have been lost. With the decentralized internet we can each choose how we make contact with it. We can use any available program to access the world wide web. We can choose among the many types of systems, in addition to the web, that use the internet as their communication medium (such as email, file transfers, various kinds of live video and video transmissions, telnet, virtual private networks). We can select our brand of computer. A central planner might have forced everyone to use the same software, the same modes of data transfer, the same hardware, at the cost of flexibility and productivity.

In any system as complex as the internet, knowledge about how its components work is scattered throughout it; no one can oversee it. According to a study by economist Hal Varian and colleagues, the world wide web contains textual content equivalent to ten to twenty million books.[14] No one comprehends the entire process by which traffic is routed through the internet. Maps charting its myriad interconnections do not exist. No one knows how many computers are connected to it, where they are all located, or what people are doing with them. The most sophisticated robotic spider programs are able to explore and record only a fraction of it. Overseeing the entire network, as it currently exists, would be infeasible. Central control requires central monitoring. Insisting that the internet be monitorable would have condemned it to perpetual underdevelopment.

A still bigger cost of central control would have been a curbing of innovation. The main failure of overcentralized systems is their inability to mobilize local knowledge. People at ground level often have the best insights into how the system could be improved. Good ideas come from hands-on users at least as often as they come from people at the center. A central authority usually is unable to harness that imaginative energy. In a system under central control, people at ground level know that if they come up with a good idea, the decision on whether or not to put it into practice will be made by some distant authority. Foreseeing the chance that their ideas will be implemented ineptly, if at all, they might not go to the trouble of trying to innovate. Conversely, if the people at the center want to promote innovation, they might not be able to find ways to motivate the people who have the necessary knowledge. The best way to motivate creative people is to give them a stake in their innovations, that is, grant them the freedom to follow their ideas as they see fit and allow them to keep a share of whatever returns they generate. This means using a decentralized system.

A wide variety of people and groups have contributed to the internet's improvement. If anyone "wants to add some kind of cool feature it doesn't matter in an internetworked world," said David Isenberg, a computer scientist who did early research on the internet. Because there is no central point of control, he continued, "you have the control way out on the edges, and anyone can do anything."[15] A remarkable capacity for innovation resulted, both in technology—for example, in generating low-cost communication devices that have revolutionized telephone, mail, and broadcasting services—and in business methods—reinventing the way goods and services are bought and sold.

The internet's growth "is not a fluke or a fad," said Christopher Anderson of the *Economist*, "but the consequence of unleashing the power of individual creativity. If it were an economy, it would be the triumph of the free market over central planning. In music, jazz over Bach. Democracy over dictatorship."[16]

*   *   *   *

Decentralization, then, is the essence of the internet. As its boosters say, it is "naturally" free. It is commonly described as a libertarian system, running without any central control or direction. Kevin O'Connor, chief executive of DoubleClick, a large internet advertising firm, for example, described the internet as a "platform for libertarianism worldwide."[17] Calling the internet libertarian has become a cliché. It is not just a cliché. It is mistaken.

Labeling the internet libertarian is at odds with how it got started and how it continues to run. According to computer entrepreneurs Sharon Eisner Gillett and Mitchell Kapor (the founder of the software giant Lotus Development Corporation), "Contrary to its popular portrayal as total anarchy, the internet is actually managed." It is not fully decentralized. While 99 percent of the internet's day-to-day operations, according to a guesstimate by Gillett and Kapor, are handled without any direction, central authorities are needed for the remaining 1 percent, consisting of various nonroutine activities. In addition, central authorities were needed to set up the system initially and continue to be needed to integrate new activities into it.[18]

Some of the internet's central decisions come from organizations run from the bottom up. Technical management and standard-setting is the responsibility of ad hoc voluntary groups such as the Internet Engineering Task Force, with open membership and democratic procedures. But self-regulation has not been the only form of central decision-making: the government has also played a role. The internet did not arise spontaneously. It was built by the government. With the internet, the government, for once, picked a winner.

Subsidies from the state got the internet started: the U.S. government spent about $125 million building the internet's predecessors.[19] In the 1960s and 1970s the U.S. military sponsored research into how to link computers so as to allow the sharing of data, and this research led to a network of university computers. Crucial technological advances were also made at the European Laboratory for Particle Physics (known by its French acronym CERN), a cooperative effort of European governments. The National Science Foundation, the U.S. government's science agency, also provided substantial funding after it took over responsibility for the computer network from the military in the 1980s. It was not until 1995 that the U.S. government ended its direct control of the internet.

Not only was government funding crucial; so was government decision-making. The very fact that the internet is so decentralized is, ironically enough, the result of a decision made centrally. The U.S. military imposed the modular structure in the early 1980s for the sake of flexibility of use. Another decision by the military, the adoption of the Internet Protocol, solved the problem that to be able to talk to each other, different kinds of computers needed a common language. Incompatibilities between networks could have arisen, otherwise making it hard to send documents and read web pages. Without a modicum of central management, the internet would not have grown into the flexible, easy-to-use tool we experience now.

Some management continues to be needed, in particular over domain names, or dot-com addresses. For the network to be able to function, each name must be unique; this could not be ensured without coordination. The domain-name servers bring an unavoidable element of centralization.

Each of these servers, one or a few for each address ending such as ".com" or ".edu," acts like a telephone directory, maintaining a master list of addresses and ensuring communications are routed accurately. The system of assigning names to internet users, also, is unavoidably centralized. Names must be in step if they are to be usable. Initially the U.S. government assigned names itself or through a subcontractor. In 1998 it established a private nonprofit corporation to do it, the Internet Corporation for Assigned Names and Numbers (ICANN). ICANN became controversial among those who see the internet as free and informal because it could prevent them from picking whatever domain names they felt like. But coordination of some sort is needed. "Like it or not, you really do need a single root to make it all work," says Vinton Cerf, an internet pioneer who became chair of ICANN. "There should be common ground rules. That's what ICANN strives to achieve."[20]

For contracting and intellectual property protection, internet commerce has relied on the existing state-supplied legal system. The regulatory apparatus of antitrust has shielded internet firms from predatory competition just as it has shielded traditional firms. The state prosecutes those who spread computer viruses.

The internet offers us, then, a conflicting pair of lessons. Its vigor is in its decentralization. The initiative and imagination of hundreds of thousands have pushed it forward. But decentralization has limits. A crucial aspect of the internet's success was its central management. This was a far smaller part of the picture than its users' freedom to make creative adaptations to it, but nevertheless it was indispensable. Without the government's help in getting it started and setting some of its rules, the internet would have been stunted. Some coordination is still needed, though it has to be strictly limited. In the internet or any other complex system, both management and autonomy are essential—the trick is to get the balance right.

Any modern economy is far more complex than the internet. The world wide web contains, it has been estimated, just 0.001 percent of the world's total information.[21] Big as the internet is, it is not all that big. All of the reasons why the internet needs to be decentralized, within the framework of some administration, apply, many times over, to the economy.

＊   ＊   ＊   ＊

Successful entrepreneurs like to believe, with Frank Sinatra, "I did it my way." This is largely true but not completely, in that usually the state lays the groundwork. In the development of the U.S. economy, the state has been ever-present. The internet, as noted, was set up by the government. High-tech industry in general—computers, telecommunications, biotechnology—would not have flourished without the government's funding of basic scientific research. The aerospace industry was built on military procurement. The interstate highway system, initiated by President Eisenhower in the 1950s, aided long-distance commerce.

Adam Smith, the most eloquent advocate of markets, recognized that they have limits. Markets cannot provide everything. The state must protect its citizens by providing national defense and a police force. In addition, the state has "the duty of erecting and maintaining those public institutions and those public works, which though they may be in the highest degree advantageous to a great society, are, however, of such a nature, that the profit could never repay the expense to any individual."[22]

These kinds of goods and services are called public goods. Pollution control and police protection are examples. Public goods have two defining characteristics. They are *nonrivalrous*, meaning one person's benefiting from a public good does not reduce the amount of it available for others. Ordinary goods, like a loaf of bread, say, get used up when consumed, but not public goods. Your enjoying clean air or the security that comes from an effective police force does not prevent others from enjoying exactly the same benefits. And they are *nonexcludable*, meaning that once the good is in existence, everyone can freely benefit from it. You can benefit from unpolluted air and police protection whether or not you helped bear the expenses of their provision. There are no property rights in public goods.

Because the benefits from public goods are widespread, they cannot be left to the market to reliably deliver. Everyone enjoys cleaner air or the absence of crime produced by effective policing or the security of national defense, so no one can be charged for it, and firms will not go to the expense of supplying it. Benefiting all whether they help pay for them or not, public goods are undersupplied unless there is some coordinated decision-making. A small, cohesive community may be able to generate its own public goods for itself, but public goods that bring benefits to many call for funding and perhaps provision from the government. Some public goods are supplied either by the state or not at all.

Health care and education have some public good aspects. Eradicating communicable diseases and ensuring the population is literate bring widespread benefits. Some state provision is therefore warranted. With other aspects, such as cosmetic surgery and business school training, most of the benefits go directly to the recipient and so these are not public goods. To what extent should health care and education come from the state, and to what extent should individuals make their own arrangements via the market? Just where the cutoff between public and private provision should be drawn brings in additional considerations. The ideas in this book are relevant to the debate on whether health care is better supplied by the government or the market, for they provide guidance on how a market for health care would be best designed and what the limitations of such a market would be. But other issues, including ethical judgments about what is equitable, are also central to that debate.

Public versus private provision is determined by more than just the technocratic consideration of whether the goods at issue are public goods. It is also determined by value judgments. The ideal scope of the state is a highly contentious issue. The ideas I am discussing help to answer it, in that they show there are upper and lower limits on the size of a workable state; countries whose governments are outside these bounds have a low standard of living. Some governments are demonstrably too big, taking on the production of goods and services better supplied by the private sector and bringing the ineptness of central control. Other governments are demonstrably too small, neglecting the basic functions of coordination and the provision of public goods that require the state, and without which sophisticated economic activities cannot thrive.

Between these clear-cut extremes lies a wide range of more activist or less activist roles for the state. Reasonable people can disagree about how big the government should be because they can disagree about how much it should redistribute from rich to poor. I am not going to take a stand on this here. Whether you believe the government should redistribute a little or a lot depends on your own personal value judgments. Ultimately it is not resolvable by economic analysis, which is about means not ends. I will confine myself to analyzing the workability of markets, and to examining the role of the state in market design.

The foregoing discussion of public goods could have come straight out of an economics textbook (the ponderous jargon of *nonexcludable* and *nonrivalrous* is a giveaway). Less examined is one of the subjects of this book: what public goods are needed for markets to work well.

Adam Smith, writing in 1776, foresaw an expansion of government as the economy grew. Public provision of what he called "institutions for facilitating the commerce of society," like roads, bridges, and ports, would be increasingly required. Being difficult to price so as to earn an adequate return on the investment, public infrastructure requires state involvement. Public provision does not necessarily mean public production, though. These facilities are sometimes most efficiently produced by the private sector, but their public-good nature calls for the government to help pay for them.

Funding roads, bridges, and ports is not the only way the modern state facilitates commerce. The state provides the foundation for market activity, by supplying the legal and regulatory infrastructure, that is, by helping to set the rules of the market game.

✵   ✵   ✵   ✵

Markets develop spontaneously, without help from the state. New York City's sidewalks are crammed with peddlers offering everything from counterfeit watches to books, tee-shirts, and flowers. They provide a useful service, as any visitor to the city notices. When it is raining, you can buy an umbrella; when it is cold, a jacket; when it is hot, sunglasses—more conveniently and inexpensively than in regular stores. Most of the ten thousand peddlers are unlicensed, the city council having made it almost impossible to operate legally by setting an arbitrary cap of 853 licenses. Being unlicensed, the peddlers are subject to harassment by the police, who from time to time arrest them and confiscate their goods. Both David Dinkins and Rudolph Giuliani as mayors tried to crack down on peddlers; Dinkins said they were "a thorn in the side of small businesses and legal vendors." But they persevere.

Street vending has even gone global. In Ecuador's Otavalo Valley, in the shadow of the Andes, indigenous artisans weave sweaters, ponchos, blankets, and rugs and ship them around the world.[23] On the streets of New York, as well as other cities from Tokyo to Amsterdam, the handicrafts are peddled by Otavalenos in their distinctive attire, the men in ponytails and fedoras and the women in long wrap skirts. After staying abroad for a few years they return home with substantial savings, to be replaced on the streets by their siblings or cousins. So productive is this trade that the Otavalo Valley has prospered. Though the manufacturing techniques are rudimentary, using old-fashioned looms to craft traditional Andean designs, the Otavalenos show a twenty-first-century responsiveness to fashion trends. Information on which colors and patterns are in vogue is faxed back to Otavalo by the peddlers, and within two weeks the artisans ship out new sweaters and ponchos in the current styles.

Firms and workers are said to be in the shadow economy if, like the New York street vendors, they are not officially registered. In developing countries, not just retailing but also production is often carried out in the shadow economy. Operating in the shadow economy means, on the one hand, being beyond the grasp of the tax collector. It also means, on the other, being outside the protection of the state. Transactions in the shadow economy do not have the benefit of the legal system and other state-provided support.

Because it is underground, exactly how much business activity is done in the shadow economy is hard to estimate. Economic detective work is required, resourcefully piecing together disparate clues. Sample surveys, using questionnaires administered to random respondents, are sometimes used to build up a picture of the entire economy from a fraction of it. Another method compares the nation's annual total expenditure with its total measured income. Because of the way the national accounts are set up, these two totals should be equal. If some income-producing activities are not reported to the authorities because they are in the shadow economy, however, measured income falls short of aggregate expenditure. The size of the shadow sector can be deduced from the discrepancy. Yet another method is to extrapolate from electricity usage. Total economic activity moves in lockstep with electricity consumption: in most countries, an increase in economic activity of 1 percent brings an increase in electricity consumption of about 1 percent. Thus, a nation's total economic activity can be inferred from its electricity consumption. Subtracting from this total the officially reported level of economic activity gives an estimate of shadow activity.[24]

From a combination of these and other methods, it has been estimated that Nigeria, Egypt, and Thailand have the world's largest shadow economies, at nearly three-fourths the size of their official national income. In countries such as Peru, the Philippines, Mexico, and Russia, the shadow economy is about half the size of the official economy. In Tanzania, Chile, and South Korea it is about a third. These countries, therefore, are far less poor than is indicated by their reported national incomes, which overlook a significant part of economic activity. In the extreme cases of Nigeria, Egypt, and Thailand, for example, if the estimates of the shadow economy are accurate, then people's incomes are roughly three-fourths higher than the official data say.

The shadow economy numbers are both good news and bad news. On the one hand, the existence of the shadow sector shows it is possible for large amounts of market activity to proceed independently of the state. The state is not essential to markets, which can thrive even under a dysfunctional or hostile government.

On the other hand, countries with large amounts of shadow activity tend to be poor. In the affluent countries of North America and Western Europe, the shadow economy is around one-tenth of national income. Shadow economy activities there comprise mainly street-vendor sales, self-employment earnings that are not reported to the tax authorities, and barter transactions. In developing countries, by contrast, the shadow economy contains many ordinary manufacturing and service firms as well. Whereas in affluent countries the vast majority of economic actors are able to call upon the state for support, in poorer countries many cannot.

What is the role of the state? The large amount of shadow activity shows that markets can function where the state is not merely absent but even disruptive. Does this mean that the state is irrelevant to markets? Would the market participants supply for themselves all the market-supporting mechanisms they need, if only the state stayed out of things?

✻   ✻   ✻   ✻

Hernando de Soto, in his deservedly famous book *The Other Path*, depicted Peru's vigorous shadow economy as a democratic system, run by the people themselves quite independently of the state.[25] Unlicensed entrepreneurs developed informal passenger transportation, to such an extent that in the 1980s officially licensed operators ran just 10 percent of Lima's mass-transit vehicles. Innumerable street vendors sold food, cigarettes, and so on without permits and without paying taxes. The authorities tried to control the street vendors, passing ordinances restricting the vendors to trading in very low-value goods. But these ordinances turned out to be unenforceable and eventually the mayor of Lima, saying the street vending was beyond his control, conceded defeat.

Many of Lima's street vendors organized themselves into groups and set up off-street marketplaces, squatting on land and building unlicensed structures to house their stalls. These marketplaces sold mostly food but also clothing and household supplies. The stallholders' investment in the fixed structure of the marketplace gave a sense of permanence. Customers had reason to believe that the vendors would be in the same location tomorrow, so trust could develop between marketplace vendors and their customers. Unlike the street vendors, the marketplace vendors began to offer guarantees and after-sales service. Goods such as household appliances, as a result, began to be traded.

Peru's shadow entrepreneurs operate their mini-economy separately from the state. By staying in the shadow economy, they evade the overbureaucratized state. To illustrate the costs of bureaucracy, de Soto's researchers went through the red tape involved in setting up a small garment factory, assiduously complying with all rules and regulations and avoiding any shortcuts obtainable by paying bribes. (On ten occasions licensing officials solicited bribes from them.) Getting the eleven different permits required to start the factory took them nearly a year.

Being in the shadow economy means avoiding taxes; but it also means missing out on any help from the state. Peru's shadow entrepreneurs have no access to the legal system. They have their own set of norms and customs that serve in place of laws. But these have shortcomings; the informal rules are not a fully adequate substitute for a legal system. Unable to make use of laws of contract, they deal only with people whose reputation they know. This puts a limit on whom they can trade with, keeping them small. Shadow businesses have ad hoc rights to the land they occupy. But these rights are not as secure as they would be under an effective legal system, for there is some risk of expropriation. As a result, entrepreneurs are reluctant to make expensive, immobile investments in plant and equipment, investments that might enable them to grow beyond simple processing into manufacturing advanced goods. Operating outside the law "involves tremendous costs," Hernando de Soto concluded. "The apparent chaos, waste of resources, invasions, and everyday courage are the informals' desperate and enterprising attempts to build an alternative system to the one that has denied them its protection." The shadow economy has its limits.

When you examine the shadow economy anywhere, from Lima to New York, what is most striking is its dynamism: its bustling, life-sustaining energy. Markets can thrive without the state. What is also noticeable is its precariousness. The businesses in it, with few exceptions, are small. They confine their activities to elementary activities like retailing, services, and small-scale manufacturing.

The shadow economy shows that spontaneous order can develop and permit markets to flourish—but only up to a point. Spontaneous order works only when transactions are simple and firms are small. Beyond that, the complete absence of government produces dysfunctional markets. It is possible to take nonintervention too far. A modern economy needs some management.

Markets that arise spontaneously, like the street markets, are not typical of markets in general in that they are relatively simple. Most of the dealings are pure exchange, with the street vendors reselling food and clothing. Any production is on a small scale. The goods being traded are simple enough that buyers can easily verify their quality, so there is little scope for a seller to cheat a buyer and little need for a buyer to be wary of being cheated. Where transactions are straightforward, markets are quite easy to run and laissez-faire is workable. In markets run purely on informal mechanisms, however, transaction costs are high and as a result many productive opportunities are lost. Where transactions are more complicated, informal mechanisms are still more limited. Markets may not spontaneously arise to take care of every-thing, and where they do arise, they may not work efficiently.

For markets to operate effectively, they need mechanisms to protect property rights and contracting and to limit third-party harm. Many of these mechanisms are provided bottom-up by the market participants themselves. But some are provided either top-down or not at all. Upholding the complex, large-scale transactions of a modern economy requires laws and regulations.

*　　*　　*　　*

Market design's most fundamental question is, Where should the scope of markets end? Most decisions in a flourishing economy are decentralized to the people who have a direct and immediate stake in them. The economy goes badly awry if the government tries to do too much or to do that for which it is ill equipped. Markets outperform central planning because they mobilize local knowledge. The Soviet Union, like other centrally run sys-tems, could not mobilize local knowledge.

The market system, by contrast, economizes on information flows. In well-functioning markets, prices serve to aggregate the information that is dis-persed among the market participants. With prices serving as a feedback mechanism, the market system coordinates the actions of millions.

The collapse of central planning is sometimes held up as proof that the government should stay right out of the economy. This is a non sequitur. Observing that something is not black, we are not impelled to infer it must be white. That governments often fail does not prove the ideal state is the minimal state. To frame the choice as planning versus completely free mar-kets is oversimple. Public goods, offering widespread benefits, must be pro-duced by the state or at least funded by it. While the government often tries to do too much, it is possible for it to do too little.

T H I R T E E N

∷

Managers of Other People's Money

A corporation can be as big as a nation. The annual production of General Motors lies between that of Uruguay and Hungary. (GM's value added, or net income plus wage bill, is $35 billion; Uruguay's gross national product is $20 billion and Hungary's is $46 billion.) Wal-Mart Stores, employing 1.1 million, has a "population" as large as Mauritius and almost as large as Estonia.

Firms are the most conspicuous landmarks in the vista of a market economy. In this lies a paradox, for firms are run by a kind of central planning. The buck does not stop until it reaches the top. A transaction within a firm is subjected, not to the market, but to hierarchical control. While firms use the market in their dealings with each other, in their internal dealings they deliberately overrule it. Planning is history in the communist economies, but in market economy firms it is still going strong.

How can Wal-Mart and GM be reasonably productive as planned economies, while Hungary and Estonia are not? For a firm, what is there to guard against the wastefulness that planning brings when it is done economy-wide?

The answer is threefold. The firm's owners have a direct stake in its performance and monitor the managers' decisions. For a large firm, however, private ownership is not enough by itself to ensure it is efficient. Market forces outside the firm prod the managers to run it effectively. Discipline comes from the product market: customers must want to buy its products.

Discipline also comes from the financial markets: a badly run firm goes bankrupt or is taken over. The discipline from the marketplace, in turn, rests in part on government actions, in the shape of antitrust and financial regulation.

* * * *

A firm is unavoidably centralized. Many large firms, to be sure, try to co-opt the benefits of the market. They set up divisions with their own profit-and-loss accounting. But a firm can mimic the market incompletely at best. While the organizational chart may push decision rights down the hierarchy, any such decentralization remains subject to ultimate control from headquarters. Firms have centrally run budgeting and reporting mechanisms. Management, not any internal market, is the final arbiter of any within-firm transactions.

Employment practices in particular highlight that firms' internal dealings are centrally directed. Employees are paid according to the firm's salary scale. The labor market outside the firm puts a floor on pay rates, but employees may be paid more than they could earn elsewhere. Pay often depends on seniority and is not as finely adjusted to each individual's current productivity as it would be in a market. The main incentives for middle managers are the carrot of promotion and the stick of firing, which means that the head office sets the managers' incentives.

Herbert Simon, economics Nobel laureate and polymath, offered a fable to illustrate how much of a modern economy is ruled not by markets but by organizations.[1] Simon imagined a visitor from Mars who "approaches the Earth from space, equipped with a telescope that reveals social structures." In the Martian's telescope, firms show as solid green areas, while market transactions show as red lines, so the economy appears as a spider's web of red lines and green areas. Most transactions occur within firms, so organizations make up most of the landscape the Martian sees. If it sent a message back home describing the scene, our Martian would not describe it as "a network of red lines connecting green spots," but as "large green areas interconnected by red lines." Simon remarked, "When our visitor came to know that the green masses were organizations and the red lines connecting them were market transactions, it might be surprised to hear the structure called a market economy."

Employees' earnings—which represent transactions inside the boundaries of firms and other organizations—account for 71 percent of Americans' aggregate income. The remainder mostly comes from market transactions, via investments and self-employment (it is the sum of proprietors' income, corporate profits, and rental and interest income).[2] In a market-oriented economy, then, intrafirm transactions predominate. Marketplace transactions account for well under a third of total income.

Large firms play a major role in any modern economy. Firms grow large because of the nature of their production processes or the demand for their products. In some industries, like steel and automobiles, larger firms gain economies through mass production. As Henry Ford discovered, manufacturing may be cheaper when done on a larger scale. The production of software such as Microsoft's Windows is an archetypical economy-of-scale activity: most of the costs are incurred in the up-front design, and the cost of servicing an extra customer is small. In the pharmaceutical industry, large sales are needed to cover research-and-development expenses. Products like breakfast cereals and household cleaners gain economies of scale through distribution and marketing. In electronic commerce, scale economics arise from network effects. At an internet auction site, having more sellers attracts more bidders, which attracts more sellers, so the site grows in a self-reinforcing spiral; new auction sites find it difficult to get started because it is hard to dislodge the users of the incumbent's site. Bigger can be better.

Economies of scale do not by themselves determine where the boundary between a firm and the market is drawn. Firms have two ways of acquiring the inputs they need: they can make them or buy them. Transactions inside the firm are mediated by the firm's hierarchical chain of command. Transactions with a separate firm are mediated by the market. Firms that contract out some of their production—buying rather than making—place their trust in the market mechanism.

If markets achieve such impressive efficiencies, why are so many transactions deliberately taken out of the market and put into the planned subeconomies that are firms? Why isn't everyone an independent contractor instead of a hired employee? The answer is that firms exist as a response to market frictions. Sometimes it is less expensive to run a hierarchy than to use the market. Whether a firm produces its inputs in-house or procures them from other firms depends on the relative costs of each form of transaction. One of the factors affecting this comparison, as Ronald Coase wrote in 1937, is the efficiency with which markets work. Where the transaction costs of using the market are high, firms tend to make inputs themselves. Where markets work smoothly, firms contract out much of the work.

Firms do not necessarily need their own in-house production capabilities to benefit from economies of scale. Cisco Systems Inc., the market leader in routers (the hardware used for managing the internet's traffic), is almost a virtual firm. It focuses on research and development at one end of the production process, and marketing at the other. The middle part—actually making the products—it mostly contracts out to other firms. For this to be feasible requires rapid communication with the manufacturing firms. Carl Redfield, who runs Cisco's manufacturing, says, "Without the internet, none of it would be possible." The internet has lowered the transaction costs of using the market. It allows instant communication of large amounts of financial, technical, and customer information between Cisco and its contractors. It permits complex transactions to be managed among multiple firms located far from each other.[3]

Given that firms are run internally by a kind of central planning, what is there to replace the incentives for efficiency that markets provide?

*   *   *   *

Private ownership is the primary reason why firms, large or small, operate efficiently. The shareholders have a direct stake in the firm; they are motivated to seek out opportunities to increase revenue and lower costs, for each dollar added to profits is a dollar more in the owners' pockets.

The rediscovery of this elementary truth is what led to the late-twentieth-century wave of privatization of state-owned firms. Massive shifts in ownership resulted, with governments in over a hundred countries raking in about a trillion dollars. After 1980, state ownership plummeted worldwide. The largest drop was in the formerly communist countries, where the state had monopolized production. In noncommunist countries, also, the state reduced its share of production: in low-income countries the output produced by state-owned enterprises fell from 16 percent of national income to 5 percent, and in industrialized countries from 9 percent to 5 percent.

The incentives from private ownership usually have led to solid if unspectacular improvements. The many studies that have been carried out on the performance of privatized firms give evidence that ownership does indeed matter.[4] Following privatization, most firms (though not all) charge their customers lower prices and offer better service than under state ownership. Output per worker is higher (by about 20 percent on average), as are investment spending (by about 5 percent on average) and profitability (by about 4 percent on average). Some firms increased their employment after they were privatized, but layoffs of workers followed in many cases, a symptom of the overstaffing that was rife under state ownership; overall, employment rose slightly following privatization (by about 1 percent on average).

Also, productivity grew faster, production costs were lower, and debt was lower. Shifting state firms to private ownership, by and large, has achieved what it was intended to. Firms perform better when they are privately owned than when they are state-owned.

Ownership is only part of the story, however. Having private owners does not guarantee a firm runs with full efficiency. There are limits to ownership. An organizational invention devised just before the Industrial Revolution was as important for subsequent worldwide economic growth as any engineering invention like the steam engine or the cotton loom. This was the limited-liability corporation. Before, a tight limit on firms' size was imposed by the risks owners faced. Business is always fraught with uncertainty. The returns earned by any firm vary unpredictably. Owners are in jeopardy of losing their investment in a downturn. The corporation serves to limit investors' risks. Limited liability and multiple owners mean that the risks carried by any individual investor are attenuated. Since no single person is bearing a significant fraction of the firm's risks, the firm can grow large enough to benefit from economies of scale. Limited risk also means, however, limited incentives. If each of the shareholders owns just a small fraction of the company, none of them is motivated to go to the trouble of checking that it is well run. How do large firms avoid becoming bloated?

Adam Smith, writing in 1776, identified what he thought was a fatal flaw in the corporate form of organization. Managers of corporations are "managers rather of other people's money than of their own." It cannot be expected that they would "watch over it with the same anxious vigilance" as if it were their own money. Smith was pessimistic about the future of corporations, for they would not be well managed. "Negligence and profusion," he warned, "must always prevail."[5]

In a corporation, ownership is separated from control. Just as the planners in Stalin's Soviet Union may not have been seeking the ends that socialism's theoreticians would have wanted, so a firm's top executives—managers of other people's money—may not always push the firm in the direction the owners would want.

In a small firm managed by its owner, private ownership can be enough by itself to ensure the firm is run well, but not in large corporations with many shareholders. Second-guessing the managers' decisions is not easy: it is a costly, time-consuming exercise. To do it right, a lot of information is needed. For a shareholder, it is rarely worth the effort, especially since most of the benefits would accrue to the other shareholders. The board of directors in principle monitors the managers on the shareholders' behalf. But the board's ability to check up on the managers is also limited, given the time and resources at their disposal.

Most large firms grant their managers a stake in the firm's performance by offering them stock options and linking the managers' pay to the firm's stock market value. These incentives partially—but only partially—align their interests with the owners'. Informational problems similar to those arising under central planning, however, still impede efficiency. Costs of operating a hierarchy arise from the dispersal of knowledge among the people in the organization—not just scientific and engineering knowledge but also more mundane information about people and local conditions. A worker on the production line might observe quality defects that are apparent only on the shop floor, or a machine that is sometimes idle, or a surplus stock of raw materials that could be used. A middle manager might be aware of engineering problems in a new process, or of a way of reassigning workers to increase productivity. Salespeople in the field learn about demand for the firm's products. Much of the information about demand and costs that the top management needs for planning must come from below. Knowledge that is valuable to an organization is acquired by people—at all levels of the organization, including the lowest—as a by-product of their day-to-day duties.

Why does it matter that the source of the information is separated from the decision-making responsibility? People take advantage of any special knowledge they have acquired. Dispersed information within a hierarchy makes conflicts of interest inevitable. Information becomes distorted because of people's incentives to exploit any informational advantages they have. "People are reluctant to share their information," observed the head of a large French company. "Managers in particular seem to think it gives them extra power." Middle managers "have an interest in husbanding information—and the power that goes with it."[6]

This hoarding of information occurs in the budgeting process in multidivisional corporations. A study of large U.S. corporations found that divisional managers built slack into their annual budgets by understating expected revenues (by using low price and sales estimates) and overstating costs (by inflating personnel requirements, proposing unneeded projects, and failing to report the adoption of cost-lowering process improvements). The padding, which was lower in years when operating conditions were adverse, averaged 20 to 25 percent of the divisions' budgets.[7] The separation of ownership and control sometimes brings wastefulness reminiscent of Soviet planning.

✳   ✳   ✳   ✳

Adam Smith was right, then, to worry about misaligned incentives inside corporations. By and large, though, corporations work remarkably well. Perceptive as he was, Smith was no better at making predictions than present-day economists. His gloomy forecast of "negligence and profusion" notwithstanding, the corporation has gone on to become the dominant means of organizing production worldwide. The total value of shares in the world's listed companies in 1999 was $35 trillion. If the corporate form of organization had worked as badly as Smith expected, it would have succumbed long ago in the competitive marketplace to alternative forms of organization: firms run by a single owner, partnerships, nonprofit firms, or even government-run firms. The corporation is, on the contrary, the only way so far discovered to run large-scale production processes with tolerable efficiency. "The modern corporation is quite possibly the highest form of human cooperation," noted Jerry Kaplan, a Silicon Valley entrepreneur. "Specialized resources in the form of labor, raw and finished materials, capital and knowledge come together in a marvelous process that transforms these components into goods and services of greater value."[8]

Smith correctly diagnosed the problem of the separation of ownership and control. He failed to anticipate the solution: market forces. The market system provides checks and balances. Pressing on the firm from outside, market forces constrain the managers' decision-making and induce them to run the firm efficiently. Discipline comes from both the product markets in which firms sell and the financial markets from which they get capital.

Well-functioning financial markets—accessible banks and a stock market—enable firms to invest and grow and then push them to perform well. A liquid stock market means owners can punish underperforming managers by selling their shares, driving down the firm's stock market valuation. Corporate raiders add to this discipline. A firm performing badly enough to have a low stock market valuation may be bought out by a corporate raider, whose first action after taking over the firm often is to fire the managers. The threat of takeover serves to induce managers to run the firm efficiently.

Product markets also provide discipline. Firms that face competition to sell their output must produce at high enough quality and low enough prices that consumers buy their products ahead of their competitors'. Firms failing to hold down their production costs lose market share and ultimately may go bankrupt. Monopolists, by contrast, lack this discipline and so tend to offer shoddy products manufactured with inflated production costs. Figuring out how to run the firm efficiently is a difficult task for managers that requires continual upgrading and rethinking. Restructuring is painful. Lacking product-market discipline, managers may not bother to try. As economist John Hicks remarked, "The best of all monopoly profits is a quiet life."

The Xerox Corporation enjoyed Hicks's quiet life in the 1960s, as its monopoly in the photocopier market was protected by patents. Initially highly innovative, it failed to maintain the flow of innovations and let its production costs become bloated. When competitors arrived in the early 1970s, its inadequacies were harshly exposed, as its share of the photocopier market plunged. David T. Kearns, president of Xerox during the subsequent restructuring, said, "We had always been successful, and we assumed that we would continue to be successful. Our success was so overwhelming that we became complacent." It took a painful decade for Xerox to remake itself into a viable competitor: it raised the quality of its products, speeded up innovation, and cut its manufacturing costs by 20 percent.[9] That such large improvements could be made shows how inefficient it had been before.

The U.S. automobile industry followed a similar path. It used to be a cozy oligopoly, with little real competition; then in the 1980s there was an upsurge of imports, mainly from Japan. The new competition forced the car makers to reorganize. By flattening their internal hierarchies, switching to just-in-time inventories, reducing in-house production by making more use of subcontractors, and revamping their product lines, they converted themselves into lean competitors. The car firms and Xerox illustrate that private ownership is not by itself enough to induce firms to be run productively; in addition, it takes the pressure of competition.

Large firms necessarily entail inefficiencies. Organizing a firm entails pursuing mutually incompatible goals. A firm should be run lean so as to keep its production costs low; but it should also be innovative, which requires using valuable resources in ways that may not yield a payoff. It must be responsive to information arising at low levels in the hierarchy but at the same time have enough central control that its various units are not working at odds with each other. Messy compromises are ubiquitous. There is no perfect form of organization—just constant vigilance from those in charge, and frequent midcourse corrections whenever one of the messy compromises tips too far in one direction. Ensuring that this vigilance is maintained requires external market discipline.

*   *   *   *

"The free enterprise system is too important to this country to be left in the hands of private individuals," a Mississippi congressman allegedly once remarked. Oxymoron as this may be, it contains an element of truth.

For markets to work well enough to discipline firms, some state action is needed.

Large firms are much more prevalent in affluent countries than in developing countries. In the United States, plants with fifty or more employees account for over 80 percent of total manufacturing employment. In Thailand they account for 30 percent of manufacturing employment, and in Indonesia and Ghana, 15 percent. In the United States, plants with less than ten employees account for a mere 4 percent of jobs, whereas in Thailand such tiny plants account for 60 percent, and in Indonesia and Ghana, about 80 percent.[10] Richer countries have larger firms.

Why does small-scale production go together with low national income? Where labor is cheap and capital is scarce, firms use simple equipment for which a small scale of production is economical. Firms in poor countries are small, in other words, because they should be small. This is part of the explanation, but not all of it. The other part is that poor countries lack the market supporting institutions that enable firms to grow and, if they do grow, to operate efficiently. In a well-functioning economy, the state is quietly helping to ensure that product-market competition continues to exist and that financial markets are working properly.

The main way the government sets the rules of the market game is by writing laws and maintaining the machinery to enforce them. Laws are needed to guard against theft and fraud, to define and protect property rights, and to support contracting. In addition, governments directly oversee economic activity via regulatory agencies. All governments regulate markets to some degree.

Why is the law not enough? Couldn't all problems be resolved by rational people bargaining in the shadow of the law? Is it not enough that people can sue when contracts are not lived up to, or fraud is perpetrated, or property rights are violated? Why do we need the extra degree of government involvement in the form of regulation? The answer is that the law is imperfect, and in some cases regulation works more effectively. Implementing laws may require more than the courts. Commercial disputes can be exceedingly complex. Regulation sometimes is needed to supplement the courts—usually not direct regulation of firms' day-to-day activities but oversight to ensure markets are doing what they are supposed to do.

A specialist agency employing experts may be better able than the legal system, which is generalist, to make decisions that require deep industry knowledge. Regulatory agencies are often called on to add detail and specificity to the laws that emerge from the legislature. A regulator can economize

on the costs of information-gathering and inspection, by avoiding the dupli-
cation of many people having to inspect a firm's activities. Bureaucracies are
not generally noted for their nimbleness, but if they are well run (an important caveat), they can move more quickly than the legislature and the courts.

*   *   *   *

Shareholding, when you stop to think about it, is a marvel. You hand over
your hard-earned money to the safekeeping of the firm's managers, in the
hope of eventually getting it all back and more. And most of the time you do
get it back. If you tried to describe this process to a Rip van Winkle, awak-
ened after sleeping through the last hundred years of history, you would be
hard-pressed to convince him you weren't just making it up. "Give me your
money and I'll multiply it for you" is the spiel of every con man. Why are we
able to trust corporations presenting the same pitch?

Whereas markets are driven by the profit motive, corporations are based
on the presumption that managers are not seeking profits for themselves:
instead, they follow their fiduciary duty and seek profits for the shareholders.
Managers are no more altruistic than the rest of us. To ensure they will act in
their shareholders' interests, they must be given incentives to do so. Creating
such incentives is not easy. Many countries have not yet succeeded.
Financial markets work well only where there is trust.

At root the problem is one of information. If investors could easily evaluate the managers' decisions, they would have little to be concerned about.
Their ability to sue the managers or in other ways punish them would deter
any inappropriate activities by those managers who are dishonest or incom-
petent. But managers usually know far more about what goes on inside the
company than their putative superiors, the shareholders.

Of the major cases of fraud suffered by corporations, according to a survey of senior executives in fifteen industrialized countries, one-fourth are perpetrated in-house by the firms' own managers. Abuse of shareholders'
trust—negligence and profusion on a scale Adam Smith could never have
dreamed of—was committed, for example, by the top executives of CUC
International, a hotel, car rental, and real estate franchising firm. In the
biggest accounting fraud ever (according to U.S. authorities), costing
investors $19 billion, they inflated earnings and projected earnings in order to
keep the stock price artificially high. Revenues were overstated by hundreds
of millions of dollars per year, and expenses were hidden by shifting funds
between accounts. An accountant employed by the firm said faking the numbers "was my job, and my superiors were encouraging me." The firm agreed

to pay its shareholders a record $2.8 billion in settling civil litigation, and the executives pleaded guilty to federal criminal charges. "This case boils down to greed, ego, and arrogance," said the FBI agent in charge of the investigation. "It's about lying, deceit, and fraud."[11]

Managerial misbehavior of this kind is rare, however, in industrialized economies. People willingly invest their money in corporations. How can they be confident the managers will not dissipate their money in "negligence and profusion"?

The devices for providing reliable information to shareholders include a range of market intermediaries. The stock exchange requires the companies it lists to report specific data by means of financial statements. Listing provides some assurance for investors, so delisting is a sanction for misreporting. Specialized firms vouch in various ways for the information reported by corporations. Accountants audit firms' financial statements. Investment banking firms underwrite share issues. Law firms approve companies' prospectuses. These intermediaries gain credibility for themselves by their own concern for their reputation, which is what keeps them in business over the long term. Additional credibility comes from membership in self-regulatory organizations. Voluntary bodies like the U.S.'s National Association of Securities Dealers provide oversight of their members, expelling any who misbehave. The business press also is part of the oversight system, with journalists exposing fraud and incompetence.

These market-based devices are reinforced by various state-provided devices. The government writes laws defining and protecting shareholders' rights, designed to ensure that investors receive accurate, timely information. It supplements the reputational incentives of accounting firms, law firms, and investment banking firms by making them legally liable for any faulty disclosures that they endorse. Laws define what managers may and may not do to benefit themselves. False disclosure and insider trading are subject to legal penalties. The law also allows individuals to sue companies or managers for losses due to illegal actions.

The United States, the United Kingdom, and similar countries do not just rely on market forces and the legal system but have in addition strong financial regulators. Adjudicating complex financial arrangements and pursuing white-collar fraud calls for an expert agency. The Securities and Exchange Commission (SEC) sets the rules governing U.S. securities markets, filling in the details of Congress's general legislation. It prosecutes cases in civil court and refers criminal cases to the Department of Justice. It oversees stock exchanges and securities lawyers and accountants. Stock prices can be manipulated in subtle ways that would easily escape legal prosecution but that might be controlled by a regulator. Only an expert could detect insider trading carried out via layer upon layer of transactions. A focused regulatory agency provides a more credible deterrent to financial misdealing than can the overstretched courts.

The system of financial market supervision does not work perfectly, despite the myriad means of oversight. CUC International's massive misreporting, for example, went undetected for at least twelve years. It was exposed only by happenstance, when CUC merged with another company and its new partner refused to keep the fraud going. The authorities went to work only after the whistle had been blown. The risk of going to jail had not been enough to deter CUC's employees from falsifying the accounts. The market-based controls did not catch it either. In their periodic audits, the firm's auditors somehow failed to notice the fictional earnings numbers or the unusual transfers of funds between accounts. In response to criticism, the accounting firm's lawyer was strangely defensive, saying, "The CUC people were so determined to fool the auditors that they could fool any audit firm."[12]

*　　*　　*　　*

False disclosure to manipulate stock prices is not the only way managers can profit at the expense of their shareholders. Inside investors—shareholders with a large block of a company's shares, and the managers who run the company—usually are well informed about, and in control of, the company's affairs. Outside investors, by contrast—those holding a noncontrolling block of shares—do not have as much access to information on the value of the company. And they find it hard to monitor and assess the managers' decisions. Outsiders therefore are vulnerable to expropriation by insiders.

Wayward managers can contrive to get their hands on much of their companies' profits. They might simply steal the money or, in what amounts to the same thing, sell the firm's assets or outputs at an artificially low price to companies of their own. They might arrange for the company to pay themselves excessively high salaries, provide them with lavish perquisites, or grant them loans on generous terms. These appropriations can be done in convoluted ways that are hard for outsiders to unravel.

The difficulty in monitoring managers is a rationale for rules restricting what managers can do. Because of the difficulty in evaluating a company's worth, governments often ban insider trading, in which the manager uses inside information to trade in the firm's shares. In the absence of such a ban, shares might be priced low, because of the outside investors' vulnerability.

Since the manager is better informed, the outside investors would expect that whatever happens they would lose out. They fear that in the event the firm is successful, their returns will be diluted by the managers' profiting early from their inside knowledge, and in the event the firm is unsuccessful, the managers' selling off their own shares early would exacerbate the fall in the share price. The outsiders therefore are willing to buy the shares only at a discount. There is less trade in shares than should occur.[13]

A ban on insider trading and self-dealing reassures the outside investors that they are not at the mercy of the better-informed insiders, improves their expected returns, and results in an increased level of investment by the outsiders. The government intervenes because of an externality (analogous to the unbalanced-competition externality in a sports labor market). Unscrupulous managers do not bear the full costs of their actions, in reducing the overall liquidity of the equity market. Honest firms, tarred with the same brush as their unscrupulous rivals, may withdraw from the securities market altogether. Everyone can become better off, in principle, by measures that alleviate the shareholders' fear of being exploited and reluctance to invest. A ban on insider trading promotes public confidence in the financial markets and makes funds more readily available to all firms.

In the U.S. regulatory structure, established in 1934 after the great crash of 1929, the emphasis is on accurate disclosure. The system of financial oversight "put the burden of telling the whole truth on the seller," as President Franklin D. Roosevelt said at the time, in order to "give impetus to honest dealing in securities and thereby bring back public confidence."

Many countries have weaker investor protections than the United States and the United Kingdom, and so firms behaving deceptively often go unpunished. Where shareholder safeguards are less strict, there is a dampening of willingness to invest. Looking across countries, we see vast variation in the liquidity of financial markets and firms' ability to raise money for investment. A measure of financial market development is the ratio of the total value of stock market–listed companies to gross domestic product. This is much larger in the United Kingdom and the United States (1.3 and 1.1, respectively) than in France and Germany (0.4) and in the developing countries (0.4 in Indonesia, 0.3 in Ghana, 0.2 in Peru). Countries with stronger investor protections have bigger capital markets. The efficacy of the stock market varies with how activist the government is in setting the platform.[14]

In countries with limited shareholder protections, shares are held by a narrow segment of the population, because investors, especially small investors, are unwilling to entrust their money to firms. Firms are relatively small and closely held because of the shortage of funds. There are few initial public offerings because investors are especially reluctant to put their money into firms without a track record. Investments do not necessarily flow to the areas with the highest returns because whether firms have access to funds depends on factors beyond the economic worth of their activities, such as their political connections.

In the typical developing country, corporate ownership is narrow. A clique runs the corporate sector. This clique is usually unfriendly to those who do not belong to it. In Indonesia, the Philippines, and Thailand, ten rich families control half of the corporate assets. The concentration of ownership in a few hands reflects the absence of formal shareholder protections. Outsiders' justifiable fears that the company will be run in the interests of the controlling family dissuade them from investing in it. The members of the clique often have special links to the government, and such crony capitalism adds to outside shareholders' defenselessness.

In Russia, there is little regulatory oversight and lawsuits are difficult to mount. Investors are told little about the state of firms, and what little they are told is unreliable. Sometimes they are even locked out of annual meetings. Managers often sell off subsidiaries and pocket the proceeds. The value of shares is routinely diluted; occasionally shares are expropriated outright. Even the largest companies refuse to publish meaningful accounts or to be audited. Fleecing shareholders is the norm. The result is that shares trade at a discount, and the total value of Russian equities is billions of dollars lower than it should be. "In Russia, shareholders today are not capable of controlling the behavior of management," complained one such shareholder. "We just don't get the full picture. So everything turns on faith—blind faith."[15]

The mechanisms that induce financial markets to operate honestly are numerous and complex. The courts, regulatory agencies, self-regulation via private sector associations, and intermediary firms all are part of the system that creates the transparency needed for investors to be willing to entrust their money to others. That securities markets exist at all "is magical, in a way," remarked the legal scholar Bernard Black. "Investors pay enormous amounts of money for completely intangible rights." But it is not really a matter of magic, he added, for this willingness of investors to trust managers "does not appear in unregulated markets."[16]

*   *   *   *

The corporation is an "ingenious device for obtaining individual profit without individual responsibility," according to Ambrose Bierce's *Devil's*

Dictionary. Formed to capture economies of scale, corporations represent a bound on the scope of markets. While they use the market for dealing with each other, for their internal dealings they use central control. Private ownership is part of what makes firms run efficiently, despite the lack of individual responsibility, but for large firms, with separated ownership and control, private ownership is not enough. It is external market pressures, coming from both product markets and financial markets, that keep firms honest.

The effectiveness of product and financial markets as disciplinary forces on firms depends in turn on institutions: the legal system and antitrust and financial regulation. Without rules designed to give shareholders reliable information about a company, investors would be reluctant to hand over their money to firms.

Even with rules in place things can go awry. The Enron scandal of 2001–2 underlined the need for mechanisms to constrain managers from abusing their trust. Hiding behind creative accounting, Enron's executives enriched themselves at their shareholders' expense.

A modern economy is almost incomprehensibly complex. Transactions require the cooperation of large numbers of people and may take years to come to fruition. Markets need a well-designed superstructure to enable them to handle such complexity. In market design, it is not a matter of markets *or* the state; it is markets *and* the state.

F O U R T E E N

⋮⋮⋮

A New Era of
Competition

"If it is feasible to establish a market to implement a policy, no policy-maker can afford to do without one," said J. H. Dales, an early proponent of enlisting market forces in the fight against pollution, writing in 1968. What do markets offer governments? Profits, after all, are not the goal of public policy. But markets are not just about money. A well-designed competitive market puts resources into the hands of those who can use them best. This is why markets can sometimes be useful in the public sector. Markets cannot supersede the government, but in some areas they can help the government do its job.

I have described already one case of market design by the government, the spectrum auctions. Let us now look at two others: California's deregulation of its electricity supply, and the U.S. government's creation of a market in rights to pollute the air.

＊   ＊   ＊   ＊

"It isn't pollution that is harming the environment," U.S. Vice President Dan Quayle remarked in 1988. "It's the impurities in our air and water."[1] Acid rain damages the environment, whether you call it impurities in the air or pollution. It causes lakes to die, as fish cannot survive in the acidified water. It blights forests and historic buildings. The grimy air harms people's health, causing respiratory and cardiac problems that can lead to premature death.

To reduce sulfur dioxide emissions, the main cause of acid rain, the U.S.

government introduced, with the Clean Air Act of 1990, a new technique of pollution control. It eliminated the command-and-control method under which each polluting firm had been regulated directly by officials from the Environmental Protection Agency (EPA), who decided how much pollution each individual firm would be permitted to emit. In its place, the EPA created a market in the rights to pollute. The act brought in emissions allowances—licenses that allow the holder to emit in one year one ton of sulfur dioxide. The allowances were freely tradeable. Anyone could buy or sell them, or bank them for future use.

The emissions allowances program was controversial. Economists had long advocated it, but political barriers delayed its introduction. The case against it, argued by some (but not all) environmentalists, was that the allowances, in assigning a right to pollute and thereby seeming to legitimate pollution, were immoral. The case for allowances was pragmatic—they would work better than the alternative ways of limiting pollution.

Protecting the environment cannot be left to the free market. Those harmed by pollution often have no influence on the polluters. Firms damaging the environment impose a cost on society that is not included in their accounting. They have no market-based incentives to limit their pollution. If the environment is to be protected, the state must step into this void.

Emissions allowances were introduced not to take the government out of pollution control, but to help it control pollution more efficiently. Emissions trading does not mean the market replaces the government; rather, the government is using the market to help it attain its policy goal. The government hands over to the market a part of its role: deciding how the emissions cutbacks are to be shared among the firms. But it retains its primary roles: assessing how much pollution in total is to be allowed, checking compliance, and fining any firms that break the rules.

To jump ahead of the story, the emissions allowances program has been, according to most who have studied it, a notable success, more effective than any earlier acid rain program. The Environmental Defense Fund, one of the program's proponents, echoes this assessment: emissions trading "is cleaning up acid rain faster and far more cheaply than skeptics had predicted. The market system is unleashing inventiveness and showing that the cleanup need not put a heavy burden on the economy."[2] The amount of pollutants emitted actually fell 30 percent below the ceiling the government had set. This was achieved at a cost to industry of billions of dollars less than the alternatives. Air quality and sulfate concentrations in rain measurably improved nationwide.

In an elegant twist, environmental groups sometimes buy emissions allowances and hold them inactive. The Clean Air Conservancy in Cleveland, Ohio, bids for allowances and then offers them for sale to the public, with the promise that each one bought and retired prevents the discharge of a ton of sulfur dioxide into the air. Sixth graders at the Glens Falls Middle School in Cleveland, among others, raised money to buy allowances. "It's been a real launching point for us, to allow individual citizens to get involved and feel like they've actually done something for the environment," said Kevin Snape of the conservancy. They reduced pollutants in the air, over a three-year period, by six to eight thousand tons.[3] The allowances are especially in demand, he remarks, for giving as Christmas presents. Similar activities occur around the nation, with ordinary people making a small but perceptible contribution to cleaning the air. (Their scale is small but not unimportant: they could be driving pollution, at a rough guess, around 1 percent below the level the government mandated.) The firms that sell allowances to environmental groups make a profit, it is safe to assume; the price more than covers their abatement costs. The environmentalists, spending their own money, get a purer environment.

Coal-burning electricity producers are the main emitters of sulfur dioxide. To reduce its emissions, a plant must either install scrubbers (which clean the sulfur dioxide out of the flue gases) or switch to cleaner fuel (lower-sulfur coal or natural gas). The costs of abatement differ widely among the different plants, depending on their location and the age and type of their equipment.

Reducing sulfur dioxide emissions by ten million tons per year by 2010 was the government's announced intention. To achieve this by the old command-and-control methods might have required micromanagement by the EPA: investigating each individual polluting plant, deciding how much it should reduce its emissions, and ordering it to install specific pollution-control equipment. Alternatively, command and control might have set uniform standards for all firms, requiring them to take the same abatement steps regardless of costs or outcomes.

With tradeable emissions allowances, flexibility is achieved without micromanagement or blunt rules. The government simply decides what total nationwide level of emissions is acceptable, and lets the market decide how much each plant cuts back. It creates a total number of licenses equal to the target level of emissions and gives the licenses to the polluting companies, which then trade the licenses among themselves. The firms that find it relatively easy to reduce their emissions sell some of their allowances and use the revenue to pay for their abatement activities (and have some profit left over). Those that find abatement relatively difficult buy extra allowances. As a result, the firms with low abatement costs clean up their operations more than the mandatory amount, and so the target reduction in total emissions is achieved at the lowest possible cost to the industry.

This theory is borne out in practice. Large numbers of allowances are bought and sold: in 1998 such trades corresponded to nearly ten million tons of emissions. Behavior varies across firms. Some sell allowances and emit less pollution than initially assigned, while others buy allowances and pollute more than their assignment. As the Environmental Defense Fund said, "Any utility that can find a way to exceed its reduction target is rewarded by being allowed to sell or trade its extra allowances to another utility that would have found it more expensive to meet its target by itself. This profit incentive has been spurring competition and innovation. For example, both energy efficiency and the use of cleaner fuels, such as natural gas, have increased, new cleanup chemicals have been developed to neutralize sulfur, and bioengineers are trying to create bacteria that will eat and metabolize sulfur in fossil fuels."

At root, what the emissions allowance market is doing, like any other competitive market, is generating information. It reveals how to reduce pollution in the lowest-cost way, as well as what the costs of reducing pollution actually are.

Why can't the government achieve whatever the emissions allowance market achieves? Smart bureaucrats, in principle, could control pollution as cost-effectively as the market by requiring extra reduction from the plants that have lower abatement costs—except that the bureaucrats do not know where abatement costs are high and where they are low. The key information is held locally. Each firm is different. It is the firms themselves that best understand their own circumstances, and in particular how much it would cost them to cut their own pollution. The EPA can know a firm's abatement costs only if the firm itself volunteers the information. The incentives under command and control worked against this. Managers, negotiating with the EPA, might exaggerate their firms' abatement costs in order to be assigned easier cleanup targets. The managers may even not have known how low their abatement costs could be driven, for under command and control they had little incentive to find out. Bureaucracy-run pollution controls were hindered by a lack of information.[4]

Under the market, by contrast, decisions are made by the people who are the best informed. Actions speak louder than words: what firms do in the marketplace provides more reliable information than anything they might tell the bureaucrats. Firms with low cleanup costs have a profit-based incentive to reveal this fact, by selling their allowances.

The prices of the allowances surprised most observers, being far lower than expected. The surprise came because command and control had left everyone (except perhaps the polluters themselves) with a distorted impression of those costs. Before emissions trading began, the EPA estimated it would cost $750 to clean up a ton of sulfur dioxide. The electric-power firms claimed it would cost them up to $1,500. The average price at which the allowances actually traded over 1994–1999 was about $150.[5] By selling an allowance for $150, a firm in effect was saying that cutting its emissions would cost it no more than $150 per ton. The EPA had believed the abatement cost to be an astonishing five times higher, and the industry had claimed it to be an even more astonishing ten times higher, than the market revealed it to be.

The emissions allowances market has turned out to be the environmentalists' ally. Under direct regulation the EPA, greatly overestimating the cost of cleanup, may have pushed for less pollution reduction than it should have. By showing how inexpensive the cleanup really is, the market has actually bolstered the case for aggressive clean-air targets.

Not everyone is convinced. While many environmentalists see the value of tradeable emissions allowances, some continue to abhor them on principle. When allowances trading went online, the Sierra Club re-raised its objections. "An online sulfur dioxide auction is putting the right to pollute on eBay," said club spokesperson Ann Mesnikoff. "It's bad no matter where you're trading, but this puts it in a starker form."[6] It is hard to argue with success, however. The allowances market lowered pollution.

Environmental programs that make use of market incentives have sprung up elsewhere: to phase out the use of leaded gasoline, to improve air quality in Los Angeles, and to limit the worldwide emissions of carbon dioxide, the source of global warming.

Does the success of emissions trading mean we can leave all pollution problems to the market? Of course not. First, command and control is still needed in some areas where markets are not workable. Acid rain is easier to address than some other forms of pollution. A market can be set up as readily as the sulfur dioxide emissions market only if the total amount of pollution matters more than where it originates. For pollution that is strictly local, with a single firm damaging a specific region, there is no way of creating a market in emissions licenses, for there would be no one to trade them with; direct regulation is still required. Markets cannot be applied to every kind of pollution. Second, even where markets work, as with the control of sulfur dioxide pollution, the government must continue to take the lead, setting the overall ceiling on emissions and monitoring compliance.

* * * *

Despite the success of the tradeable pollution licenses, when they were introduced, the market design issue was not fully faced. The government put in place an auction for the allowances that was flawed. The flaw is interesting, for it shows the importance of apparently innocuous features of the rules of the market game.7 The issue is convoluted, but it illustrates the chess-like reasoning that markets of all kinds often induce in their participants, and the need for market rules to anticipate the participants' decision-making.

The EPA implemented a double auction; that is, both potential buyers submit bids and potential sellers submit price offers. Bids and offers are sealed. Prices are set as follows. The EPA arrays the bids from highest to lowest, and the offers from lowest to highest. It then matches the highest bidder with the lowest offerer, the second-highest bidder with the second-lowest offerer, and so on, until the last buyer-seller pair for whom the bid exceeds the offer is reached. The prices paid are equal to the buyers' bids, so each transaction occurs at a different price. The firm bidding the highest pays the price it bid to the seller offering the lowest price; the second-highest bidder pays its bid to the second-lowest offerer, and so on. This pricing rule perhaps might look reasonable at first glance, but it induces perverse incentives. By lowering its offer, a seller gets to be matched with a higher bidder and so increases the price it receives. Sellers therefore do best by offering low prices. Buyers, paying their own bids, do best by bidding low, just above the (low) level they foresee for the sellers' offers. The sellers and the buyers quickly understand this logic, and all offers and bids are low.

The EPA's auction design gets things the wrong way around: a seller does better by offering a lower price. Fortunately, the poor design of the auction turned out to have no ill effects. Bottom-up market creation compensated for the flaws in the top-down market design. The emissions allowances program was rescued by the emergence of a private market alongside the EPA auction. (In fact, the EPA envisaged its auction as a way of jump-starting the private market, and in this it succeeded.) Intermediaries took on the role of market makers, buying and selling allowances on behalf of clients and sometimes speculating on their own account. Although sellers may be deterred by the prospect of low prices from offering their allowances in the

EPA auction, they have the alternative of the private market. The private market handles most of the transactions.

The secondary market in emissions allowances is easy to operate. One allowance is identical to another: it is simply the right to emit one ton of sulfur dioxide in a year. Because of the simplicity of what is being traded, it was not difficult to create a smoothly operating secondary market in emissions allowances. For this reason, in the case of emissions allowances, getting the market design wrong turned out to be inconsequential. With pollution allowances, it was just a matter of leaving it to the market. Next we will turn to another example of a new market designed by the government, where design flaws were grave.

*　　*　　*　　*

The lights went out in California in 2001 after a market in electricity was created. According to the California Assembly bill that initiated it, deregulation would create "a market structure that provides competitive, low cost, and reliable electric service." It didn't.

The attempt to build a market in electricity went badly awry. The price of wholesale electricity soared to ten times what it had been. Blackouts ensued. Governor Gray Davis labeled the experiment with electricity markets "a colossal and dangerous failure."

The electric utilities once produced most of the power themselves. Production costs were high because, as regulated monopolies, the utilities could pass any cost increases on to their customers in higher rates and so had little incentive to hold their costs down. A competitive market, it was hoped, would bring more efficient production and cheaper electricity. To create a wholesale-electricity marketplace, the regulators asked the utilities to sell off their generating plants. In the new deregulated system, the utilities were purely retailers of electricity, buying wholesale electricity from the independent generators. Signing the bill enacting deregulation in 1996, Governor Pete Wilson said, "We've pulled the plug on another outdated monopoly, and replaced it with the promise of a new era of competition."

It was "the most complex transition of an industry done anywhere in the world," according to Steve Peace, the chair of the Senate energy committee and an architect of the new market.[8] The special features of electricity as a commodity make the performance of the market unusually sensitive to its design. Since electricity is costly to store, it must be produced as needed. Demand fluctuates widely from hour to hour and from season to season. At peak demand times, all but a handful of generators are operating at their maximum capacity, and at such times the few marginal producers are able to bid the price high. In most markets, high prices bring about their own demise, as they attract new producers into the industry, who then push the prices down. With electricity, however, even in the long run and even with the pull of high prices, supply can expand only slowly to meet demand. Building a new generating plant takes years—in part because of the engineering required, and in part because of not-in-my-backyard objections.

An online auction was implemented to set the prices. Each day, companies wanting to buy electricity submit bids stating the amount of electricity they want the next day and the price they are willing to pay. Companies wanting to sell submit offers of quantity and price. A bank of computers array the bids and offers and, hour by hour, calculate the price at which supply meets demand. (Such an auction would not have been feasible a few years earlier, by the way, for powerful computers are needed to instantly compare the bids, compute the market-clearing price, and allocate the quantity orders to the buyers and sellers.)

The auction prices rose higher and higher. "We are so far into the realm of extraordinary gouging we are orders of magnitude off the chart," California Assembly Speaker Fred Keeley told the Federal Energy Regulatory Commission in 2001. Why did prices rise following deregulation, rather then fall as they were supposed to?

The primary reason for California's electricity problems, it must be said, predated deregulation. You cannot defeat supply and demand. In the years leading up to deregulation, California's robust economic growth had brought increases in electricity usage. Meanwhile, no significant new generating plants were built; generation capacity actually declined by 2 percent between 1990 and 1999. With or without deregulation, California would have suffered electricity shortages. California had bad luck, being hit shortly after deregulation by two unpredictable events, either of which alone might have been manageable but together were damaging. Below-normal rainfall and snowfall meant low water levels for hydro-electric generation and increased the need to use natural gas to generate electricity. At the same time there was a big increase in the price of natural gas.

The high prices were in part an ordinary market response to high demand. What determines the competitive market price is the marginal cost (that is, the cost of generating one additional megawatt of power). When a large supply is needed, it is the high-cost gas-fired plants, and not the low-cost hydro-electric plants, that are the pivotal suppliers. When demand hits a peak, therefore, marginal cost is high and so price is high. As the price of natural gas rose, generation costs rose and so did the price of electricity.

This is not the whole of the story, though, for at times prices far exceeded the generation costs. Some of the generating companies after deregulation were able unilaterally to set the price. Gray Davis, saying the generators were earning "unconscionable profits," slammed them as pirates and price-gougers.

"There is evidence that some generators may be withholding electricity," the governor said, "to create artificial scarcity and drive up the price astronomically."[9] Such manipulation of the market is illegal. It is for the courts to decide whether it actually occurred. Making such a judgment requires a detailed examination of the firms' accounting records, which calls for the power to subpoena. But whether or not the generators illicitly colluded to cause artificial scarcity, part of the explanation for the high prices is merely the natural scarcity arising from limited supplies. It was easy for the generators to game the system. At peak demand, most generators cannot expand their output because they are already producing at full capacity. The remaining generators, only a handful, determine how much power gets produced. Each of those pivotal generators is aware that the quantity the system purchases will not vary with the price. Charging what the market will bear means bidding very high.

Proving that prices were excessive is hard because the marginal cost of generation varies widely from hour to hour, depending on what fraction of the generation capacity is being used at each point in time. To establish whether prices have been marked up over costs and by how much entails gathering very detailed data on generation costs and examining many thousands of individual transactions. According to a careful estimate by economists Severin Borenstein, James Bushnell, and Frank Wolak, wholesale prices in 1998–1999 were an average of 16 percent above marginal cost. Then in 2000 prices soared a further 500 percent. In just ten months in 2000–2001, according to an estimate by the Independent System Operator, which runs the state's power grid, the prices the generators charged the utilities exceeded competitive prices by $6.2 billion.[10] During a period of less than a year, in other words, the overpricing added up to roughly $500 for each household in the state.

*   *   *   *

It was the design of the new market that caused it to malfunction. Before deregulation, the system was centrally controlled. Decisions all the way from generating the power to delivering it to homes and businesses were made inside each utility, under regulatory supervision. The old system worked; power was reliably supplied. But it did not work efficiently: the costs of generation were high. Given the limitations of central control, it worked about as well as could be expected. It is difficult if not impossible to efficiently run a system as complex as a large state's power supply from the center.

The deregulation, by interposing a market between the generation and distribution stages, eliminated the central control. There was a catch, though. No alternative set of controls was installed in its place. The control mechanism in a normal market is the price system. It is the movement of prices that makes a market work. When supply is short, the price rises. Consumers have an incentive to use less. Demand falls and the shortage is averted. Price movements make the system self-correcting. In the deregulated electricity market, this simple mechanism was thwarted. Prices were not allowed to do their job.

Although the wholesale price at which the utilities bought power was set by the market, the regulators fixed the retail price the utilities could charge their customers. When wholesale prices shot up, retail prices stayed put. The utilities were squeezed, paying far more to buy electricity than what they were permitted to sell it for. Pacific Gas and Electric, the company supplying northern California's power, filed for bankruptcy in 2001, claiming it had amassed debts of $9 billion because of this gap between its costs and the price it could charge.

If the retail price had varied month by month to reflect wholesale prices, not only could the utility have avoided indebtedness, but also consumers would have been motivated to conserve electricity. They might have installed energy-saving light bulbs, acquired the habit of switching appliances off when they are not being used, or turned the air-conditioning down a little.

A thoroughgoing deregulation would have allowed retail prices to fluctuate not just month to month but hour to hour. For business customers, especially, sophisticated meters allowing real-time pricing could have been installed. If the retail price had followed the wholesale price in its roller-coaster fluctuations, then power users would have had an incentive to reduce their consumption in high-demand hours and increase it in low-demand hours. Businesses could shut down when prices were high, and run extra shifts when they were low. Thus, peak-time power would be saved for other uses such as in homes.

The Californian electricity market tripped up, then, on the most elementary requisite of market design: prices should reflect production costs. With the retail price fixed, the system had no way of responding to shortages—of which there turned out to be plenty.

Normal market mechanisms also were prevented from doing their job in a further sense. The regulators required the utilities to buy all power when needed. Long-term supply contracts with generators were prohibited; power could be bought only in the spot market. The ability to buy ahead would have helped ease the day-to-day volatility of the wholesale prices and diminish the generators' peak-time market power. This regulatory mistake served to exaggerate the day-to-day price fluctuations.

California deregulated by half measures. The mix of controls and market-set prices was incompatible: it made no sense to free up wholesale prices while keeping retail prices fixed. This is not to say, however, that California should have deregulated completely. Ongoing government regulation of the electricity market is needed.

Prices could have been far above generation costs even under a more thoroughgoing reform. At times of peak demand, when a handful of generators are able to hold the system for ransom, the price is bid very high. Competition by itself cannot always be relied on to hold the price down close to generation costs. Overpricing is an ever-present possibility in an electricity market. Some regulatory oversights on pricing keep in check egregious price-gouging.

The transmission grid—the high-voltage lines that carry the power—is by its nature a monopoly, so it cannot be left to an unregulated market. Because of the physics of electricity, the operator of the grid constantly must monitor it to ensure its reliability. The amount of power being pumped into the grid by the generators must always equal the amount being tapped by electricity users. The transmission system would be destabilized, bringing blackouts around the state, if there were a sudden uncompensated surge in the amount of electricity either being put in or being drawn out. No matter how smoothly the retail and wholesale electricity markets operate, therefore, the grid needs continuing regulation.

Some critics say California's deregulation did not go far enough; it should have moved to fully free markets. Others say there should have been no deregulation, for markets for electricity cannot work. Both sides have some truth, but both are oversimplifying the sitution. The deregulation fell short in retaining retail-price controls and preventing prices from signaling scarcity; it went too far in eliminating restraints on overpricing by the generating companies. The problem was not too much or too little use of markets, but bad market design.[11]

The main lesson from Californian electricity is that no matter how badly deregulation is needed, the details of how it is done matter. Elsewhere, such as in Norway and Australia, electricity markets have been introduced successfully. In those markets, most of the power is traded in long-term contracts, not in the day-ahead market, and retail prices move with generation costs. Moreover, their market designs were not put through the same kind of trials as California's, for electricity was in plentiful supply.

The design of a market must be watertight, especially when large sums of money are at stake. Any oversight in market design can have harmful repercussions, as smart people can be counted on to seek ways to outfox the mechanism. A newly instituted market achieves what it is supposed to only if it is well designed. The rules of the market matter.

This is the case with most markets, but especially with electricity. Because demand is insensitive to price and the consequences of a shortfall in supply are severe, a few producers are sometimes in the position, as we have seen, of being able to bid prices far above production costs. These high prices do not immediately call forth new sources of supply, since new generation facilities take years to come on line. Unlike the case of the pollution allowances, private sector intermediaries cannot step in to correct the official market's failings by starting their own marketplaces, for all the power must travel through the grid. Because of electricity's particular properties, the market's performance is highly sensitive to its design.

In understanding the breakdown of the California electricity market, the blame need not be placed on the fact that the market designers were in the public sector. The private sector is equally prone to market design mishaps. Trial and error is the usual way for most markets to develop: learning from errors is the chief way of correcting any design flaws. Of the companies offering novel methods for online buying and selling that were floated in the late 1990s, for example, a few prospered but most perished. The internet industry shakeout of 2000–2001 winnowed out the less promising online marketers. The difference between public sector and private sector market design is that the government's exercises can be on a very large scale and are carried out in the glare of news media, so when things go wrong, we hear about it.

* * * *

The Swedish parliament in 1992 passed a bill ordering that market forces be used to schedule the railroad network. Like everywhere else, railroads were centrally managed. Seeking the efficiencies of decentralized decision-making—the market's ability to elicit information and to discover optimal allocations—Sweden proposed creating a market in which the railroad company would retain ownership of the tracks but sell access to private firms, who would then offer the passenger and freight services.

There is a snag: tracks merge. If the scheduling is decentralized to the separate decisions of multiple rail users, there is a risk that two trains will reach the same point at the same time, and collide. Skeptics contended that scheduling by auction would be impossible. As one consultant put it, "There are no independent units of capacity to bid for. The viability of every bid to operate a train service depends on the specification of every other train service which has been bid for." Externalities, in other words, are ubiquitous. A market in railroad routes, it was claimed, simply could not work.

Responding to this challenge, economists Paul Brewer and Charles Plott designed an ingenious auction.[12] Railroad companies submit bids for any individual route. Only the highest current bid for a particular route is retained; lower bids are discarded. A computer program combines the bids into feasible schedules (in which collisions are avoided and safety margins are respected). The program then adds up the bid total for each schedule and declares the schedule with the highest total the provisional winner. Then, the process is repeated, with a new round of bids in which all the bidders may participate. It continues until no new bids are submitted. The highest-value feasible schedule is then adopted.

In experimental simulations this auction outperforms centrally planned scheduling, since it is responsive to the railroad companies' own information about their needs, as expressed in their bids. Routes are awarded to the railroad companies that can extract the most value from the routes. The externalities—the risk of collisions—mean that decentralization to a market-based system could not be absolute. Some coordination is needed. But that does not mean the benefits of decentralization are unobtainable. It just means that the design of the market mechanism has to recognize the interdependencies, which it does via the computer program that ascertains which bid combinations give rise to feasible schedules. The railroad-scheduling example shows that it is possible for a market to handle large externalities, provided the auction's rules are carefully designed to encompass them.

*   *   *   *

In picking winners, governments have a bad track record. Picking winners is exactly what the government is called upon to do when it makes allocation decisions such as which firm gets the right to use a publicly owned resource.

A market-based allocation leaves the government to do what only it can do, while turning over to the market the job of picking winners. Competitive markets, if well designed, can reveal the information that is needed for allocating the resources.

For electricity and emissions allowances, new markets were deliberately designed, their rules written in detail. Where a single, specific market is to be built, this can be done. Designing an entire economy, with its full set of interconnected markets, as I will discuss next, is a far more daunting task than designing a single market.

FIFTEEN

⋮⋮⋮

Coming Up for Air

Economic reform swept the world in the 1980s and 1990s. In ex-communist countries like Russia and China, markets were created from scratch. In countries with market economies like Britain and New Zealand, privatization and deregulation extended the span of markets. The shift away from state control has a lot to teach us about how markets work. It is history's biggest-ever experiment in economics.

"The market spells liberation, openness, access to another world. It means coming up for air." This is how the historian Fernand Braudel portrayed the emergence of markets in medieval Europe. Braudel's sentiment applies as well to their emergence in countries that used to be under state control.

The changes were painful for many who lived through them. Reform is difficult no matter how badly it is needed. How should it be managed so as to correct the inefficiencies of an overregulated economy without inflicting too much pain? By comparing the reform experiences of three very different countries, New Zealand, Russia, and China, we can extract lessons on what it takes to build well-functioning markets.

How can a sluggish, state-dominated economy change course? Warren Christopher, as U.S. secretary of state, advocated economic shock therapy. You should "look at economic reform as a passage over a ravine," he said. "You cannot do it by taking several little steps; only one giant leap will get you across."[1] He happened to be visiting Vietnam when he said this, though he would probably have offered the same advice to reformers anywhere.

The shock therapy prescription gravely underestimates the task of reform. An economy is a complex, hard-to-predict system. Shock therapy—like the state control that went before it, ironically enough—presumes the economy is more amenable to management than it actually is. The ravine-leaping analogy is inapt. Designing an entire economy is unlike designing a single market. You don't know where you are going and you don't know how to get there.

*   *   *   *

New Zealand's economy was never centrally planned, but for fifty years it had heavy state intervention. Then, between 1984 and 1992, it restructured its economy more rapidly and more deeply than any other affluent democratic country. It transformed itself from one of the most regulated of the developed economies to one of the least regulated. Since the full range of market-supporting institutions were in place at the outset, most prices were free, and most of the economy was privately owned, New Zealand provides a favorable test case for shock therapy.

The impetus for reform was chronically low growth together with unsustainable budgetary imbalances. From 1950 to 1980, New Zealand slipped from having the world's third-highest income per capita to twenty-second. The reforms were needed, therefore, and most observers agree that moving rapidly was justified in the circumstances. But the reforms were slow to show a return, and they brought severe social costs.

In the 1960s and 1970s, the government's knee-jerk response to any external shock was to impose controls on imports, prices, wages, profits, and interest rates. Restraints on markets abounded. Government officials or government-sanctioned monopolies made many decisions regarding resource allocation. Wheat was assigned to mills by the Wheat Board, aiming to guarantee each mill a profit; this resulted in milling capacity being twice the demand. Long-distance trucking was controlled by the railway company (which was state-owned): anyone who wished to truck goods more than 150 kilometers needed the railways' permission. Apple growers were barred from selling their apples at the farm gate, for to do so would have impinged on the producer board's monopoly. Shopping hours were strictly regulated. Margarine had to be an unappetizing off-white color, for it was deemed that yellow margarine would pose undue competition for butter producers. As journalist Marcia Russell summarized it, "What business you could be in, the prices you charged, the hours you worked, the wages you were paid, what you could buy and when were all controlled by the state."[2]

The bizarre nature of the old New Zealand economy is illustrated by an anecdote from the industrialist Alan Gibbs. For the sake of employment, the government required television sets to be assembled locally. When Gibbs went to Japan to negotiate a price for the components, he was greeted with disbelief. Because of the way the production lines were set up, the Japanese television makers could supply the separate components only by placing workers at the end of the assembly line to take apart the completed televisions. Gibbs's firm had to pay 5 percent more for the pieces than it would have for the whole television set. The parts were shipped to New Zealand, reassembled in a specially built factory, and sold for twice the world price.

The low productivity reflected market distortions from subsidies and price controls, as well as import controls and tariffs. These not only were high but also varied widely across industries, preventing the price system from allocating resources to their best uses. Low productivity further reflected misaligned incentives: a centralized labor market, compulsory union membership, and pay based on occupation rather than performance. The income tax schedule, with a top marginal rate of 66 percent, inhibited effort, except in tax avoidance. Import controls meant that, with the small population, in many industries only one or two firms served the entire market. There were just two brands of washing machine, for instance, both made by the same firm. "Every area of our economy was licensed," said Gibbs, "and if you had a licence you were protected and no one could break into your market." The lack of competition meant firms had little incentive to innovate or to lower their costs.

By the early 1980s there was inflation, unemployment, a government deficit, a trade deficit, and a foreign-exchange crisis. New Zealand was living, literally, on borrowed time. The reforms, when they finally came, were broad. In addition to macroeconomic reforms, there were reforms designed to make markets work better: slashing barriers to international trade; corporatizing state-owned firms and opening them to competition, then privatizing them; abolishing price supports and other agricultural interventions; injecting price incentives into natural resource management; and changing the labor laws to make individual contracts paramount in labor markets.

The reforms became bitterly controversial among New Zealanders, for they brought social dislocation. Unemployment shot up during the reform period. Inequalities widened and poverty increased. For the first time, homeless people began to be seen on the streets. The Trade Union Federation complained that the "deregulation policies have contributed to the growing inequalities in New Zealand society." Law professor Jane Kelsey said that the radical structural change had made New Zealand into "a highly unstable and polarised society."[3] Incomes stagnated: there was virtually no economic growth during the first eight years of reform. Only after this protracted transition did growth pick up, averaging a little over 4 percent, in the first half of the 1990s, then slipping back to 2 or 3 percent.

Since market-oriented reforms were sorely needed, why did the economy respond so slowly? Much of the pain should not be attributed to the reforms but to the previous policies. The procrastination of the earlier governments meant that a recession was inevitable regardless of what policies were adopted in the 1980s. But some of the pain came from the reforms.

The clearest and quickest reform success came in macroeconomic stabilization. The government's budget was balanced and an inflationary spiral was broken. These macroeconomic stabilization policies were needed to correct the severe imbalances left by the pre-reform policies. But they also impeded the economy's response to the other reforms. The pain, as well, was inherent in the program of deep reform. In the reformed environment, with more competition and less government intervention, workers and firms had to make major adjustments. New ways of running markets, of organizing firms and doing business, arose to supplant the old. This necessarily took time.

Many New Zealand firms at the start of the reforms were inefficient. Shaped by controls on prices and profits, and sheltered from imports, they faced little product-market competition. After reform shattered their quiet life, firms had to reduce slack by restructuring—changing their lines of business and finding new ones, redesigning internal hierarchies, offering stronger incentives to workers, finding new managers better able to handle the changed environment, imposing new financial oversights, locating new trading partners, and revamping customer and supplier networks.

Firms' immediate response to the new market incentives was to cut back their production. They rationalized their output mixes, shutting down their higher-cost plants and focusing on a narrower range of products in which they had some competitive advantage. Only by the early 1990s could real improvements be observed: firms began moving into new products and engaging in the technological and market research that new products necessitated. Turnover of top managers increased, and there is some evidence that the new managers were better qualified than their predecessors. There was an increase in the use of performance-based pay for workers, with either individual or team incentive-pay plans. Firms became leaner by reducing the number of layers in the managerial hierarchies. The larger firms began outsourcing an increased amount of work, and so became more specialized and more efficient. It took a decade or so for firms to adapt to the new environment so that production picked up again. Rapid as the policy changes were, industry's responses were slow.

The nation's stocks of labor, capital, and natural resources came to be managed better than before. Productivity grew in manufacturing and agriculture. Firms responded to the increased competition by becoming leaner, by shutting down their higher-cost plants and focusing on a narrower range of lines of business. Reductions in trade barriers reoriented the pattern of production, increasing both imports and exports, rationalizing production, and broadening the range of export-competitive industries. The corporatization and privatization of public enterprises induced more efficient operation. The reforms did have their intended effects, then, in improving the economy.[4] The reforms had effects beyond the purely economic. The nation was invigorated. "This land is simply seething," said Catherine Tizard, the governor-general, twelve years after the reforms began. "There is a whole geyserland of achievement."[5]

Reform is usually difficult, but New Zealand's reforms were even more difficult than most would have predicted. Shock therapy was arguably the right choice for New Zealand. The magnitude of the problems justified a radical cure. The main argument against using shock therapy in general—that it hinders the development of needed economic and political institutions—did not apply to New Zealand, for all the institutions were already in place. Well designed as New Zealand's reforms were, the transition to better functioning markets was painfully slow.

*   *   *   *

Russia chose the one-giant-leap approach when it began its transition from planning to markets. Its shock therapy had three components: the balancing of the government's budget, the immediate decontrol of prices, and the rapid privatization of firms. The aim was to tear down the existing economic institutions and to build new ones from scratch. Lawrence Summers, then the World Bank's chief economist, said at the start of Russia's reforms, "Make no mistake, this is one of the greatest economic challenges in history."

On New Year's Day of 1992, the Russian government abolished price controls on almost all goods (controls remained only on prices of energy and transportation). Between October 1992 and June 1994, state-owned firms were privatized by granting vouchers to citizens. In an amazingly large transfer of assets, two-thirds of Russian industry, around fifteen thousand firms, suddenly became privately owned. The attempt to balance the government's budget began firmly, then faltered, but was eventually somewhat successful. In 1992, inflation was 2,500 percent for the year. By 1996, inflation was under control, at 22 percent, though it still threatened to break out.

With Russia's political and economic institutions imploding, the government saw no other course than to move fast on all fronts. Anatoly Chubais, who as deputy prime minister was responsible for the reforms, believes he had no alternative; he said, "There is no doubt that the gradual approach is always best—except for circumstances where a country faces immediate collapse, as Russia did." Shock therapy's more effusive advocates, however, did not rest their argument on political necessity. They saw it as simply the best way to reform any economy.[6]

Russia's reforms were deeply unpopular. A sardonic joke went the rounds: "Everything the communists told us about communism was a complete and utter lie. Unfortunately, everything the communists told us about capitalism turned out to be true." In a 1997 nationwide public opinion poll that asked Russians whether the privatization policies had had a "bad" effect, 70 percent said they had.[7] Some believed that shock therapy was an American plot to destroy their economy.

Living standards crashed. National income in 1994, two years into reform, was just over a half what it had been in 1989. The reported drop in incomes somewhat overstated the actual drop, because some of the new businesses that arose in response to the reforms operated in the shadow economy, to avoid bribes and taxes, and the income they generated did not show in the official data. But even after a correction for that there was a disastrous decline in living standards, bringing a drop in life expectancy and an increase in family breakups.

The decline in living standards was in part the inevitable hangover from communism, with its combination of inflation, shortages, and gross inefficiencies. Some of the hardship—it is impossible to know how much—was caused by the attempts to carry out the first plank of shock therapy, balancing the government's budget. The previous government's spending had so far exceeded its revenues that urgent attempts to balance the budget were unavoidable. But part of the disruption was attributable to the other two planks of shock therapy, price liberalization and mass privatization.

On the first day of free prices, food prices shot up by 250 percent. Most salaries did not rise, so suddenly many people found themselves desperately poor. Lifetimes' savings became almost worthless. Many survived only by growing their own food.

Prices rose after liberalization because the planners had routinely set prices too low, resulting in unsatisfied demands. In a normal market, when prices rise, more product comes to be offered for sale. But in Russia of the 1990s, with its stunted market mechanisms, the price rises were followed by a sharp decrease in output. Although there was overall inflation, with the ruble prices of most manufactured goods rising, there was less change in the ruble prices of labor and energy, two of the main factors of production. In 1993, the ratio of output prices to industrial wages was three times higher than in 1992; by 1995 it was ten times higher. This increase in the price of outputs relative to wages should have called forth more output. It didn't. The economy's total production fell 19 percent in 1992, the first year of shock therapy, a further 12 percent in 1993, and a further 15 percent in 1994. It took years for production to start to climb back. The price liberalization exemplifies the flaws of shock therapy. Setting prices free is counterproductive if the response of supply to price goes in the wrong direction.

All Russian firms at the start of the reform period were state-owned. They needed deep restructuring to become responsive to price signals. They needed better decision making procedures, performance-based pay, and modernized accounting practices. They had to raise capital to pay for restructuring, and to find new products and customers. "Most of these problems can be ameliorated by rapid privatization," economist Jeffrey Sachs said at the time.[8] Unfortunately, they weren't.

In the worldwide wave of privatization, more than a hundred countries from the United Kingdom to Malaysia to Mexico converted state firms to private enterprises, and the process mostly achieved what was intended. The incentives from private ownership usually led to better performance—except in Russia. Little restructuring occurred in Russia's firms immediately following privatization, because privatization preceded, by years, the development of market-supporting institutions.[9] In a normal economy, as we have seen, private ownership is not the only force inducing firms to operate productively. Market pressures of various kinds also discipline managers: pressure from shareholders and the stock market, customers, and competitors.

Russia's newly privatized firms lacked these disciplines. Because the Soviet planners thought bigger was always better, many firms were monopolies and so, even after privatization, they continued to be free from the checks that normally come from competition. Even in industries with multiple firms, competition was slow to develop because with few channels of market information, it was hard for firms to reach new customers. Privatization put ownership mostly in the hands of insiders: in a typical firm, managers and workers ended up holding two-thirds or so of the shares. The incumbent managers were entrenched, and outside shareholders were unable to influence them. The absence of effective bankruptcy laws meant that the ultimate sanction for bad managers was missing; the state continued to bail them out. In 1994 Anatoly Chubais said that privatization had not changed the way the managers ran the firms. "There remain the same instincts, habits, and connections, and the same bend in the spine. It's a rare director who does not rush off to the government, who doesn't seek connections with high-placed officials, who doesn't beg for subsidized credits, tax breaks, quotas, and privileges."[10]

A further reason for Russia's output drop was that shock therapy shattered the relationships among firms.[11] In any economy, manufacturing is a cooperative process; firms tailor their products to the needs of other firms. Before the reforms, who sold to whom was dictated by the planners, and matches between firms were often inappropriate. With reform, firms suddenly became free to seek out better-suited trading partners, but establishing relationships from scratch was not easy. The search for new trading partners took time, during which the firms were reluctant to invest, for they did not know what goods they should produce or for whom. With the market for their output in turmoil, it paid to wait and see.

A domino effect magnified the problem. The manufacture of, say, a car involves a large number of different firms. If each is producing a part that no other firm in the chain is producing (as tended to be the case in the planned economies), then a failure by one firm to deliver can affect many others. If a firm loses a supplier of a crucial input, it cannot supply its customers, who in turn cannot supply theirs. Just as a storm that closes Chicago airport can delay a flight from New York to Dallas, because the plane was scheduled to fly first through Chicago, so a breakdown in the relationship between one pair of firms affects other firms. Airline delays can be resolved in hours; with firms it can take years to rebuild the chain.

Russia's shock therapy created an institutional vacuum. Private ownership matters, but not enough to produce efficient firms. Also needed are functioning product and financial markets. Shock therapy privatized the firms before the market support they needed had time to develop. It demolished the old institutions and it took years to build the new ones. The reforms outpaced the economy's ability to adjust.

*   *   *   *

China took a different reform path. Not trying to leap any ravines, China adopted gradualist reforms. They worked. In contrast to the free-falling incomes Russians suffered under reform, China maintained immediate and rapid economic growth: around 8 percent per capita annual growth over two decades from 1980. The gains spread widely, as living standards rose for most citizens. New firms blossomed, bringing a major shift in employment away from the state-owned enterprises. Most of China's economy was being run by markets within less than a decade.[12] China achieved what most countries could not: virtually painless reform.

Part of the reason for the success was particular to China. Large gains came quickly after agricultural reform, as we saw earlier, freeing labor to move into new manufacturing firms. Agriculture accounted for three-fourths of the workforce, so this gave the reform process a jump start, without which China's reform path would have been rockier. But there was more to China's success than agriculture.

China's reforms were similar to Russia's in one of the three components of shock therapy: keeping a lid on inflation. Hyperinflation would have undercut any attempt to restructure firms or to create markets. But macroeconomic stability does not in itself generate growth. Building a market economy means transforming incentives and property rights. In the other two components of shock therapy the Chinese and Russian approaches differed. Where Russia immediately privatized its state firms, China procrastinated. Where Russia freed prices in one dramatic stroke, China freed them by stealth.

Prices were reformed in an unconventional way. Under planning, the state-owned firms were required to sell their output to the state at fixed prices. Under reform, this aspect of the plan stayed in place, but they were allowed to produce extra output to sell in markets. There were dual prices; the market price was usually far higher than the official price. The fraction of state-firm output sold on markets rose progressively.

With dual prices, a firm's decisions on how much to produce, what inputs to use, and what investment to undertake were unaffected by the state's output quota, as long as that quota was less than the total output. What mattered for such decisions was the price received for any extra output, which was the market price. Although a gradual form of price reform, dual pricing therefore had an instantaneous impact, for it induced firms to become market-oriented. Dual pricing avoided the chain-reaction disruption that shock therapy generated. Permitting the state-owned firms to sell extra outputs and to buy extra inputs in markets allowed new interfirm relationships to grow around the stable platform of the existing ways of doing business.

There were growing pains. Dual pricing enabled illicit profiteering by well-connected people, like the children of important officials, who could obtain goods at the low plan price and sell them at the higher market price. Anger at such corrupt practices was one of the sparks that ignited the 1989 demonstrations in Tiananmen Square. Dual pricing was a temporary expedient to smooth the reform process, and it should have been replaced by full market pricing as soon as was feasible, that is, by the late 1980s, rather than when it happened in the early 1990s. Although it outlived its usefulness, dual pricing was a clever device to achieve price reform with little disruption.

Rather than privatizing its state-owned firms, China left them under state control, doing little privatization until the late 1990s. It did restructure them, however, achieving respectable productivity gains. Initially highly inefficient, the state firms significantly improved their productivity in response to a range of incentives. The government allowed firms to retain some of their profits, which were used to fund worker bonuses, benefits such as housing and health care, and investment in new plant and equipment. Managers' pay came to be based on their firm's performance. In some cases they were required to post a bond, to be forfeited if the firm underperformed. Managers obtained autonomy to decide what to produce, how much to produce, and how to produce it, and were permitted to pay workers bonuses. New methods of appointing managers were introduced, and there was considerable managerial turnover; as a result better managers were appointed.[13] Because of their strengthened incentives and improved organization, by the end of the 1980s the state firms were much less inefficient than they used to be, and they contributed to China's growth.

Instead of privatization, China fostered the formation of new firms. Although barely noticed in the first few years of reform, the new industrial firms grew remarkably quickly, and within twelve years were producing half of industrial output. This entrepreneurship occurred despite the impediments of inadequate laws of contract, weak property rights, and underdeveloped capital markets.

The new firms had a novel organizational structure. Most were not private firms. To anyone schooled in Western concepts of corporate control, these firms look strange. Mostly located in rural areas, they were run by village governments. Their ownership was vague, and there were no clear rights to residual returns. They had few of the usual instruments of corporate control: no shareholder controls and no threat of takeover. To our accustomed ways of thinking, these firms simply should not have worked. Yet they functioned efficiently.

These township and village enterprises turned out to be well adapted to the peculiarities of the transition economy. They did not need access to credit markets (which did not exist anyway), because their owners, the village governments, had the power to raise funds locally. They ran efficiently, despite being publicly owned, because they operated in intensely competitive product markets and had to be efficient to survive. The new firms were the main source of China's dynamism under reform.

The deplorable lack of progress in human rights and political freedoms clouds China's economic success. Twenty years into its economic reforms, China was only slightly less authoritarian than before they began. Freedoms of expression, assembly, and religion were curtailed. Political prisoners, held in brutal conditions, probably numbered in the tens of thousands. Even given these weighty caveats, however, tripling the incomes of a billion poor people is a creditable achievement.

⁂　⁂　⁂　⁂

The experiences of China and Russia could hardly have been more different. In China, reform was followed by world-record growth for twenty years. In Russia, incomes plummeted. Differences in their initial conditions—China was poor and agricultural, Russia was middle-income and industrial—account for some of the differences in responses to reform. But much of it is accounted for by their policies.

The most conspicuous difference between China and Russia is in the form of government. Throughout its reform period, China remained under communist control, whereas Russia became democratic. Does this political difference rule out the possibility of general economic lessons from China? Did China need its authoritarian government in order to follow its economic path, or could it have reformed as successfully under a democratic government? This is impossible to determine. There are reasons to believe, however, that China's economics is separable from its politics, and that it could have followed a similar economic path if it had been democratic.

China's reforms were those of a relatively weak state. Formidable political barriers stood in the way of economic reform. The reformers had to craft a political coalition that favored reform: they had to engage in ordinary politicking to get their policies enacted.[14] Having discarded Marxism and Maoism, the Communist Party had little legitimacy beyond its ability to deliver economic growth. The political commitment to reform came not from any inherent strength of the state but from the early and cumulative reform successes.

Russian shock therapy differed from Chinese gradualism, at root, in the degree of government activism. Paradoxically, newly democratic Russia chose a reform path that demanded a strong state, while authoritarian China chose one that did not. "The crucial requirement for success" of shock therapy, said economist Robert Skidelsky, one of its advocates, "is also the most difficult: a strong and legitimate state." Russia's privatization program was implemented by presidential decree (apart from initial legislation, passed by the parliament).¹⁵ Because of the need to move quickly, shock therapy meant bypassing the democratic processes of debate and deliberation.

Whereas in Russia the government controlled the transition, or tried to, in China the government was largely passive. Its main role was to repeal prohibitions: it removed the ban on farmers working individual plots, the ban on entrepreneurs forming new firms, and the ban on state firms trading on markets. It left in place the existing mechanisms by which the economy was running, and let people build the new economy around the old. Bottom-up changes drove China's reforms. The new economy arose more from the initiatives of the Chinese people, who built new firms and created new ways of doing business, than from changes imposed by the government.

Some top-down changes were needed also; in fact more than what occurred. The government was unduly laggard in acting to correct China's hopelessly inadequate financial and legal systems; undoubtedly some of the growth was based on misallocated investment. Privatization was delayed too long. But what China's success shows is that a transition economy does not have to set everything right all at once. It can get by with temporary solutions, devices like the township and village enterprises that may not exist in Western practice or in economic textbooks.

In any of the planned economics, the starting point for transition was misaligned prices, unproductive firms, and unfilled market niches. Such inefficiency offered large scope for improvement. Introducing a few incentives and some competition into a highly distorted economy could have dramatic effects, as the situation in China illustrates. It was hard to predict, however, just which incentives would work in the peculiar circumstances of the transition economy. It follows that it is prudent to take an experimental approach, and be willing to live for a while with unconventional institutions, if they work. These band-aid solutions may well not be discovered in a finance ministry, let alone in the World Bank or a Western university. They are more likely to be discovered by people whose livelihoods are on the line.

The amount of reliance on foreigners' advice highlights the difference between shock therapy and gradualism. Russia leaned on lawyers, economists, and bankers from the West for advice on how to privatize state firms, develop capital markets, and reform the legal system. The U.S. government spent $2.3 billion in grants for technical assistance and exchanges to support reform in Russia.[16] China by contrast called little on foreign consultants. This was not a matter of Chinese xenophobia versus Russian open-mindedness. It went to the very nature of the reforms. In China many of the important decisions were made in the local regions. Beijing had less use for experts than Moscow because it was deciding less.

*   *   *   *

Reflecting on the first eight years of China's reforms, paramount leader Deng Xiaoping said, "All sorts of small enterprises boomed in the countryside, as if a strange army appeared suddenly from nowhere." The rapid growth of the new township and village enterprises "was not something I had thought about. Nor had the other comrades. This surprised us."[17]

These new firms were arguably the single most important factor in China's reform success. They were a prime contributor to China's reform momentum and economic growth. They strengthened the nascent market economy by creating jobs, supplying needed consumer goods, mobilizing savings, and ending the state firms' monopoly on industry. As Deng said, however, their growth was "not the achievement of our central government." The reformers had failed to foresee, by Deng's admission, the pivotal feature of their own reforms.

The township and village enterprises were, on the face of it, a strange way of organizing firms. The planned economy had failed because of public ownership, yet China's path away from the planned economy, it turned out, involved creating additional publicly owned firms. With hindsight, we can explain the new firms' success. Each was subject to intense product-market competition from the many similar firms. Since they were owned by local governments, they could raise funds without a financial market yet could not expect to be bailed out by the government if they failed. They effectively co-opted the local Communist Party officials, who otherwise might have sabotaged the reforms, by giving them a stake in the emerging economy. The fear of failure induced the managers to run the firms efficiently. But these explanations came after the fact; these firms' success was not foreseen.

The township and village enterprises highlight the single most important feature of any program of deep economic reform—its unpredictability. The transition cannot be planned because we cannot know in advance what policies will work. There is much for reformers to do. They must design new institutions for the transition economy (and experts can provide valuable help in this). Top-down decisions are needed for creating private ownership, writing laws of contract, and building the mechanisms of financial regulation. But the example of China suggests that the reformers should also let solutions emerge bottom-up, and be willing to accept novel solutions that do not conform to preconceived views. The Chinese experience further suggests that not all top-down mechanisms have to be created at the start of the reforms.

When the conventional institutions are missing or dysfunctional, people can sometimes devise workable substitutes. In place of laws of contract, relational contracting allows deals to be made and promises to be kept. Since credit markets were unavailable, firms invest out of trade credit and retained earnings. Markets and entrepreneurship are more robust than they are usually given credit for. The economy can get surprisingly far without some of the institutions usually regarded as prerequisites for market activity.

There are, however, limits to the bottom-up mechanisms. There is one set of institutions for which there is no bottom-up substitute: property rights need to be secured, for corruption can derail the economy. These rights cannot be achieved bottom-up, since what is needed is constraints on the people at the top. Furthermore, the bottom-up mechanisms do not work well for large firms. A striking contrast is seen in the transition economies between the success of the start-up firms (at least in countries where corruption is not out of control) and the poor performance of the privatized firms. One of the sources of this difference is simply size. Large firms need the support of market institutions. Adjudicating complex commercial disputes requires a sophisticated legal system, which only the state can supply. For a firm to grow large enough to benefit from economies of scale, it must make large investments that have long-delayed returns. Such investments require legal protection, to prevent the government or other firms from expropriating them. Also, where laws are inadequate, firms tend to deal with firms they know, rather than with strangers, but this limits their range of customers and suppliers, so their growth is constrained.

If the economy is to develop, top-down rules are eventually needed. Bottom-up mechanisms turned out to work surprisingly well, nevertheless, in supporting transacting in the early stages of transition. Muddling through works better than grand schemes.

*   *   *   *

The countries undertaking market-building reforms started from very different points. New Zealand was an affluent but overregulated market economy.

China and Russia were both planned communist economies; Russia was a middle-income and industrialized country, and China was much poorer and mostly agricultural. Despite their differences, these three countries' responses to reform have some common elements. Designing the market economy entails restructuring the existing firms, creating new firms, and building labor, product, and financial markets—it is difficult in any country.

"Plodding wins the race," as the tortoise said to the hare in Aesop's fable. China's gradualism turned out to be a speedier route to markets than Russia's shock therapy. After eight years of reform, markets were working more effectively in China than in Russia. By 1986, China's agriculture had been marketized, a vast number of new firms were thriving, prices generally were aligned with costs, and per capita income had risen sharply. In each of these respects the China of 1986 was ahead of the Russia of 2000.

The fastest route from a planned economy to functioning markets, it turns out, was not frenetically tearing down the old institutions, starting with a clean slate, and enacting top-down reforms. It entailed letting the new economy grow up around the old one, maintaining some stability to let people create new ways of doing business.

In different circumstances, however, shock therapy could be warranted. In a country like New Zealand where market-supporting institutions already exist—secure property rights, well-defined laws of contract, and active financial markets—the main case against shock therapy loses its force.

Well-functioning markets rely on a judicious mix of formal and informal controls. While the government helps to set the rules for the market, so do the market participants. An economy cannot be designed from above. If it were possible to plan the reforms, it would have been possible to plan the economy.

SIXTEEN

⋮⋮⋮

Antipoverty Warriors

Human rights activists, labor union members, revolutionaries, religious groups, environmentalists, and animal rights advocates assembled in December 1999 on the streets of Seattle. What brought this incongruent coalition together was their hatred of globalization, symbolized for them by a meeting of the World Trade Organization.

The protesters turned on street theater. Singers and rappers, dancers and jugglers entertained the crowds. Environmentalists dressed up in costumes: there were sea turtles and dolphins, and a "genetically modified" man. Black-clad anarchists, scarves covering their faces, smashed the windows of McDonald's and Niketown, stores they saw as signifying American world dominance. The confrontation turned violent when the police reacted, perhaps overreacted, to the anarchists' provocations, spraying tear gas, firing rubber bullets, and wielding truncheons. The spectacle flashed nightly on the world's television news. After a similar set of protests in Genoa in June 2001, the *Economist* remarked that the protesters had done "what the public relations departments of the WTO, the IMF, the World Bank and the EU have failed to do in half a century: they have made economics exciting."

To the protesters, globalization was to blame for a host of evils: the widening income disparities between rich and poor nations and within rich nations, environmental degradation, the excessive power of the multinational corporations, the homogenization of national cultures. Globalization denoted Bangladeshi children working grindingly long days making soccer balls; Salvadorian women sewing designer jeans in sweatshops; Indonesian workers making athletic shoes in hot, airless factories while breathing toxic glue fumes. Vandana Shiva, an Indian activist, said globalization was "a new kind of corporate colonialism visited upon poor countries and the poor in rich countries."[1]

Globalization arises from the ever-closer linking of the world's markets. Changes in technology helped initiate it. With containerized ships and jumbo jets, the cost of transporting goods plummeted. Networked computers now shift money instantaneously. Changes in policy also played a role, as governments around the world abolished restrictions on trade and barriers to foreign investors. Globalization has even transformed the way its foes organize themselves: the internet links them via sites such as the appositely named www.protest.net.

Let us think about the most fundamental of the antiglobalization protesters' concerns: the impoverishment of the developing world. The protesters made some compelling points. Imposing Western-style intellectual property protections on developing countries, for example, can damage the poor, as the case of the AIDS drugs discussed earlier illustrates. Overall, though, are the world's poor the victims of globalization? Why are poor countries poor?

*　　*　　*　　*

Nearly half the world's people, 2.8 billion, live on less than $2 a day. This blunt, shameful fact underlies what angered the Seattle protesters. The child labor, the sweat shops, the environmental problems will not go away until extreme poverty disappears.

The gap between rich and poor countries is vast. In China, the average income is about one-tenth that in the United States. In India it is one-fourteenth. In Tanzania, to take an extreme case, it is one-sixtieth. A typical American spends in less than a week what a Tanzanian must eke out over a whole year. (These comparisons are done in purchasing-power-parity terms, which take account of the cross-country variations in the cost of living; without such an adjustment, the disparities would be still bigger.)[2]

The world's millionaires number seven million, according to the firm Gemini Consulting. Millionaires therefore make up just over one-thousandth of the world's population. Their assets total $25 trillion.[3] Most of those earning less than $2 per day are in Africa and Asia; most of the millionaires are in Western Europe and North America. The total annual income of the poorest 2.8 billion is about $1.5 trillion. If we assume the millionaires' annual consumption amounts to 6 percent of their wealth (probably an underestimate), then their consumption is $1.5 trillion. The richest 0.1 percent of the world consumes about as much as the poorest 45 percent.

Is sharing the wealth an option to ease the misery of the poor? Let us do some hypothetical arithmetic. Imagine that the wealth of the millionaires is confiscated and distributed to everyone earning less than $2 per day. Dividing $25 trillion among 2.8 billion people would give $9,000 to each.

Such a drastic redistribution would require authoritarian methods. It would be infeasible for many reasons, one of which is that taxing income at 100 percent would squash any incentive to earn it. It is not going to happen. But putting aside all the obvious objections, even if this redistribution could be done, it would not eliminate poverty. The sum of $9,000 is a large sum for a Tanzanian or Bangladeshi, but it is a once-only transfer, since in our thought experiment it is wealth that is confiscated. If the recipients invested their windfall and earned ten percent per year from it, in addition to what they already are earning, their annual incomes would be about $1,500· the per capita income of Algeria or Ecuador. While this redistribution would markedly reduce extreme poverty, the poor would still be poor.

Global poverty cannot be eliminated by sharing the wealth. The poor outnumber the rich by too much, and the income gaps are too wide. Even if a massive worldwide redistribution could be implemented, any gains to the poor countries would be limited. The only real solution, therefore, is economic growth, to expand the world's total resources. Growth simply means an increase in a nation's income. That poverty reduction entails growth is almost tautological, but not quite, for the effects on poverty depend on how evenly the growth is distributed.

Growth is effective: it has brought major improvements in living standards. The average American today earns six times more than a century ago. A typical American family in 1900 lived in a house the size of a two-car garage today. Then, people spent most of their money on the necessities of food, clothing and shelter; now much of it is freed for more discretionary uses. (In 1900, the average American spent over a third of his or her income on food; by 2000 this had dropped to just one-seventh.) Ordinary people in the United States and Western Europe today are better off in material terms than everyone bar the very wealthiest who ever lived prior to the twentieth century.

The good news is that the majority of the world's people, not just those in the West, are steadily becoming better off. Most countries, rich and poor, most of the time are growing. India, for example, grew slowly but consistently between 1950 and 1980 (about 1.5 percent real per capita growth), and somewhat faster in the 1980s and 1990s (4 percent or more). As a result, the average person in India in 2000 was more than twice as well off than in 1950.

While most countries have been growing, the growth is uneven. The countries that were relatively rich at the start of the twentieth century have for the most part continued to grow. The countries that started out poor have followed widely differing growth patterns. Some have grown very fast and many have grown steadily, but some of the poorest have grown little or not at all. The current inequality among countries is the consequence of differing rates of growth in the past. Countries are poor because they have been growing slowly or not at all over a long period of time. Shrinking the global inequalities necessitates speeding these countries' growth.

It can be done. Impressive success has been achieved by the Asian tigers—Hong Kong, South Korea, Singapore, and Taiwan—as well as, notably, Botswana. From 1960 to 1990 these five countries grew at per capita annual rates of 6 percent or more, meaning that people's incomes doubled every twelve years. (You can calculate roughly how many years it takes for income to double by dividing the growth rate into 72.) By 2000, per capita income in Botswana was seven times higher than the average for sub-Saharan Africa. Botswana was lucky, in having diamond mines; but it was not simply luck, for some other mineral-rich countries have failed to grow.

The potency of compound growth is shown by the example of Singapore. In the mid-1960s the average person earned a measly U.S.$500 (equivalent to less than U.S.$3,000 in 2000 dollars). The future looked bleak on both political and economic grounds. Singapore had just been ejected from a federation with Malaysia, and it faced a risk of a communist coup. It had no natural resources and little industry. Overcoming its unpromising beginnings, it grew to genuine affluence. By 2000, with a per capita national income of more than U.S.$30,000, Singapore had caught up with the world's richest countries. Prime Minister Goh Chok Tong boasted, "We have come this far on nothing."

Most of the world's poor countries have become less poor over time, though more gradually than Singapore. In some of the poorest countries, however, such as Guyana, Chad, Mali, and Zambia, per capita incomes have fallen over time.[4]

*   *   *   *

Let us look now at the effects of economic growth within a given country. Who gains from growth? Does it benefit the poor or only the rich? This is a question of fact, not ideology. We must look at the data.

Goethe said, "It has been asserted that the world is governed by figures. I do know this: figures tell us whether it is being governed well or badly." Research in economics has become increasingly empirical of late, as advances in computers have put massive amounts of data-crunching power on every economist's desk, and new statistical techniques have produced sharper ways of making inferences from the data. Facts about the economy do not come to us in a clean form. Drawing lessons from the data involves judgment as well as technique, and to the extent that judgment is involved, reasonable people can disagree. But one of the main achievements of modern economics has been refinements in statistical techniques that narrow the range of judgment needed.

A better understanding of economic growth is one of the results. Huge data sets covering many countries over many years—showing growth rates, investment levels, school enrollment, fertility rates, indexes of corruption and the rule of law, the incidence of poverty, and so on—have been brought to bear on economic growth. Later we will look at what this research has found about the sources of economic growth. For now, let us see what the data tell us about the effects of growth on the poor.

Distributed evenly, a 5 percent increase in a nation's income would mean everyone in the country has that much extra. But growth need not be spread evenly. To study the effect of growth on individuals, economists use two distinct measures: poverty and inequality. Poverty is an absolute measure: the number of people who earn less than the minimum necessary to purchase basic food and shelter. Inequality is a relative measure: the breadth of the gap between the poor and the rich.

Inequality is calculated in various ways; one simple measure is the fraction of national income going to the poorest 20 percent of the population. Poverty is measured by a somewhat arbitrary line. Studies of global poverty customarily take income of $1 or $2 per day as the cutoff. Rich countries set their own poverty line higher. In the United States in 2000, the Census Bureau defined as poor any family of four with an annual income of less than $17,761. (There are two ways of looking at this number. On the one hand, one-fourth of it exceeds the per capita income of most developing countries. On the other, most Americans cannot conceive how a family of four can get by on less than $20,000.)

To see the distinction between the two concepts, inequality and poverty, suppose the income of tenant farmers in India, who are barely getting by, has risen 12 percent over the past two years. Has this change improved things? By the poverty criterion, the outcome is more fair than before, for the poor can buy more and better food for their families. By the inequality criterion, in contrast, it depends on what happened to the incomes of the affluent. If rich landlords at the same time also become 12 percent richer, the nation is no better off. Perhaps in affluent countries inequality may be salient, but in poor countries, in most economists' view, poverty is the more pressing concern.

Poverty is usually reduced, the data show, by economic growth. The rising tide tends to raise all boats. By the $1-a-day definition of poverty, the fraction of the world's population who are poor fell from 24 percent in 1987 to 20 percent in 1999. Poverty has fallen almost everywhere growth has occurred. It is most persistent in countries that fail to grow. An analysis of data from eighty countries over four decades finds that while the effects of growth vary a lot from country to country, the poor usually share in the fruits of growth. The incomes of the poorest 20 percent of the population, in a typical country, rise one for one with overall economic growth.[5] The poor become better off in lockstep with everyone else.

The degree of inequality within a country, in other words, tends to stay constant over time, so any growth means some reduction in poverty. But this is a statement about averages; how much growth helps the poor varies across countries and over time.

The amount of poverty reduction depends on the degree of inequality. In countries with low inequality, growth has a bigger impact on poverty than in very unequal countries.

In the United States over the second half of the twentieth century, growth brought uneven gains. Inequality widened as the rich got richer, mainly from technological changes that increased the wages of the skilled relative to the unskilled. But growth still brought widespread gains. The robust growth of the 1990s reduced the incidence of poverty, mainly by creating jobs. Over a fifth of the people living below the official poverty line in 1992 had been lifted above it by 1999. (The number below the poverty line fell from 15.1 percent of the population to 11.8 percent.) Rebecca Blank, an expert on poverty in the United States, concluded that the "most important lesson for anti-poverty warriors from the 1990s is that sustained economic growth is a wonderful thing."[6]

In China, as we saw, economic growth and poverty reduction on a massive scale followed the restructuring of agriculture. China is not unique. In India also, the productivity of farms rose—not as in China from a radical reform of a deeply inefficient economic system, but from technological advance. The green revolution, with its improved seed varieties, spurred increases in food production. The fruits of the economic growth that followed from India's higher farm productivity have been widely spread.[7] Over a thirty-five-year period, absolute levels of poverty were significantly reduced. Many millions were lifted out of extreme poverty.

*　　*　　*　　*

This is not to say that growth alone can eliminate poverty, or that redistribution from rich to poor is necessarily unwarranted. Growth is not the whole of the solution to poverty. But it is an indispensable part of it.

One reason why growth by itself may not solve poverty is that extreme poverty might actually prevent any growth from getting started. While growth usually brings benefits to the poor as well as the rich, the data show that inequality affects the rate of growth—in a direction that runs counter to conventional wisdom. Countries that have a more equal distribution of income grow faster on average than those with wider income gaps. In countries with extreme inequality, conversely, the inequality in itself can be a hindrance to growth.[8]

Poor countries on the whole are more unequal than rich countries. A measure of inequality is the ratio of the average income in the richest 40 percent of the population to the average income in the lower 60 percent. In the industrialized countries this ratio lies between 2 and 3 (in Germany it is 2.4, in the United Kingdom 2.5, in France 2.7, in the United States 2.9). While in some of the developing countries the degree of inequality is similar (in Pakistan it is 2.2 and in Egypt 2.5), in most it is much higher (in the Philippines it is 4.3, and in Brazil it is as high as 6.4).[9]

Why is inequality an obstacle to growth? One reason is that wide inequality generates unrest and political instability, harming the economy. Another is that in countries that are both poor and unequal, large numbers of people live in extreme poverty. The poor are unable to take advantage of investment opportunities. Potential entrepreneurs cannot borrow or save the capital they would need to start firms. The children of the poor cannot afford an education and so are excluded from skilled employment. Where there is extreme inequality of opportunity, growth is slow simply because much of the nation's talent is wasted.

In Taiwan in the early 1950s, for example, just before the start of its rapid growth spurt, the government enacted a major land reform, redistributing the nation's farming assets toward the poor. The ensuing drop in inequality— Taiwan by then had one of the world's least unequal income distributions— arguably helped to jump-start the economy in its growth to affluence.[10] Other poor countries remain trapped in a vicious cycle of inequality causing low growth, which perpetuates the inequality.

Economic growth is not an end in itself, but a means to the end of higher living standards. More is needed than growth to end the misery of the world's poor. Growth is not a sufficient condition for correcting social wrongs—but it is a necessary condition. Having more resources does not automatically make people's lives better, but it helps.

Health is one measure of living standards. As a country's income rises, its people become measurably healthier. Measures like calorie intake, protein intake, and hospital beds per capita are significantly higher where income is higher. As a result, life expectancy is longer. Child mortality falls when national income rises. It is not just income that affects health levels, to be sure; public-health programs and new knowledge about diseases are crucial. But richer countries are healthier countries.

Gender inequities also tend to fall as the economy grows. Discrimination is largely cultural, but culture can respond to economic changes. In the poorest countries like Bangladesh and Somalia, girls spend about half as many years in school on average as boys. In lower-middle-income countries like the Philippines and Botswana, girls and boys receive about equal schooling. (In Middle Eastern and North African countries like Tunisia, Algeria, and Iraq, though, girls consistently average about two years less in school than boys.) Women workers also benefit from growth: gender pay differentials tend to be narrower in richer countries. Growth helps shrink the gender gap.[11]

*   *   *   *

The consequences of economic growth for human welfare, said Nobel laureate Robert Lucas, "are simply staggering: Once one starts to think about them, it is hard to think of anything else."[12] Understanding how to achieve successful economic performance is urgent. We are far from having all the answers, but we have some.

Investment—broadly defined to include investment in equipment and machinery, in people through education, and in ideas through research and development—is the direct route to growth. Countries that invest more in equipment grow faster, as the statistical studies of growth show. Investment in ever more machines, however, eventually hits diminishing returns. A country that already has a large stock of capital gets a smaller boost from any additional investment, other things equal, than a country with little capital. This implies that poor countries should be growing faster than rich countries because investments should yield larger returns in poor countries. Countries' income levels should be converging. But they aren't.

The rich countries have been able to avoid diminishing returns to physical investment by means of technological progress. New and better ideas offer an escape from the limits of growth. Further, a country can benefit from the world's stock of ideas only if it educates its people. Education, or investment in human capital, is a major source of growth, in addition to investment in machines and equipment. Countries that spend more on education grow significantly faster. Education spurs growth.[13]

The rapid growth in Singapore, for example, is sometimes described as a miracle, but it actually has a straightforward explanation. Singapore simply mobilized its resources. The primary source of growth was massive investment in physical capital. Singaporeans saved and invested as much as 40 percent of their income. A further source of growth was investment in people. In 1966, more than half the workforce had no formal education; by 1990 two-thirds had completed secondary education.[14] Singapore's growth, far from a miracle, was based on cumulative investment.

Investment in machines, people, and ideas is not enough to ensure growth. The investment must be well directed if it is to be productive. For this, markets are needed.

We can obtain a measure of the scope of markets by calculating the fraction of national income that is spent by the government; the remaining fraction passes through the private sector. Big government, it turns out, is statistically related to its rate of growth, in the way most would expect. Large government expenditure is associated with slow growth. A government that controls too much of the economy's resources slows down the economy.[15]

Two further measures of a country's reliance on markets are its openness to international trade and the degree of development of its financial markets. High trade barriers signify government intervention in the everyday workings of the economy. Prohibiting trade across borders means not letting markets operate fully. Price signals are distorted, so investment goes into unproductive areas, such as capital-intensive projects in a capital-poor country. The absence of competition from overseas means firms can be lazy monopolists, rather than being forced to make themselves lean to survive. Low trade barriers, on the other hand, foster an efficient domestic industry. The statistical growth studies corroborate this: countries that are relatively open to international trade tend to invest more and grow faster.

Financial markets promote growth. Where the financial system is inadequate, it is hard for firms to grow large enough to benefit from economies of scale, as industry tends to be owned and run by a politically favored clique. Financial markets allow the entry and growth of new firms. The statistical growth studies find that countries that have workable banks and stock markets tend to invest more and grow faster. Also, controlling inflation is part of financial health. Inflation makes doing business uncertain, by increasing the risks of borrowing and lending and by making prices unreliable signals of demands and supplies. Low inflation turns out to be correlated with faster growth.[16]

*　　*　　*　　*

Markets are needed, then, to generate investment that is both at a sufficient level and directed in the right areas to sustain economic growth. Contrary to the assertions of the more fervent fans of the free market, however, markets are not all that is needed.

If the government is small, then by default much of the economy is left to markets. Small government does not necessarily mean fast growth. Government spending has a negative effect on growth, as noted, but only up to a point. When the government is a large part of the economy, smaller government tends to go with faster growth—but not when it is a very small part.[17] To foster growth, the government must not be absent. Some investment is needed from the government. Growth is faster, the data show, in countries that build workable public infrastructure such as roads, railroads, bridges, ports, and telephone and electricity networks. If a country's infrastructure is sparse, congested, or unreliable, it is hard to do business and growth is impeded. Government can be too small.

Allowing markets to encompass most of the economy is no guarantee of economic success. Some of the poorest countries are predominantly market economies. They fail to grow despite leaving most decisions to markets. In the sub-Saharan African countries, for example, government expenditure accounts for just 26 percent of national income, little more than in the other developing countries. (In East Asia, South Asia, and Latin America this figure is between 20 and 24 percent.) During the 1980s and 1990s the African countries overall had negative economic growth, despite the fact that their governments accounted for only one-fourth of their economies.

Somalia is an extreme case of small government: in Amnesty International's phrase, it is a country without a state. It was devastated in the early 1990s by civil war. As of the year 2000, five years after the United Nations peacekeepers left, admitting failure to stabilize the country, the economy had started to bounce back. By then it was a pure free-market economy. No taxes were collected. Business boomed, with firms competing fiercely for customers. But the economy did not run smoothly. Firms faced high transaction costs. "You have to provide everything for yourself," said

Abdi Muhammad Sabria, a Mogadishu businessman. "You have to collect the garbage on your own street."[18] With no police force, firms had to pay armed thugs to protect their property. They generated their own electricity and found their own sources of water. The lack of a working port meant it was hard to get imported inputs. Competition among the three telephone companies had driven rates low, but they did not interconnect, so a firm needed three telephone lines. The ubiquity of markets, and the absence of government, did not lead to an efficient economy.

Markets do not automatically bring growth. It is not enough that the government stays out of the economy and just leaves things to markets. The sustained high investment needed for long-term growth requires more than that. The statistical evidence further indicates that a country grows if it has sound institutions. Growth is faster in countries that have secure property rights, workable rules preventing corruption, functioning laws of contract, and political stability.[19]

The links between growth and these institutional variables are easy to see. Political instability both discourages economic activity by raising the risks of doing business and diverts firms' resources away from productive activities into a quest for political favors. Corruption discourages investment. Insecure property rights and unreliable contract enforcement impede markets.

What is cause and what is effect? Do countries grow faster because their officials are honest, or does corruption fall as a consequence of increasing affluence? Are effective laws a cause or a consequence of growth? The causality goes both ways, the evidence indicates: most of these variables both lead and follow economic growth.[20] Growth, as a result, can be self-reinforcing. A country may grow because it educates its people; the growth then means it can afford a higher level of education, which brings still further growth. A country that succeeds in lowering corruption boosts its growth, with the result that it is able to devote still more resources to fighting corruption, and so it grows still more. Growth benefits from virtuous feedbacks. By the same logic in reverse, however, the very poorest countries can become trapped. Their dysfunctional institutions mean they are poor, and their poverty means they cannot afford to do what it would take to improve their institutions.

The variables that economists have found to be associated with increases in per capita income, to sum up, fall under two headings: *investment* and *institutions*. Economic growth requires not only that markets be extensive but also that they be well designed. A sturdy platform is needed: mechanisms to protect property rights and contracting, accessible financial markets, a competitive environment for firms, bounds on government expenditure, stable politics and low inflation to limit the uncertainties of doing business, and adequate public infrastructure for transportation and communication. Given this platform, markets generate growth.

That some countries are comfortably affluent while others are grindingly poor is explained in large part by the quality of their institutions. The economic and political environment determines the efficiency of market activity: manufacturing, inventing, investing, buying, selling. If the platform for markets is inadequate, the nation's scarce resources are wasted.

*　　*　　*　　*

Globalization has turned out to be a sideshow as far as poverty is concerned. It neither impoverishes poor countries nor enriches them. Countries are poor because they fail to grow. Globalization does not prevent them from growing: some developing countries, after all, succeeded in growing fast while globalization proceeded. Neither does it necessarily do much, though, to help them grow. Many countries were growing as slowly in 2000 as in 1970; globalization had passed them by.

Globalization could help the poor countries if it made markets in rich countries accessible to their products. Hypocritically preaching the virtues of the global economy, the United States and Western Europe have been notably reluctant to expose their own firms to competition from third-world producers. Some poor countries have obtained an alternative benefit from globalization. By lowering their own trade barriers, they have both widened the range of consumer goods for their citizens and induced their own firms, now facing foreign competition, to become more efficient. Countries with lower trade barriers, the data show, do tend to grow faster. Openness to trade is just one of the sources of growth success, however, and not the chief one.

Poverty need not be a trap. Growth can be achieved, and when it is, impressive poverty reduction follows. China's rapid growth of the 1980s and 1990s resulted, according to the World Bank, in more than 200 million people escaping poverty.[21] It is homegrown policies that make the difference between fast growth and no growth. Successful economic performance reflects the country's own internal policy decisions. Handicaps left over from history aside, countries can affect their own destiny.

Fixing an underperforming economy, as Russia shows, is a lengthy and sometimes painful process. There is uncertainty about what policies will work. We still have a lot to learn about what a country must do to achieve economic growth. "There is not some glorious theoretical synthesis of capitalism that you can write down in a book and follow," as Nobel economist Robert Solow said. "You have to grope your way."[22]

While there is no recipe book for economic success, the broad-brush growth studies summarized in this chapter and the more close-up analyses in the earlier chapters yield some lessons. Growth requires getting the institutions right. This means the state must take appropriate actions. It also means letting markets do what they do best. For this, the market system must be well designed, so that market information flows smoothly, trading relationships can develop, contracts are enforced, property rights are assured, harmful externalities are controlled, and competition is fostered.

The deepest justification for the market economy is that where it works, it is the best remedy we have for poverty. The deepest reason for studying market design is that markets can work badly and thus fail to do away with poverty.

S E V E N T E E N

:::

Market Imperatives

Williilliam F. Buckley, the pundit of free-market conservatism and guru of the American right, was asked at age seventy-four to imagine what views he would espouse were he to be reborn as a college student of today. "I'd be a socialist," he told the startled interviewer. "I'd even say a communist."[1] He ran down a list of causes, including global poverty and AIDS, that would give his young counterpart misgivings about the free market. The genuineness of his qualms is intimated by a further remark he made in the same interview. The emphasis on the market by conservatives, he said, "becomes rather boring. You hear it once, you master the idea."

What Buckley or anyone else is able to "master" of the economy in a single hearing is at best a caricature. In the real world, one size does not fit all. The caricature trips up on a crisis like AIDS or poverty that does not fit into a one-dimensional worldview.

The economy is a highly complex system, as we have seen. It is at least as complex as the systems studied by physicists and biologists. (The economic system has an additional layer of complexity: its components are people, who react intelligently to it and even reshape it.) No one would expect to be able to comprehend physics or biology with ease. Both pro-market and anti-market ideologues—who are to economics what flat-earthers are to physics—like to reduce the market system to a few universally applicable precepts. They can do this only by grossly oversimplifying it.

*   *   *   *

To answer any question about the economy, you need some good theory to organize your thoughts and some facts to ensure they are on target. You have to look and see how things actually work or do not work. That might seem so trite as not to be worth saying, but assertions about economic matters that are based more on preconceptions than on the specifics of the situation are still regrettably common.

The low-fact or fact-free genre is exemplified by a 1999 book *The Origin of Capitalism* by Ellen Meiksins Wood (according to the book's blurb, "one of the most important Marxist thinkers of our time"). Wood said, "wherever market imperatives regulate the economy and govern social reproduction, there will be no escape from exploitation." By "depressing the conditions of great multitudes of people," the market brings "mass unemployment and poverty."[2] No evidence that markets lead to poverty is presented: no data on poverty rates in market economies or on how they vary across countries or have changed over time. That markets bring misery is, for some, an article of faith—misplaced faith for, as we have seen, the evidence denies it. The belief that markets inevitably hurt the poor is plainly and dangerously wrong.

A similarly unworldly mode of reasoning, though opposite on the political spectrum, is used by the libertarians. Ayn Rand viewed economics as philosophy; indeed, *philosophy* was one of her favorite words. Her libertarian disciples today build shrine-like web sites, squabble over fine points of doctrine, and evangelize her creed. As one of them said, they believe "in the truth according to Ayn Rand and only Ayn Rand."

The titles of Rand's books, like *The Virtue of Selfishness* and *Capitalism: The Unknown Ideal*, evoke her themes. Free markets are the ideal way to organize any society; the best government is one that governs least. Arguing that the only function of the state is to provide law and order to "protect men from those who initiate the use of physical force," she advocated "the abolition of any and all forms of government intervention in production and trade." The government should not regulate the economy or redistribute wealth. "In a system of full capitalism, there should be (but, historically, has not yet been) a complete separation of state and economics, in the same way and for the same reasons as the separation of church and state."[3]

Free markets constrained only by laws are unfair, say the critics of libertarianism, because they provide no safety net to those who, through no fault of their own, cannot cope with unrestrained market competition. This criticism is moot. It is not only the poor who would be harmed if libertarian ideas were ever to be put into practice, but the rich as well. There would be economic dislocation. A modern economy simply cannot run on libertarian principles. For it to function, as I have argued, more is called for from the state than just supplying laws to protect people against violence, theft, and fraud. Rand's ideal world, with its "complete separation of state and economics," is an unworkable fantasy.

Two ironies summarize my message. Those on the far left of the political spectrum, who abhor poverty, espouse policies that would entrench it. The fervent proponents of laissez-faire, who esteem markets, advocate a system that would trigger their collapse.

*   *   *   *

I have been arguing for a pragmatic approach to the market, against the quasi-religious views that it is always right or fundamentally evil. The market system is not an end in itself but an imperfect means to raise living standards. Markets are not magic, nor are they immoral. They have impressive achievements; they can also work badly. Whether any particular market works well or not depends on its design.

People's opinions about the market system often can be inferred from their general political orientation. Conservatives view it through rose-tinted glasses. Those on the left are cynical about it. There is no logical necessity to this, however. A conviction about what is just and fair is separable from an appraisal of the effectiveness of markets. One is a matter of core values, on which reasonable people can disagree. The other is a matter of weighing the evidence. In the messy real world of economics the evidence often is not transparent. I have tried to show, however, that it is more conclusive than is generally recognized. We have built up some real understanding of markets.

The evidence, it turns out, supports views across the political spectrum. Economic growth is good for the poor; the incomes of the poor usually rise when incomes rise overall. This finding supports a standard conservative point of view: it could justify policies that foster an efficient economy with incentives for productive effort. On the other hand, the growth studies show that equality is good for growth; countries with a more equal distribution of income tend to grow faster than less equal countries.[4] In this respect the evidence pushes in a politically liberal direction.

Markets are not intrinsically antithetical to social concerns, as we have seen. Market incentives have been enlisted to help conserve endangered fisheries and produce cleaner air. Market mechanisms, properly designed, are the most effective spur to the invention of life-saving drugs against AIDS and other diseases. For nations that are poor, the market system is the only reliable route of escape out of poverty.

Markets cannot do everything, however, and should not be expected to. Externalities and public goods test the scope of markets. An externality like pollution, affecting third parties, calls for some coordinated decision-making; there is a need for rules designed to forestall any third-party harm. Setting up the rules may involve some centralized action by the state or some other organization. Public goods like basic scientific knowledge, benefiting all whether they help pay for them or not, are undersupplied unless there is some coordinated decision-making. A small, cohesive community may be able to generate its own public goods for itself, but public goods that bring benefits to many call for funding and perhaps provision by the government. The state helps to set the rules of the market game in ways that go beyond simply maintaining the legal system. Regulation sometimes has a part to play to help markets work, by underpinning financial arrangements or by guarding against monopolization.

The best way to understand the interaction of state and market is not to debate it in the abstract but to examine how real economies with varying degrees of government intervention actually work. Whether intervention is warranted, and by how much, is best decided case by case. It requires looking into the details of the specific market, while taking into account any distortions the government's action would bring. It is a technocratic issue, not one of high principle.

Economic analysis has its limits, of course. It cannot resolve the major question of whether, and by how much, the government should redistribute income. How you believe the fruits of economic success should be shared comes down to your own values. It is not solely a value judgment, for we can measure the downside of redistribution: the extent to which taxing the better-off discourages them from working and investing and thus hampers the economy. Debates between the left and right sometimes come down to claims, often implicit, that the disincentives from taxation are small or are large. Economists can usefully contribute to such debates, by empirically assessing the consequences of redistribution.[5] But better data cannot settle the central question about redistribution — what is a society's obligation to its poor? — for the answer rests on what is fair and just. An economist has no more to say about this than anyone else.

*   *   *   *

The "main merit" of the market economy, the free-market economist F. A. Hayek said, is that it is "a system in which bad men can do least harm."[6] The market design approach endorses Hayek's claim—and tempers it. The market puts a check on harmful or antisocial behavior. It does not always succeed in preventing "bad men" from doing harm, but it usually does, provided its design is set right.

John le Carré said in an interview that the gruesome tales of corporate shenanigans that he wrote about in his novel *The Constant Gardener* reflected his "total frustration" with the "extraordinary belief," which he believes is widely held, that "at the center of corporations lies a moral purpose, some humanitarian self-restraint. It's nonsense." The market design approach takes le Carré's point as given. It cannot be presumed that people or corporations will behave well.

The desire for profits is not the most appealing of human traits. It can have untoward consequences, as in Arthur Miller's *Death of a Salesman*, in which tragedy results from Willy Loman's desperate need "to end up big," his frantic pursuit of the million-dollar idea. Attractive or not, the profit motive is extremely potent. Any economy is driven by it. The challenge of market design is to devise mechanisms, or to allow mechanisms to evolve, that channel the pursuit of profits in a socially productive direction.

For a market to function well, you must be able to trust most of the people most of the time; you must be secure from having your property expropriated; information about what is available where at what quality must flow smoothly; any side effects on third parties must be curtailed; and competition must be at work. A multitude of mechanisms sustain these five key requisites of effective markets. Your trust in your trading partner rests on both the formal device of the law and the informal device of reputation. Your property rights are protected by the law and, in the case of your investments, by regulation. For you to be able to take your business elsewhere, there are channels for the flow of information, so you can locate others to deal with, and there are few impediments to starting up and running firms.

A market's design, supporting these features, may evolve from below or be imposed from above; usually there is a bit of both. A workable structure provides rewards for good behavior and checks and balances to deter bad behavior, so people act honorably while following their self-interest. When markets are well designed—but only then—we can rely on Adam Smith's invisible hand to work, harnessing dispersed information, coordinating the economy, and creating gains from trade.

"Democracy is the worst form of government," Winston Churchill observed, "except all the other forms that have been tried from time to time." This was in a speech to the British Parliament just after World War II, which was, among other things, a fight for democracy. At around the same time E. M. Forster offered "Two cheers for democracy: one because it admits variety and two because it permits criticism. Two cheers are quite enough: there is no occasion for three."7

The market system is like democracy. It is the worst form of economy, except for all the others that have been tried from time to time. It succeeds because, precisely as in Forster's view of democracy, it admits variety and permits criticism. We should cheer it because it solves some all-but-intractable problems, which have been tackled by none of the alternative forms of economic organization. It generates wealth. It alleviates poverty. But it has its limits. There are things it cannot do. It does not necessarily do even what it is supposed to; it works well only if it is well designed. Two cheers are enough.

ACKNOWLEDGMENTS

Thanks to the following for comments, suggestions, and information: Daniel Berkowitz, Simon Board, Roger Bohn, Ashok Desai, Lewis Evans, Beth Goldberg, Avner Greif, Brad Handler, Eiichiro Kazumori, Kurt Lauk, Patrice Lord, Preston McAfee, Eva Meyersson, Paul Milgrom, Barry Naughton, John Roberts, Paul Romer, Michael Rothschild, Suzanne Scotchmer, Yoav Shoham, Matthew Shugart, Joel Sobel, Dale Squires, Steven Tadelis, Romain Wacziarg, Sonia Weyers, Matthew White, Bryce Wilkinson, Robert Wilson, Christopher Woodruff, Muhamet Yildez, and Jeffrey Zwiebel. At W. W. Norton, I especially thank my editor, Drake McFeely, as well as Eve Lazovitz and Jack Repcheck. Stanford University's Graduate School of Business supported the writing of this book. Most of all, I thank Patti for her warm and wise support.

ENDNOTES

Preface

1. Vargas Llosa said this in reference to the story of how Peru's poor make a living through black markets (in his foreword to de Soto (1989) p. xi).

Chapter One. The Only Natural Economy

1. Data from Bloemenveiling Aalsmeer, www.vba.nl, accessed January 2001.

2. This description of the history and evolution of football draws on Dunning and Sheard (1979) and Denney and Riesman (1954); the quote from the spectator is from Macrory (1991, p. 9).

3. On trade in the Fertile Crescent, see Weiss (1998). On the utilitarian origins of writing, see Green (1989) and Postgate, Wang, and Wilkinson (1995), and of mathematics, see Aczel (1996, pp. 11-12, 41). On the Agora, see Thompson (1976).

4. From *Merriam-Webster Online Collegiate Dictionary*, www.m-w.com, accessed November 2000.

5. The household production number is from Sharp, Ciscel, and Heath (1998).

6. Havel (1992, p.62)

7. Cox (1999, p. 19). The Fuentes quote is from *World Press Review*, November 1995, p. 47. Gilder is quoted by Borsook (2000, pp. 150, 151). On the Reverend Whately, see Rashid (1998, p. 219).

8. The Nobel laureates' quotes are from Swedberg (1994). The Nobel citation is from www.nobel.se/economics/laureates/2001/press.html.

9. Simmel (1978, p. 175).

10. The giant in developing the new theory of markets is Kenneth Arrow; see Arrow (1974a). Other landmark works include Stigler (1961), Vickrey (1961), Akerlof (1970), Spence (1973), Rothschild and Stiglitz (1976), and Wilson (1977).

11. The significance of transaction costs for markets and firms was first emphasized by Ronald Coase and Oliver Williamson; see Coase (1937, 1960) and Williamson (1985, 2000). The work of Coase and Williamson underlies many of the ideas discussed in this book. For more on the various kinds of transaction costs, see in particular Williamson (1985).

12. Dawkins (1986).

13. World Bank estimate, www.worldbank.org/poverty/data/trends/income.htm, accessed January 2001.

Chapter Two. Triumphs of Intelligence

1. The Hanoi sidewalk markets are described by Templer (1999, p. 233); the Rwandan refugee camps by Wrong (2000, p. 239); and the prison camp by Radford (1945).

2. Robertson (1983); the quotes are from pp. 469, 490. See also Clark (1988). The Adam Smith quote is from Smith (1971, vol. 1, pp. 477–478).

3. Lockhart (1996, p. 151). On consumption levels, see Miron and Zwiebel (1991).

4. The economic changes brought by advances in computer and communications technology are detailed by Shapiro and Varian (1999).

5. The eBay story is told by Holloway and Morgridge (2000). Quotes from *Business Week*, April 12, 1999, p. 33, and the *Economist*, June 24, 1999, p. 67.

6. *New York Times Magazine*, January 30, 2000, p. 18.

7. Spulber (1996, p. 137).

8. On Marshall Field, see Twyman (1954, pp. 3–4, 179).

9. On the New York Stock Exchange, see Sobel (1970) and Banner (1988).

10. On the Osaka futures market, see Schaede (1989) and West (2000).

11. *San Jose Mercury News*, June 26, 2000, and December 30, 2000, p. 11C; and *Upside Today*, December 15, 2000.

12. On Rembrandt, see Alpers (1988, ch. 4); the quotes are from pp. 101, 105. On the German composers, see Baumol and Baumol (1944) and Scherer (2000); the quote is from Gardner (1944, p. 48).

Chapter Three. He Who Can't Pay Dies

1. UNAIDS (2000, p. 25).

2. *New York Times*, June 17, 2000, p. A6, and July 10, 2000, p. A1.

3. Trouiller and Olliaro (1999). For more information, see the web site for Doctors Without Borders: www.accessmed.msf.org/.

4. *New York Times* May 21, 2000, p. A1, and February 9, 2001, p. A1. The *Times* ran a thoroughly researched series of articles in 2000–2001 on the drug industry, culminating in a moving article by Tina Rosenberg, "Look at Brazil," *New York Times Magazine*, January 28, 2001, pp. 26–31.

5. Schweitzer (1997, ch. 2); *New York Times*, May 21, 2000, p. A1, April 23, 2000, p. 1-1, and April 24, 2001, p. C1.

6. le Carré (2001, pp. 164, 176, 324, 370, 459); interview in the *Observer*, December 17, 2000.

7. Quotes from *New York Times*, July 9, 2000, p. 4-1, and May 21, 2000, p. A8.

8. Cost estimates from Trouiller and Olliaro (1999), and Schweitzer (1997, p. 27). Research spending data from www.phrma.org/publications/publications/profile00/tof.phtml, accessed February 2001.

9. Comaner (1986), Scherer (1993). *The Fortune 500* data are at www.fortune.com/fortune/fortune500/.

10. *New York Times* May 21, 2000, p. A1; Zwi, Söderland, and Schneider (2000).

11. See Pritchett and Summers (1996), Easterly (1999), and Ranis, Stewart, and Ramirez (2000).

12. On the successes of the drug industry, see the web site for the Pharmaceutical Research and Manufacturers of America, www.phrma.org.

13. *New York Times*, November 4, 2000, p. B1.

14. Cockburn and Henderson (1997, p. 2); Chirac et al. (2000); Narin, Hamilton, and Olivastro (1997); *New York Times*, April 23, 2000, p. 1-20. World Health Organization quote from *New York Times*, March 11, 2001, p. 4-3.

15. *New York Times*, July 10, 2000, p. A1, and July 19, 2000, p. A1.

16. Berndt et al. (1995). Similarly, an estimate of the demand for patented drugs by Ellison et al. (1997) finds relatively little price sensitivity for patented drugs, though they estimate price sensitivity to be substantial for generic (that is, off-patent) drugs.

17. *Economist*, September 30, 2000, p. 69. India is required by international agreement to conform to Western-style patent laws by 2005.

18. *Washington Post*, September 17, 2000; Chirac et al. (2000); UNAIDS (2000, p. 101); Cardoso quote from *New York Times* March 31, 2001, p. A4.

19. *San Jose Mercury News*, December 24, 2000, p. 6A; UNAIDS (2000, pp. 101–103); *Far Eastern Economic Review*, February 17, 2000. Sullivan quoted in *New Republic*, March 5, 2001. PhRMA spokesman quoted in *Washington Post*, September 17, 2000.

20. On Cipla, see *New York Times*, February 7, 2001, p. A1. The Kenyan politician quoted in *New York Times*, June 17, 2000, p. A6, and the drug company spokesperson in *Toronto Star*, September 18, 1999.

21. *New Zealand Herald*, April 20, 2001.

22. *Financial Times*, March 8, 2001, and March 14, 2001.

23. See Kremer (1998, 2000).

Chapter Four. Information Wants to Be Free

1. Geertz (1978). The quotes are from pp. 29–31.

2. Weiss (1998, p. 43).

3. This logic is from Diamond (1971).

4. Quoted in the *Journal of Economic Perspectives*, Summer 2000, p. 238.

5. Hsing (1999). The quote is from p. 106.

6. Brand (1987, p. 202).

7. "All Things Considered," National Public Radio, February 8, 2000.

8. *San Jose Mercury News*, July 16, 2000, p. 5A.

9. *New Zealand Herald*, September 12, 2000.

10. Salop and Stiglitz (1997).

11. On books and compact discs, see Brynjolfsson and Smith (2000); on cars, see Scott Morton, Zettelmeyer, and Risso (2000); and on life insurance, see Brown and Goolsbee (2000). The most thorough account of the economics of the internet economy is by Shapiro and Varian (1999).

12. Akerlof (1970).

13. Klitgaard (1991, p. 51–55). The quote is from Desai (1999, pp. 171–172).

Chapter Five. Honesty Is the Best Policy

1. *New Yorker*, March 5, 2001.

2. On signaling, see Spence (1973), Rothschild and Stiglitz (1976), Kreps and Sobel (1991), and Riley (2001). On advertising as a signal, see Milgrom and Roberts (1986).

3. On signaling in biology, see Bergstrom (2001) and Zahavi and Zahavi (1997).

4. *Telecommunications Policy Review*, October 8, 1995, p. 9.

5. Quoted by Abolafia (1996, p. 172).

6. Quotes on GoFish are from National Public Radio, "Morning Edition," January 29, 1999.

7. Bernstein (1992).

8. Woodruff (1998), Greif, Milgrom, and Weingast (1994). For more on these and other private sector mechanisms that provide contractual assurance, see McMillan and Woodruff (2000).

9. *Red Herring*, November 1999, p. 178.

10. This account of Vietnamese entrepreneurs draws on interviews and a survey done in Hanoi and Ho Chi Minh City in 1995–1997, reported in more detail by McMillan and Woodruff (1999a, 1999b); the sources of the quotes are given there.

11. *New York Times*, June 1, 2000, p. A1. For some theory of how formal and informal contracting interact, see Baker, Gibbons, and Murphy (1994).

12. Williamson (1985, 2000).

13. Quotes from *Fortune*, February 21, 1994, pp. 60–64; *Purchasing*, July 17, 1997, p. 127, and November 6, 1997, p. 16; and Macaulay (1963, p. 61).

14. Quotes from Hume (1978, p. 546), and Arrow (1974b, p. 357).

Chapter Six. To the Best Bidder

1. On the Tsukiji market, see Bestor (1998) and the auction's web site, www.tsukiji-market.or.jp.

2. On the theory of the transaction cost of bargaining, see Myerson and Satterwaite (1983) (on bargaining breakdown) and Sobel and Takahashi (1983) (on delays to agreement). On the theory of bidding, see McAfee and McMillan (1987). For a comparison of bargaining and competition, see Johansen (1979) and Bulow and Klemperer (1996), and on competition as a process for revealing information, see Hayek (1978).

3. Roth, et al. (1991).

4. Renoir and FitzGerald quotes from FitzGerald (1995, pp. 7, 17). Fung quote from *Far Eastern Economic Review*, July 22, 1993, p. 74.

5. Gibbon (1946, pp. 83–84).

6. On bidding to avoid the winner's curse, see Wilson (1969) and Milgrom and Weber (1982). For the experiments, see Garvin and Kagel (1994)

7. The quotes from John Sterling, Elyse Cheney, David Rosenthal, Molly Friedrich, and Carol Reidy are from *New York Times*, May 17, 2001, p. B3, and *New Yorker*, January 8, 2001, p. 31.

8. Hendricks, Porter, and Boudreau (1987).

9. The prices paid for the television contracts are from *Regional Review*, September 1999, and *Financial Times*, June 15, 2000.

10. That competition works as a "discovery procedure" was first noted by Hayek (1978); on the theory of it, see Wilson (1977).

11. The costs for setting up businesses come from a painstaking study by Djankov et al. (2000). This study, covering 75 countries, found that the official costs of entry tend to be higher in countries with higher levels of corruption and less democratic governments.

12. The quotes from Judge Jackson's rulings are from *New York Times*, April 4, 2000, p. A1.

13. Chekhov (1978, p. 51).

Chapter Seven. Come Bid!

1. Words by W. H. Auden and Chester Kalman.

2. Skoll quote from *Stanford Business*, February 2001, p. 14.

3. Milgrom and Weber (1982), McAfee and McMillan (1987).

4. Myerson (1981), Riley and Samuelson (1981).

5. This account of internet auctions draws on Bajari and Hortacsu (2000), Lucking-Reiley (2000), and Roth and Ockenfels (2000).

6. Whitman quote from *San Jose Mercury News*, April 8, 2001, p. 1G.

7. www.perfect.com.

8. This discussion draws on McAfee and McMillan (1996). The sources of all the quotes pertaining to this discussion are documented there. For more on the

process of designing the FCC auctions, see Milgrom (2000). For up-to-date information, see the FCC's auction site, www.fcc.gov/wtb/auctions. Many of the ideas used in designing the auction trace their origins to Robert Wilson; see his Econometric Society presidential address, Wilson (1999).

9. The idea behind the simultaneous ascending auction was originated by Preston McAfee, Paul Milgrom, and Robert Wilson.

10. For more on auction design, see the web site of Market Design Inc.: www.market-design.com.

11. *Financial Times*, November 2, 2000.

12. McCain quote from *New York Times*, October 16, 2000; Fritts quote from *Washington Post*, December 17, 2000, p. H1.

13. McAfee and McMillan (1986).

14. *MSJAMA Online*, www.ama-assn.org/sci-pubs/msjama, September 1, 1999.

15. Roth (1984), Roth and Peranson (1999). The details of the matching algorithm are given in Roth (1996).

16. *MSJAMA Online*, March 3, 1999.

17. Plott (2000).

Chapter Eight. When You Work for Yourself

1. Hart (1995), Williamson (1985).

2. Kellek (1992). The quoted sentences, from the Hadith, the book of the Prophet's sayings, were translated by Muhamet Yildez.

3. *Financial Times*, January 27, 2000, p. 15; *Economist*, January 6, 2000, p. 62.

4. On the theoretical trade-offs of doing research and development in an integrated versus an independent firm, see Aghion and Tirole (1994).

5. Zhou (1996, pp. 56, 58). The history of the end of the communes is told in Zhou's fascinating book, and in Yang (1996); its effects on productivity are estimated by McMillan, Whalley, and Zhu (1989). Some of the quotes are from the *New York Times*, September 19, 1998, p. A4; others are from Zhou (1996, p. 59).

6. The MacLaine story is told in the *New York Times*, February 23, 1997, p. E4, and the *Irish Times*, October 18, 1997, p. 8.

7. Jin (1999, p. 10).

8. Nyberg and Rozelle (1999, p. 95).

9. Robinson (1976, pp. 8, 38).

10. This story is from Lyons (1984).

11. Reported by Nyberg and Rozelle (1999, p. 63) and Brandt et al. (2000).

12. *New York Times*, April 20, 2001, p. A1.

13. Deininger and Feder (1998), Nyberg and Rozelle (1999). The Jefferson quote comes from a letter to Isaac McPherson, August 13, 1813, available at http://etext.lib.virginia.edu/jefferson/.

Chapter Nine. The Embarrassment of a Patent

1. On McDonald's: *Economist*, July 15, 2000, p. 60; *Toronto Star*, October 25, 1987, p. F7; *Sunday Telegraph*, June 27, 1993, p. 41; *Daily Telegraph*, September 24, 1996; *Scotsman*, April 14, 1998, p. 4.

2. See Romer (1986).

3. On the law and economics of patents, copyright, and trademarks, see Besen and Raskind (1991) and Gallini and Scotchmer (2002). The quotes on copyright are from the U.S. copyright law; see Besen and Raskind (1991, p. 6).

4. This trade-off was highlighted by Arrow (1962).

5. For examples of software that was arguably developed with a view to patenting, see Heckel (1992). Data on software research and development before and after patenting are given by Bessen and Maskin (2000, Fig. 5).

6. These patents can be found under Class 705, Subclass 37 on the patent office's web site, www.uspto.gov. Quote from *New Scientist*, November 25, 2000.

7. *San Jose Mercury News*, January 3, 2001, p. 1C.

8. On the Grateful Dead, see Jackson (1999, p. 277); *Atlantic Monthly*, September 1998.

9. The testimony is at www.napster.com/pressroom/legal.html and www.riaa.com/Napster_Legal.cfm. The numbers for compact disc sales are at www.riaa.com/pdf/year_end_2000.pdf.

10. The story of the purloined program and the quotes come from Manes and Andrews (1993, pp. 81, 91), Levy (1994, pp. 227–229), and *New York Times*, March 26, 2000, p. 3-1, and September 18, 2000, p. C1. The analysis of Silicon Valley is drawn from Saxenian (1994) and Gilson (1999).

11. Managers' quotes from Saxenian (1994, pp. 36, 54, 55).

12. On setting the buyout price, see Kremer (1998), and Shavell and van Ypersele (1999).

13. On research tournaments, see Taylor (1995) and Fullerton and McAfee (1999); the examples are from the latter.

14. The Casablanca story is from Marx (1994, p. 14). The St. Petersburg story is from *Moscow Times*, January 27, 2000.

15. *St. Petersburg Times* (Russia), August 29, 2000.

Chapter Ten. No Man Is an Island

1. Glickman (2001). The data on time lost in traffic are from a study by Texas A&M University's Texas Traffic Institute: *New York Times*, May 9, 2001, p. A14.

2. The tax needed to correct the congestion externality is estimated by Edlin and Mandic (2001). The effect of the alcohol tax on road deaths is estimated by Ruhm (1996).

3. Vickrey (1963).

4. *Deutsche Presse-Agentur*, April 1, 1998.

5. On negotiated solutions, see Coase (1960). On taxes and subsidies, see Pigou (1947); the quote is from p. 42.

6. Steinbeck (1996, p. 1).

7. Botsford, Castilla, and Peterson (1997) (quotes are from p. 509); Jackson et al. (2001) (quote is from p. 636). For an excellent account of the economics of the fisheries crisis, see Grafton, Squires, and Kirkley (1996).

8. *Calgary Herald*, June 15, 1997, p. A2; *Ottawa Citizen*, April 1, 1995, p. B3.

9. The World Wildlife Fund report is summarized in *Monterey County Herald*, August 19, 1998. Sorlien was quoted in *New York Times Magazine*, August 27, 2000, p. 38.

10. *Regulation*, Spring 1998, p. 10.

11. Bender, Kagi, and Mohr (1998), Sethi and Somanathan (1996), *New York Times Magazine*, August 27, 2000, p. 40.

12. Grafton, Squires, and Kirkley (1996), Grafton, Squires, and Fox (2000).

13. Leal (2000). The Garvey quote is from *New York Times Magazine*, August 27, 2000, p. 41.

14. Grafton, Squires, and Fox (2000).

15. On monitoring, see Batkin (1996) and Squires, Kirkley, and Tisdell (1995). The number for illicit crayfish is from *New Zealand Herald*, Febuary 17, 2000.

16. *Japan Economic Newswire*, August 27, 1999; *New Zealand Herald*, August 23, 1999; *Global Information Network Interpress Service*, September 3, 1999.

17. *New York Times*, November 11, 1999, p. A25, April 7, 2000, p. A1, and July 1, 2000, p. B17. Costas is quoted in *New York Times Book Review*, July 2, 2000, p. 14, in a review of his book *Fair Ball*.

18. On the size of competitive balance effects in baseball, see Rascher (1999); in American football, see Welki and Zlatoper (1999); in Australian-rules football, see Borland and Lye (1992); in cricket, see Hynds and Smith (1994); and in soccer, see Szymanski (2001).

19. Noll (1991), Scully (1995, ch. 1).

20. *New York Times* August 8, 2000, p. C23.

21. This account of competitive balance policies draws on Fort and Quirk (1995), Kahn (2000), Rosen and Sanderson (2001) (the quote from the latter is from p. 25), and Weiler (2000).

22. Weiler (2000, pp. 190–191).

23. *New York Times*, November 1, 2000, p. C27, and November 21, 2000, p. C21.

24. *Financial Times*, October 27, 2000.

25. Cheung (1973).

26. Smith (1975). Sugimoto quote from *Business Daily*, February 13, 1998.

Chapter Eleven. A Conspiracy against the Public

1. On Mobutu's Zaire, see Wrong (2000).

2. Estimates from Levin and Satarov (2000).

3. The information on Russian corruption comes from Brady (1999, p. 187),

Handelman (1995, pp. 378–379), Johnson et al. (2000), and Waller and Yasmann (1995). The quotes are from Brady (1999, p. 187) and *New York Times*, April 18, 2000, p. A31.

4. Johnson, McMillan, and Woodruff (2001).

5. The computations on growth rates if corruption were reduced are based on Wei (1998), using estimates from Mauro (1995); similar estimates are in Knack and Keefer (1995).

6. *New York Times*, January 16, 1998, p. A1; *Washington Post*, January 25, 1998, p. C1; *New York Times*, October 12, 1999, p. A1; *Financial Times*, June 27, 2000; Vatikiotis (1998, pp. 43–45, 151-152).

7. Private sector investment data are given in Glen and Sumlinski (1999).

8. www.transparency.de/, accessed November 2000.

9. Shleifer and Vishny (1993). The logic bears a close resemblance to the logic of overfishing the ocean discussed in chapter 10.

10. Handelman (1995, pp. 39, 286).

11. The account of Suharto's Indonesia is borrowed from MacIntyre (2000).

12. For the sources of the information on how companies organize and carry out *dango*, and the quotes associated with this discussion, see McMillan (1991). The Adam Smith quote is from Smith (1976, vol. 1, p. 144).

13. *New York Times*, November 25, 1999, p. A1.

Chapter Twelve. Grassroots Effort

1. The Havel quote is from the *New York Times*, August 23, 2000, p. A8.

2. Reprinted in Einstein (1995, p. 158).

3. Estimates of the number of deaths during the Great Leap Forward are summarized by Yang (1996, pp. 37–39).

4. Productivity estimates are in Bergson (1992) and McMillan, Whalley, and Zhu (1989).

5. Wilson (1940, pp. 480, 483).

6. Planning's computational failures were perceptively analyzed by Hayek (1945). The quote is from Wilson (1940, pp. 451–452).

7. The *Dictionary of Occupational Titles* is published by the Department of Labor, at www.oalj.dol.gov/libdot.htm.

8. The informational failures of planning are described in fascinating detail by Berliner (1957). The quote is from p. 161.

9. Scott (1998); the quote is from p. 313. Scott gives numerous examples of the failure of centralized schemes, though he does not advocate markets as the solution. Scholars of diverse ideological views have pointed to the failure to utilize local knowledge as the fatal flaw of centralized schemes; see also Hayek (1945) and Stiglitz (1994).

10. This paragraph describes what Smith is generally taken to have meant by the "invisible hand." In fact, he seems to have meant something rather different; see Grampp (2000). What is relevant here, however, is not textual exegesis but the

ideas that have become associated with Smith. Quotes from Smith (1976, vol. 1; pp. 18, 477).

11. Arrow and Debreu (1954). The quote is from Debreu's citation on the Nobel Prize web site, www.nobel.se.

12. See Smith (1982) and Plott (2000).

13. The Quarterman quote comes from Gromov (1998); the Berner-Lee quote is from *San Jose Mercury News*, January 30, 2001, books section, p. 2.

14. Lyman et al. (2000).

15. *New York Times*, February 10, 2000, p. C1.

16. The Anderson quote comes from Gromov (1998).

17. *New York Times* November 21, 1999, p. 3-1.

18. On the internet's origins and its decentralization, see Abbate (1999), Claffy, Monk, and McRobb (1999), and Gillett and Kapor (1997).

19. Press (1996, Table 3).

20. *San Jose Mercury News*, January 14, 2001, p. 6F.

21. Lyman et al. (2000).

22. Smith (1976, vol. 2, p. 244).

23. On the New York peddlers and the Dinkins quote: *New York Times*, June 14, 1983, p. B1; *Financial Times*, June 3, 1998, p. 4. On the Otavalo network: *Los Angeles Times Magazine*, November 14, 1993, p. 30.

24. On the methods of measuring the shadow economy, and for the sources of the estimates cited, see Schneider and Enste (2000).

25. The information on Peru's shadow economy is based on de Soto (1989), especially chs. 3, 5. The quote is from p. 152.

Chapter Thirteen. Managers of Other People's Money

1. Simon (1991, pp. 27–28). On the firm as a nonmarket form of allocation, see Holmström (1999) and Goldman and Gorton (2000).

2. The data, for 1999, are from the Bureau of Economic Analysis, www.bea.doc.gov/bea/dn1.htm.

3. For more on the theory of the firm, see Milgrom and Roberts (1992). On Cisco, see the *Economist*, February 12, 2000, pp. 61–62.

4. Megginson and Netter (2001) summarize the evidence that private ownership does matter.

5. Smith (1976, vol. 2, pp. 264–265).

6. *Economist*, February 27, 1993, p. 70.

7. Schiff and Lewin (1970).

8. Kaplan (1995, p. 21).

9. The Xerox quote and data are from McQuade and Gomes-Casseres (1991). Hicks quote from Hicks (1935, p. 8).

10. Tybout (2000, pp. 15–18).

11. On CUC International: *New York Times*, December 8, 1999, p. C1, and June 15, 2000, p. C1. The survey on corporate fraud is discussed in Sherwin (2000).

12. *New York Times*, June 16, 2000, p. C1.
13. Akerlof (1970), Ausubel (1990), Black (2000), Johnson et al. (2000).
14. See Shleifer (2000, ch. 7). The statistical studies on the efficacy of different countries' stock markets include Levine (1997), Demirgüç-Kunt and Maksimovic (1998), Claessens, Djankov, and Lang (2000), La Porta et al. (1997, 2000), and Wurgler (2000).
15. *New York Times*, February 12, 2000, p. B4.
16. Black (2000, p. 1565).

Chapter Fourteen. A New Era of Competition

1. *Detroit News*, November 9, 1999, p. A9. The Dales quote is from Dales (1968, p. 100).
2. This section on the emissions allowances program draws facts from Ellerman et al. (2000), Bohi and Burtraw (1997), and the Environmental Protection Agency (1999). The quotes from the Environmental Defense Fund here and later are from its March 1995 newsletter, at www.edf.org. See also the EPA site, www.epa.gov/acidrain.
3. *Columbus Dispatch*, December 1, 1999, p. 4D; *Buffalo News*, August 27, 1997, p. 16C.
4. A technical side point: It is theoretically possible to devise a mechanism that induces firms to reveal their private information, along the lines of Baron and Myerson (1982). This would involve subsidizing the plants that reveal themselves to be low cost (and so are asked to do the most cleanup) and taxing the others. Such a mechanism is, however, difficult if not impossible to implement in practice.
5. The $1,500 figure was stated in the 1990 Clean Air Act as the price of direct sales of allowances by the EPA, and the $750 figure was cited by the EPA in 1990 as its best guess of the price at which allowances would trade (Bohi and Burtraw, 1997, p. 8). The allowance prices ranged between $70 and $220 over 1994–1999 (see www.epa.gov/acidrain/ats/prices). The price of low-sulfur coal fell in a way that could not have been anticipated, and this explains part of the fivefold to tenfold difference between actual and predicted prices; see Bohi and Burtraw (1997) and Ellerman et al. (2000). Much of it, though, is due to information.
6. *Forbes ASAP*, August 21, 2000.
7. Cason and Plott (1996) pointed out this flaw in the EPA auction.
8. Quotes from *Los Angeles Times*, January 11, 2001, and January 14, 2001; *Economist*, August 24, 2000; *San Jose Mercury News*, April 11, 2001, p. 1A.
9. *San Jose Mercury News*, April 11, 2001, p. 1A.
10. Borenstein, Bushnell, and Wolak (2000); *New York Times*, March 23, 2001, p. A14. For further such estimates, see Joskow and Kahn (2001).
11. Wilson (1999) gave the authoritative account of the principles of electricity market design.
12. See Brewer and Plott (1996) for the details of this auction mechanism and

the experiments with it. An alternative auction mechanism is proposed by Nilsson (1999).

Chapter Fifteen. Coming Up for Air

1. *New York Times*, August 9, 1995, p. A3. An argument that gradualism would work better than shock therapy in the ex-communist countries was made by McMillan and Naughton (1992). The Braudel quote is from Braudel (1982, p. 26).

2. Russell (1996, p. 12). The next quote, from Alan Gibbs, is from the same page.

3. Kelsey (1995, pp. 254, 350).

4. For detailed evaluations of the reforms, see Evans et al. (1996) and Silverstone, Bollard, and Lattimore (1996).

5. *National Business Review*, December 15, 1995, p. 18.

6. For a careful statement of the view that the crisis forced the use of shock therapy, see Boycko, Shleifer, and Vishny (1995). For the view that shock therapy was simply the best approach, see Skidelsky (1996). Chubais is quoted in *Australian Financial Review*, December 22, 1999, p. 9, and Summers in *Transition Newsletter*, January 2001, p. 17.

7. *Economist*, March 15, 1997.

8. Sachs (1992, p. 43).

9. On the effects of privatization around the world, see Megginson and Netter (2001), and in Russia, Boycko, Shleifer, and Vishny (1995), Brown and Earle (2000), Djankov (1998), and Earle, Estrin, and Leshchenko (1995).

10. Gustafson (1999, p. 37).

11. That shock therapy shattered relationships between firms is argued by Blanchard and Kremer (1997) and Roland and Verdier (1999).

12. The best account of China's reforms is provided by Naughton (1995).

13. On state firm reforms, see Groves et al. (1994, 1995).

14. Shirk (1993, p. 334).

15. Skidelsky (1996, p. 142), Boycko, Shleifer, and Vishny (1995, p. 5).

16. U.S. General Accounting Office (2000, p. 10).

17. The quote is from Zhou (1996, p. 106).

Chapter Sixteen. Antipoverty Warriors

1. *Economist*, June 23, 2001, p. 13. The Shiva quote is from www.gn.apc. org/resurgence/articles/mander.htm, accessed September 26, 2001.

2. World Bank purchasing-power-parity data for 1999, www.worldbank. org/data/databytopic/GNPPC.pdf.

3. The data on millionaires, for 1999, are at www.gemcon.com/fs/wealth 2000.htm. The number of the poor, an estimate for 1998, is reported at www.worldbank.org/poverty/data/trends/income.htm.

4. Data from Temple (1999) and Pritchett and Summers (1996). The Goh Chok Tong quote is from the *Economist*, August 22, 1992, p. 25.

5. The cross-country evidence is given by Dollar and Kraay (2000), whose study covers 80 countries over four decades; Timmer (1997) and Easterly (1999) report similar results.

6. On the United States, see Blank (2000) (the quote is from p. 10) and Haveman and Schwabish (1999). The data on poverty rates are from www. census.gov/hhes/poverty/histpov/hstpov5.html.

7. Datt and Ravallion (1998); Desai (1999, p. 40).

8. Aghion, Caroli, and Garcia-Penalosa (1999), Barro (2000), Benabou (1996).

9. Data from Albanesi (2000).

10. Fei, Ranis, and Kuo (2000).

11. On health and growth, see Pritchett and Summers (1996), Easterly (1999), and Ranis, Stewart, and Ramirez (2000). On gender inequalities, see Forsythe, Korzeneiwicz, and Durrant (2000), Hill and King (2000), and Tzannatos (1999).

12. Lucas (1988, p. 5).

13. On ideas as a source of growth, see Romer (1986), and on education, see Krueger and Lindahl (2001).

14. Krugman (1996, p. 175).

15. On the statistical link between government expenditure and growth, see Alesina (1997), Barro (1991), Levine and Renelt (1992), and Kneller, Bleaney, and Gemmell (1999).

16. Levine (1997), Temple (1999), Wacziarg (2001).

17. That smaller government tends to go with faster growth when the government is a large part of the economy is argued by Barro and Sala-i-Martin (1992). On infrastructure: Temple (1999).

18. *New York Times*, August 10, 2000, p. A3.

19. See, among others, Alesina (1997), Barro (1991), Hall and Jones (1999), Keefer and Knack (1997), Levine (1997), Mauro (1995), and Temple (1999).

20. Chong and Calderón (2000), Mauro (1995).

21. Nyberg and Rozelle (1999, p. 95).

22. *New York Times*, September 29, 1991, p. E1.

Chapter Seventeen. Market Imperatives

1. Robin (2001).

2. Wood (1999, pp. 119–121).

3. Rand (1988, p. 4). The other quotes about Rand come from the *Chronicle of Higher Education*, April 9, 1999. For a more recent statement of similar views on limited government, see Murray (1997).

4. On growth and poverty: Dollar and Kraay (2000), Easterly (1999), and Timmer (1997). On equality and growth: Aghion, Caroli, and Garcia-Penalosa (1999), Barro (2000), and Benabou (1996).

5. For an overview of the ongoing work on the consequences of redistributive

taxation, see Slemrod (2000). The results are mixed. Lower taxes appear to induce some more investment in businesses, but they have little effect on the labor supply decisions of the affluent. The evidence does not seem to support the claim, sometimes made in political debates, that cutting income taxes below their current U.S. level would spur a large increase in work effort.

6. Hayek (1948, p. 11). The le Carré quote is from the *Observer*, December 17, 2000.

7. Forster (1951, p. 70).

REFERENCES

Abbate, Janet. 1999. *Inventing the Internet*, Cambridge, MIT Press.

Abolafia, Mitchel Y. 1996. *Making Markets: Opportunism and Restraint on Wall Street*, Cambridge, Harvard University Press.

Aczel, Amir D. 1996. *Fermat's Last Theorem*, New York, Delta.

Aghion, Philippe, Caroli, Eve, and Garcia-Penalosa, Cecilia. 1999. "Inequality and Economic Growth: The Perspective of the New Growth Theories." *Journal of Economic Literature* 37, 1615–1660.

Aghion, Philippe, and Tirole, Jean. 1994. "The Management of Innovation." *Quarterly Journal of Economics* 109, 1185–1210.

Akerlof, George. 1970. "The Market for 'Lemons': Quality Uncertainty and the Market Mechanism." *Quarterly Journal of Economics* 84, 488–500.

Albanesi, Stefania. 2000. "Inflation and Inequality." Unpublished, Northwestern University, Chicago.

Alesina, Alberto. 1997. "The Political Economy of High and Low Growth." In B. Pleskovic and J. Stiglitz, eds., *Annual World Bank Conference on Development Economics*.

Alpers, Svetlana. 1988. *Rembrandt's Enterprise*. Chicago, University of Chicago Press.

Arrow, Kenneth J. 1962 "Economic Welfare and the Allocation of Resources for Invention." In R. R. Nelson, ed., *The Rate and Direction of Economic Activity*. Princeton, Princeton University Press.

———. 1974a. *Essays in the Theory of Risk-Bearing*. Amsterdam, North-Holland.

———. 1974b. "Gifts and Exchanges." *Philosophy and Public Affairs* 1 (4), 343–362.

Arrow, Kenneth J., and Debreu, Gerard. 1954. "On the Existence of an Equilibrium for a Competitive Economy." *Econometrica* 22 (July) 2265–2290.

Ausubel, Lawrence M. 1990. "Insider Trading in a Rational Expectations Equilibrium." *American Economic Review* 80, 1022–1041.

Bajari, Patrick, and Hortacsu, Ali. 2000. "Winner's Curse, Reserve Prices and Endogenous Entry: Empirical Insights from eBay Auctions." Typescript, Stanford University, Stanford.

Baker, George, Gibbons, Robert, Murphy, Kevin J. 1994. "Subjective Performance Measures in Optimal Incentive Contracts" *Quarterly Journal of Economics* 109, 1125–1156.

Banner, Stuart. 1998. "The Origin of the New York Stock Exchange, 1791–1860." *Journal of Legal Studies* 27, 113–140.

Baron, David P., and Myerson, Roger B. 1982. "Regulating a Monopolist with Unknown Costs." *Econometrica* 50, 911–930.

Barro, Robert. 1991. "Economic Growth in a Cross Section of Countries." *Quarterly Journal of Economics* 106, 407–444.

———. 2000. "Inequality and Growth in a Panel of Countries." *Journal of Economic Growth* 5, 5–32.

Barro, Robert, and Sala-i-Martin, Xavier. 1992. "Public Finance in Models of Economic Growth." *Review of Economic Studies* 59, 645–661.

Batkin, Kirsten M. 1996. "New Zealand's Quota Management System: A Solution to the United States' Federal Fisheries Management Crisis?" *Natural Resources Journal* 36 (4), 855–880.

Baumol, William J., and Baumol, Hilda. 1994. "On the Economics of Musical Composition in Mozart's Vienna." In J. M. Morris, ed., *On Mozart*. New York, Cambridge University Press.

Benabou, Roland. 1996. "Inequality and Growth." In B. S. Bernanke and J. J. Rotemberg, eds., *NBER Macroeconomics Annual 1996*. Cambrdge, MIT Press.

Bender, Andrea, Kagi, Wolfgang, and Mohr, Ernest. 1998. "Sustainable Open Access: Fishing and Informal Insurance in Ha'apai, Tonga." Unpublished, Institute for Economy and the Environment, St. Gallen, Switzerland.

Bergson, Abram, 1992. "Communist Economic Efficiency Revisited." *American Economic Review Papers and Proceedings* 82, 27–30.

Bergstrom, Carl. 2001. "A Introduction to the Theory of Costly Signaling." http://calvino.biology.emory.edu/handicap.

Berliner, Joseph S. 1957. *Factory and Manager in the USSR*. Cambridge, Harvard University Press.

Berndt, Ernst R., Bui, Linda, Reiley, David R., and Urban, Glenn L. 1995. "Information, Marketing, and the U.S. Antiulcer Drug Market." *American Economic Review Papers and Proceedings* 85, 100–105.

Bernstein, Lisa. 1992. "Opting out of the Legal System: Extralegal Contractual Relations in the Diamond Industry." *Journal of Legal Studies* 21, 115–157.

Besen, Stanley M., and Raskind, Leo J. 1991. "An Introduction to the Law and Economics of Intellectual Property." *Journal of Economic Perspectives* 5, 3–27.

Bessen, James, and Maskin, Eric. 2000. "Sequential Innovation, Patents, and Imitation." Working paper 00-01, MIT, Cambridge.

Bestor, Theodore C. 1998. "Making Things Clique: Cartels, Coalitions, and Institutional Structure in the Tsukiji Wholesale Seafood Market." In M. W. Fruin, ed., *Networks, Markets, and the Pacific Rim*, New York, Oxford University Press.

Black, Bernard, 2000. "The Core Institutions That Support Strong Securities Markets." *Business Lawyer* 55, 1565–1607.

Blanchard, Olivier, and Kremer, Michael. 1997. "Disorganization." *Quarterly Journal of Economics* 111, 1091–1126.

Blank, Rebecca. 2000. "Fighting Poverty: Lessons from Recent U.S. History." *Journal of Economic Perspectives* 14, 3–19.

Bohi, Douglas R., and Burtraw, Dallas. 1997. "SO_2 Allowance Trading: How Experience and Expectations Measure Up." Discussion paper 97-24, Resources for the Future, Washington, D.C., February.

Borenstein, Severin, Bushnell, James, and Wolak, Frank. 2000. "Diagnosing Market Power in California's Restructured Wholesale Electricity Market." Working paper 7868, National Bureau of Economic Research, Cambridge, Mass.

Borland, Jeff, and Lye, Jenny. 1992. "Attendance at Australian Rules Football." *Applied Economics* 24, 1053–1058.

Borsook, Paulina. 2000. *Cyberselfish*. New York, Public Affairs.

Botsford, Louis W., Castilla, Juan Carlos, and Peterson, Charles H. 1997. "The Management of Fisheries and Marine Ecosystems." *Science* 277 (July), 509–515.

Boycko, Maxim, Shleifer, Andrei, and Vishny, Robert. 1995. *Privatizing Russia*. Cambridge, MIT Press.

Brady, Rose. 1999. *Kapitalizm: Russia's Struggle to Free Its Economy*. New Haven, Yale University Press.

Brand, Stewart. 1987. *The Media Lab: Inventing the Future at MIT*. New York, Viking Penguin.

Brandt, Loren, Huang, Jikun, Li, Guo, and Rozelle, Scott. 2000. "Land Rights in China: Facts, Fictions, and Issues." Unpublished, University of Toronto, Toronto.

Braudel, Fernand. 1982. *Civilization and Capitalism*, Vol. II: *The Wheels of Commerce*. London, Collins.

Brewer, Paul J., and Plott, Charles R. 1996. "A Binary Conflict Ascending Price (BICAP) Mechanism for the Decentralized Allocation of the Right to Use Railroad Tracks." *International Journal of Industrial Organization* 14, 857–886.

Brown, J. David, and Earle, John S. 2000. "Competition and Firm Performance: Lessons from Russia." Unpublished, Stockholm School of Economics, Stockholm.

Brown, Jeffrey R., and Goolsbee, Austan. 2000. "Does the Internet Make Markets

More Competitive? Evidence from the Life Insurance Industry." Working paper 7996, National Bureau of Economic Research, Cambridge, Mass.

Brynjolfsson, Eric, and Smith, Michael D. 2000. "Frictionless Commerce? A Comparison of Internet and Conventional Retailers." *Management Science* 46, 563–585.

Bulow, Jeremy, and Klemperer, Paul. 1996. "Auctions vs. Negotiations." *American Economic Review* 86, 180–194.

Cason, Timothy N., and Plott, Charles R. 1996. "EPA's New Emissions Trading Mechanism: A Laboratory Evaluation." *Journal of Environmental Economics and Management* 30, 133–160.

Chekov, Anton. 1978. *The Cherry Orchard.* Translated by Michael Frayn. London, Eyre Methuen.

Cheung, S. N. S. 1973. "The Fable of the Bees." *Journal of Law and Economics* 16, 11–33

Chirac, Pierre, von Schoen-Angerer, Tido, Kasper, Toby, and Ford, Nathan. 2000. "AIDS: Patent Rights versus Patient Rights." *Lancet* 356 (August 5).

Chong, Alberto, and Calderón, César. 2000. "Causality and Feedback between Institutional Measures and Economic Growth." *Economics and Politics* 12, 69–81.

Claessens, Stijn, Djankov, Simeon, and Lang, Larry H. P. 2000. "The Separation of Ownership and Control in East Asian Corporations." *Journal of Financial Economics* 58, 81–112.

Claffy, K., Monk, Tracie E., and McRobb, Daniel. 1999. "Internet Tomography," *Nature* (January 7). http://helix.nature.com/webmatters/tomog/tomog.html.

Clark, Gracia. 1988. "Price Control of Local Foodstuffs in Kumasi, Ghana, 1979." In G. Clark, ed., *Traders versus the State: Anthropological Approaches to Unofficial Economies.* Boulder, Colo., Westview Press.

Coase, R. H. 1937. "The Nature of the Firm." *Economica* 4, 386–405.

———. 1960. "The Problem of Social Cost." *Journal of Law and Economics* 3, 1–44.

Cockburn, Iain, and Henderson, Rebecca. 1997."Public-Private Interaction and the Productivity of Pharmaceutical Research" Working paper no. 6018, National Bureau Economic Research, Cambridge, Mass.

Collier, Paul, and Gunning, Jan Willem. 1999. "Explaining African Economic Performance." *Journal of Economic Literature* 37, 64–111.

Comaner, William S. 1986. "The Political Economy of the Pharmaceutical Industry." *Journal of Economic Literature* 24, 1178–1217.

Cox, Harvey. 1999. "The Market as God." *Atlantic Monthly* 283 (March), 18–23.

Dales, J. H. 1968. *Pollution, Property and Prices.* Toronto, University of Toronto Press.

Datt, Gaurav, and Ravallion, Martin. 1998. "Farm Productivity and Rural Poverty in India." *Journal of Development Studies* 34, 62–85.

Dawkins, Richard. 1986. *The Blind Watchmaker.* New York, W. W. Norton.

Deininger, Klaus, and Feder, Gershon. 1998. "Land Institutions and Land Markets." Policy research working paper 2014, World Bank, Washington, D.C.

Demirgüç-Kunt, Asli, and Maksimovic, Vojislav. 1998. "Law, Finance, and Firm Growth." *Journal of Finance* 53, 2107–2137.

Denney, Reuel, and Reisman, David. 1954. "Football in America: A Study in Culture Diffusion." In David Riesman, *Individualism Reconsidered*. Glencoe, Ill., Free Press.

Desai, Ashok V. 1999. *The Price of Onions*. New Delhi, Penguin.

de Soto, Hernando. 1989. *The Other Path*. New York, Harper and Row.

Diamond, Peter A. 1971. "A Model of Price Adjustment." *Journal of Economic Theory* 3, 156–168.

Djankov, Simeon. 1998. "Ownership Structure and Enterprise Restructuring in Six Newly Independent States." Unpublished, World Bank, Washington, D.C.

Djankov, Simeon, La Porta, Rafael, Lopez-de-Silanes, Florencio, and Shleifer, Andrei. 2000. "The Regulation of Entry." Working paper 7892, National Bureau of Economic Research, Cambridge, Mass.

Dollar, David, and Kraay, Aart. 2000. "Growth Is Good for the Poor." Unpublished, World Bank, Washington, D.C.

Dunning, Eric, and Sheard, Kenneth. 1979. *Barbarians, Gentlemen and Players*. Oxford, U.K., Martin Robertson.

Earle, John S., Estrin, Saul, and Leshchenko, Larisa L. 1995. "Ownership Structures, Patterns of Control and Enterprise Behavior in Russia." Unpublished, Central European University, Prague.

Easterly, William. 1999. "Life during growth." *Journal of Economic Growth* 4, 239–276.

Edlin, Aaron, and Mandic, Pinar Karaca. 2001. "The Accident Externality from Driving." Unpublished, University of California, Berkeley.

Einstein, Albert. 1995. "Why Socialism?" In *Ideas and Opinions*. New York, Crown.

Ellerman, A. Denny, Joskow, Paul L., Schmalensee, Richard, Montero, Juan-Pablo, and Bailey, Elizabeth M. 2000. *Markets for Clean Air*. Cambridge, U.K., Cambridge University Press.

Ellison, Sara Fisher, Cockburn, Iain, Griliches, Zvi, and Hausman, Jerry. 1997. "Characteristics of Demand for Pharmaceutical Products." *Rand Journal of Economics* 28, 426–446.

Environmental Protection Agency (EPA). 1999. *Progress Report on the EPA Acid Rain Program*. Washington, D.C., EPA. www.epa.gov/acidrain.

Evans, Lewis, Grimes, Arthur, Wilkinson, Bryce, and Teece, David. 1996. "Economic Reform in New Zealand 1984–95: The Pursuit of Efficiency." *Journal of Economic Literature* 34, 1856–1902.

Fei, John C., Ranis, Gustav, and Kuo, Shirley W. Y. 2000. "Economic Growth and Income Distribution in Taiwan, 1953–64." In G. M. Meier and J. E.

Rauch, eds., *Leading Issues in Economic Development*. New York, Oxford University Press.

FitzGerald, Michael C. 1995. *Making Modernism: Picasso and the Creation of the Market for 20th Century Art*. New York, Farrar, Straus, and Giroux.

Forster, E. M. 1951. *Two Cheers for Democracy*. San Diego, Harcourt Brace Jovanovich.

Forsythe, Nancy, Korzeneiwicz, Roberto Patricio, and Durrant, Valerie. 2000. "Gender Inequalities and Economic Growth." *Economic Development and Cultural Change* 48, 573–617.

Fort, Rodney, and Quirk, James. 1999. "Cross-Subsidization, Incentives, and Outcomes in Professional Team Sports Leagues." *Journal of Economic Literature* 33, 1265–1299.

Fullerton, Richard L., and McAfee, R. Preston. 1999. "Auctioning Entry into Tournaments." *Journal of Political Economy* 107, 573–605.

Gallini, Nancy, and Scotchmer, Suzanne. 2002. "Intellectual Property: When Is It the Best Incentive System?" In A. Joffe, J. Lerner, and S. Stern, eds., *Innovation Policy and the Economy*, Cambridge, MIT Press.

Gardner, Howard. 1994. "How Extraordinary Was Mozart?" In J. M. Morris, ed., *On Mozart*. New York, Cambridge University Press.

Garvin, Susan, and Kagel, John H. 1994. "Learning in Common-Value Auctions." *Journal of Economic Behavior and Organization* 25, 351–372.

Geertz, Clifford. 1978. "The Bazaar Economy: Information and Search in Peasant Marketing." *American Economic Review* 68, 28–32.

Gibbon, Edward. 1946. *The Decline and Fall of the Roman Empire*. New York, Heritage Press.

Gillett, Sharon Eisner, and Kapor, Mitchell. 1997. "The Self-Governing Internet: Coordination by Design." In Brian Kahin and James H. Keller, eds., *Coordinating the Internet*. Cambridge, MIT Press.

Gilson, Ronald J. 1999. "The Legal Infrastructure of High Technology Industrial Districts: Silicon Valley, Route 128, and Covenants Not to Compete." *New York University Law Review* 74, 575–629.

Glen, Jack D., and Sumlinski, Mariusz. 1999. "Trends in Private Investment in Developing Countries: Statistics for 1970–96." Discussion paper 34, International Finance Corporation, Washington, D.C.

Glickman, Mark M. 2001 "Beyond Gas Taxes," Redefining Progress. www.rprogress.org.

Goldman, Eitan, and Gorton, Gary. 2000. "The Visible Hand, the Invisible Hand, and Efficiency." Working paper 7587, National Bureau of Economic Research, Washington, D.C.

Grafton, R. Quentin, Squires, Dale, and Fox, Kevin J. 2000. "Private Property and Economic Efficiency: A Study of a Common-Pool Resource." *Journal of Law and Economics* 43, 679–714.

Grafton, R. Quentin, Squires, Dale, and Kirkley, James E. 1996. "Private Property Rights and Crises in World Fisheries." *Contemporary Economic Policy* 14, 89–99.

Grampp, William D. 2000. "What Did Smith Really Mean by the Invisible Hand?" *Journal of Political Economy* 108, 441–465.

Green, W. M. 1989. "Early Cuneiform." Wayne W. Senner, ed., In *The Origins of Writing*. Lincoln, University of Nebraska Press.

Greif, Avner, Milgrom, Paul, and Weingast, Barry. 1994. "Coordination, Commitment, and Enforcement: The Case of the Merchant Guild." *Journal of Political Economy* 102, 745–776.

Gromov, Gregory R. 1998. "The Roads and Crossroads of Internet History." www.internetvalley.com/intvalconcl.html.

Groves, Theodore, Hong, Yongmiao, McMillan, John, and Naughton, Barry. 1994. "Autonomy and Incentives in Chinese State Enterprises." *Quarterly Journal of Economics* 109, 183–209.

———. 1995. "China's Evolving Managerial Labor Market." *Journal of Political Economy* 4, 873–892.

Gustafson, Thane. 1999. *Capitalism Russian-Style*. Cambridge, U.K., Cambridge University Press.

Hall, Robert E., and Jones, Charles I. 1999. "Why Do Some Countries Produce So Much More Output per Worker Than Others?" *Quarterly Journal of Economics* 114, 83–116.

Handelman, Stephen. 1995. *Comrade Criminal*. New Haven, Yale University Press.

Hart, Oliver. 1995. *Firms, Contracts, and Financial Structure*. Oxford, U.K., Clarendon Press.

Hayek, F. A. 1945. "The Use of Knowledge in Society." *American Economic Review* 35, 519–30.

———. 1948. *Individualism and Economic Order*. Chicago, University of Chicago Press.

———. 1978. "Competition as a Discovery Procedure." In *New Studies in Philosophy, Politics, Economics, and the History of Ideas*. London, Routledge and Kegan Paul.

Havel, Vaclav. 1992. *Summer Meditations*. New York, Alfred A. Knopf.

Haveman, Robert, and Schwabish, Jonathan. 1999. "Economic Growth and Poverty: A Return to Normalcy?" *Focus* 20 (Spring), 1–7. www.ssc.wisc.edu/irp/focus.htm.

Heckel, Paul. 1992. "Debunking the Software Myths." *Communications of the ACM*.

Hendricks, Kenneth, Porter, Robert H., and Boudreau, Bryan. 1987. "Information, Returns, and Bidding Behavior in OCS Auctions: 1954–1969." *Journal of Industrial Economics* 35, 517–542.

Hicks, John. 1935. "Annual Survey of Economic Theory: The Theory of Monopoly." *Econometrica* 3. 1–20.

Hill, M. Anne, and King, Elizabeth M. 2000. "Women's Education in Developing Countries." In G. M. Meier and J. E. Rauch, eds., *Leading Issues in Economic Development*, 7th ed. New York, Oxford University Press.

Holloway, Charles, and Morgridge, John. 2000. "eBay: Managing Hypergrowth." Teaching case, Graduate School of Business, Stanford University, Stanford.

Holmström, Bengt. 1999. "The Firm as a Sub-Economy." *Journal of Law, Economics, and Organization* 15, 74–102.

Hsing, You-tien. 1999. "Trading Companies in Taiwan's Fashion Shoe Networks." *Journal of International Economics* 48, 101–120.

Hume, David. 1978 [1739]. *A Treatise of Human Nature*, 2nd ed., Oxford, U.K., Oxford University Press.

Hynds, Michael, and Smith, Ian. 1994."The Demand for Test Match Cricket." *Applied Economics Letters* 1, 103–106.

Jackson, Blair. 1999. *Garcia: An American Life*. New York, Viking.

Jackson, Jeremy C., et al. 2001. "Historical Overfishing and the Recent Collapse of Coastal Ecosystems." *Science* 293 (July 27), 629–638.

Jin, Ha, 1999. *Waiting*. New York, Pantheon.

Johansen, Leif. 1979. "The Bargaining Society and the Inefficiency of Bargaining." *Kyklos* 32, 497–522.

Johnson, Simon, Kaufmann, Daniel, McMillan, John, and Woodruff, Christopher. 2000. "Why Do Firms Hide? Bribes and Unofficial Activity after Communism." *Journal of Public Economics* 76, 495–520.

Johnson, Simon, La Porta, Rafael, Lopez-de-Silanes, Florencio, and Shleifer, Andrei. 2000. "Tunneling." *American Economic Review Papers and Proceedings* 90, 22–27.

Johnson, Simon, McMillan, John, and Woodruff, Christopher. 2001. "Property Rights and Finance." Unpublished, MIT, Cambridge.

Joskow, Paul, and Kahn, Edward. 2001. "A Quantitative Analysis of Pricing Behavior in California's Wholesale Electricity Market during Summer 2000." Paper 8157, National Bureau of Economic Research, Washington, D.C.

Kahn, Lawrence M. 2000. "The Sports Business as a Labor Market Laboratory." *Journal of Economic Perspectives* 14, 74–94.

Kaplan, Jerry. 1955. *Startup: A Silicon Valley Adventure*. New York, Penguin.

Keefer, Philip, and Knack, Stephen. 1997. "Why Don't Poor Countries Catch Up?" *Economic Inquiry* 35, 590–602.

Kellek, Cengiz. 1992. *The State and Market in the Prophet's Time* [in Turkish]. Istanbul, Bilim ve Sanat Vafki Yayinlari.

Kelsey, Jane. 1995. *The New Zealand Experiment*. Auckland, Auckland University Press.

Klitgaard, Robert. 1991. *Adjusting to Reality*. San Francisco, ICS Press.

Knack, Stephen, and Keefer, Philip. 1995. "Institutions and Economic Performance: Cross-Country Tests Using Alternative Institutional Measures." *Economics and Politics* 7, 207–228.

Kneller, Richard, Bleaney, Michael F., and Gemmell, Norman. 1999. "Fiscal Policy and Growth: Evidence from OECD Countries." *Journal of Public Economics* 74, 171–190.

Kremer, Michael. 1998. "Patent Buyouts." *Quarterly Journal of Economics* 113, 1137–1167.

———. 2000."Creating Markets for New Vaccines." Unpublished, Harvard University, Cambridge.

Kreps, David, and Sobel, Joel. 1991. "Signaling." In R. Aumann and S. Hart, eds., *Handbook of Game Theory with Economic Applications*. Amsterdam, North-Holland.

Krueger, Alan, and Lindahl, Mikael. 2001. "Education for Growth: Why and for Whom?" *Journal of Economic Literature* 39, 1101–1136.

Krugman, Paul. 1996. "The Myth of Asia's Miracle." In *Pop Internationalism*. Cambridge, MIT Press.

La Porta, Rafael, Lopez-de-Silanes, Florencio, Shleifer, Andrei, and Vishny, Robert. 1997. "Legal Determinants of External Finance." *Journal of Finance* 52, 1131–1149.

———. 2000. "Investor Protection and Corporate Governance." *Journal of Financial Economics* 58, 3–27.

le Carré, John. 2001. *The Constant Gardener*. New York, Scribner.

Leal, Donald R. 2000. "Homesteading the Commons." Paper PS-19, Political Economy Research Center, Bozeman, Mont.

Levin, Mark, and Satarov, Georgy. 2000. "Corruption and Institutions in Russia." *European Journal of Political Economy* 16, 113–132.

Levine, Ross. 1997. "Financial Development and Economic Growth." *Journal of Economic Literature* 35, 688–726.

Levine, Ross, and Renelt, David. 1992. "A Sensitivity Analysis of Cross-Country Growth Regressions." *American Economic Review* 82, 942–963.

Levy, Steven. 1994. *Hackers*. New York, Delta.

Lockhart, Robert Bruce. 1996. *Scotch*, 7th ed. Glasgow, Neil Wilson Publishing.

Lucas, Robert E. 1998. "On the Mechanics of Economic Development." *Journal of Monetary Economics* 22, 3–42.

Lucking-Reiley, David. 2000. "Auctions on the Internet: What's Being Auctioned, and How?" *Journal of Industrial Economics* 48, 227–252.

Lyman, Peter, Varian, Hal R., et al. 2000. "How Much Information?" www.sims.berkeley.edu/how-much-info.

Lyons, Thomas P. 1994. "Economic Reform in Fujian: Another View from the Villages." In T. P. Lyons and V. Nee, eds., *The Economic Transformation of South China*. Ithaca, N.Y., Cornell University Press.

Macaulay, Stewart. 1963. "Non-Contractual Relations in Business: A Preliminary Study." *American Sociological Review* 28, 55–67.

MacIntyre, Andrew. 2000. "Investment, Property Rights, and Corruption in Indonesia." In J. E. Campos, ed., *Corruption: The Boom and Bust of East Asia*. Manila, Ateneo University Press.

Macrory, Jennifer. 1991. *Running with the Ball*. London, Collins Willow.

Manes, Stephen, and Andrews, Paul. 1993. *Gates*. New York, Doubleday.

Marx, Groucho. 1994. *The Groucho Letters*. New York, Da Capo Press.

Mauro, Paolo. 1995. "Corruption and Growth." *Quarterly Journal of Economics* 110, 681–712.

McAfee, R. Preston, and McMillan, John. 1986. "Bidding for Contracts: A Principal-Agent Analysis." *Rand Journal of Economics* 17, 326–338.

———. 1987. "Auctions and Bidding." *Journal of Economic Literature* 25, 699–738.

———. 1996. "Analyzing the Airwaves Auction." *Journal of Economic Perspectives* 10, 159–176.

McMillan, John. 1991. "*Dango*: Japan's Price-Fixing Conspiracies." *Economics and Politics* 3, 201–218.

———. 1992. *Games, Strategies, and Managers*. New York, Oxford University Press.

McMillan, John, and Naughton, Barry. 1992. "How to Reform a Planned Economy: Lessons from China." *Oxford Review of Economic Policy* 8, 130–143.

McMillan, John, Whalley, John, and Zhu, Lijing. 1998. "The Impact of China's Economic Reforms on Agricultural Productivity Growth." *Journal of Political Economy* 97, 781–807.

McMillan, John, and Woodruff, Christopher. 1999a. "Dispute Prevention without Courts in Vietnam." *Journal of Law, Economics, and Organization* 15, 637-658.

———. 1999b. "Interfirm Relationships and Informal Credit in Vietnam," *Quarterly Journal of Economics* 114, 1285–1320.

———. 2000. "Private Order under Dysfunctional Public Order." *Michigan Law Review* 98, 2421–2458.

McQuade, Krista, and Gomes-Casseres, Benjamin. 1991. "Xerox and Fuji Xerox." Case 9-391-156, Harvard Business School, Boston.

Megginson, William L., and Netter, Jeffry M. 2001. "From State to Market: A Survey of Empirical Studies on Privatization." *Journal of Economic Literature* 39, 321–389.

Milgrom, Paul. 2000. "Putting Auction Theory to Work: The Simultaneous Ascending Auction." *Journal of Political Economy* 108, 245–272.

Milgrom, Paul, and Roberts, John. 1986. "Price and Advertising Signals of Product Quality." *Journal of Political Economy* 94, 796–821.

———. 1992. *Economics, Organization, and Management*. Englewood Cliffs, N.J., Prentice-Hall.

Milgrom, Paul R., and Weber, Robert J. 1982. "A Theory of Auctions and Competitive Bidding." *Econometrica* 50, 1089–1122.

Miron, Jeffrey A., and Zwiebel, Jeffrey. 1991. "Alcohol Consumption during Prohibition." *American Economic Review Papers and Proceedings* 81, 242–247.

Murray, Charles. 1997. *What It Means to Be a Libertarian*. New York, Broadway Books.

Myerson, Roger. 1981. "Optimal Auction Design." *Mathematics of Operations Research* 6, 58–73.

Myerson, Roger B., and Satterthwaite, Mark A. 1983. "Efficient Mechanisms for Bilateral Trading." *Journal of Economic Theory* 29, 265–281.

Narin, Francis, Hamilton, Kimberly S., and Olivastro, Dominic. 1997. "The Increasing Linkage between U.S. Technology and Public Science." *Research Policy* 26, 317–330.

Naughton, Barry. 1995. *Growing out of the Plan*. New York, Cambridge University Press.

Nilsson, Jan-Eric. 1999. "Allocation of Track Capacity: Experimental Evidence on the Use of Priority Auctioning in the Railway Industry." *International Journal of Industrial Organization* 17, 1139–1162.

Noll, Roger G. 1991. "Professional Basketball: Economic and Business Perspectives." In P. D. Staudohar and J. A. Mangan, eds., *The Business of Professional Sports*. Urbana: University of Illinois Press.

Nyberg, Albert, and Rozelle, Scott. 1999. *Accelerating China's Rural Transformation*. Washington, D.C., World Bank.

Pigou, A. C. 1947. *Socialism vs. Capitalism*. London, Macmillan.

Plott, Charles R. 2000. "Markets as Information Gathering Tools." *Southern Economic Journal* 67, 1–15.

Postgate, Nicholas, Wang, Tao, and Wilkinson, Toby. 1995. "The Evidence for Early Writing: Utilitarian or Ceremonial?" *Antiquity* 69, 549–580.

Press, Larry. 1996. "Seeding Networks: The Federal Role." *Communications of the ACM* 39 (October), 11–18.

Pritchett, Lant, and Summers, Lawrence H. 1996. "Wealthier Is Healthier." *Journal of Human Resources* 31, 841–868.

Radford, R. A. 1945. "The Economic Organisation of a P.O.W. Camp." *Economica* 12, 189–201.

Rajan, Raghuram, and Zingales, Luigi. 1999. "The Politics of Financial Development." Typescript, University of Chicago, Chicago.

Rand, Ayn. 1988. "Introducing Objectivism." In *The Voice of Reason*. New York, New American Library. Also at www.aynrand.org.

Ranis, Gustav, Stewart, Frances, and Ramirez, Alejandro. 2000. "Economic Growth and Human Development." *World Development* 28, 197–219.

Rascher, Daniel. 1999. "A Test of the Optimal Positive Production Network Externality in Major League Baseball." In J. Fizel, E. Gustafson, and L. Hadley, eds., *Sports Economics*. Westport, Conn., Praeger.

Rashid, Salim. 1998. *The Myth of Adam Smith*, London, Edward Elgar.

Riley, John. 2001. "Silver Signals." *Journal of Economic Literature* 39, 432–478.

Riley, John, and Samuelson, William. 1981. "Optimal Auctions." *American Economic Review* 71, 381–392.

Robertson, Claire C. 1983. "The Death of Makola and Other Tragedies." *Canadian Journal of African Studies* 17, 469–495.

Robin, Corey. 2001. "The Ex-Cons." *Lingua Franca* 11.

Robinson, Joan. 1976. *Economic Management in China*. London, Anglo-Chinese Educational Institute.

Roland, Gérard, and Verdier, Thierry. 1999. "Transition and the Output Fall." *Economics of Transition* 7, 1–28.

Romer, Paul M. 1986. "Increasing Returns and Long-Run Growth." *Journal of Political Economy* 9, 1002–1037.

Rosen, Sherwin, and Sanderson, Allen. 2001. "Labor Markets in Professional Sports." *Economic Journal* 111, 47–68.

Roth, Alvin E. 1984. "The Evolution of the Labor Market for Medical Interns and Residents." *Journal of Political Economy* 92, 991–1016.

———. 1996. "Report on the Design and Testing of an Applicant Proposing Matching Algorithm, and Comparison with the Existing NPRM Algorithm." www.economics.harvard.edu/~aroth/phase1.html.

Roth, Alvin E., and Ockenfels, Axel. 2000. "Last Minute Bidding and the Rules for Ending Second-Price Auctions." Unpublished, Harvard University, Cambridge.

Roth, Alvin E., and Peranson, Elliot. 1999. "A Redesign of the Matching Market for American Physicians: Some Engineering Aspects of Economic Design." *American Economic Review* 89, 748–780.

Roth, Alvin E., Prasnikar, Vesna, Okuno-Fujiwara, Masahiro, and Zamir, Shmuel. 1991."Bargaining and Market Behavior in Jerusalem, Ljubljana, Pittsburgh, and Tokyo: An Experimental Study." *American Economic Review* 81, 1068–1095.

Rothschild, Michael, and Stiglitz, Joseph E. 1976. "Equilibrium in Competitive Insurance Markets: An Essay on the Economics of Imperfect Information." *Quarterly Journal of Economics* 90, 629–650.

Rozelle, Scott, Zhang, Linxiu, and Huang, Jikun. 1999. "China's War on Poverty." Typescript, University of California, Davis.

Ruhm, Christopher J. 1996. "Alcohol Policies and Highway Vehicle Fatalities." *Journal of Health Economics* 15, 437–456.

Russell, Marcia. 1996. *Revolution: New Zealand from Fortress to Free Market*. Auckland, Hodder Moa Beckett.

Sachs, Jeffrey. 1992. "Privatization in Russia." *American Economic Review Papers and Proceedings* 82, 43–48.

Salop, Steven, and Stiglitz, Joseph E. 1977. "Bargains and Ripoffs: A Model of Monopolistically Competitive Price Dispersion." *Review of Economic Studies* 44, 493–510.

Saxenian, Annalee. 1994. *Regional Advantage*. Cambridge, Harvard University Press.

Schaede, Ulrike. 1989. "Forwards and Futures in Tokugawa-Period Japan." *Journal of Banking and Finance* 13, 487–513.

Scherer, F. M. 1993. "Pricing, Profits, and Technological Progress in the Pharmaceuticals Industry." *Journal of Economic Perspectives* 7, 97–115.

———. 2000. "Free Markets and Entrepreneurship in Music Composition, 1650-1900." Unpublished, Harvard University, Cambridge.

Schiff, Michael, and Lewin, Arie Y. 1970. "The Impact of People on Budgets." *Accounting Review* 45, 259–268.

Schneider, Friedrich, and Enste, Dominik. 2000. "Shadow Economies Worldwide: Size, Causes, Consequences." *Journal of Economic Literature* 38, 77–114.

Schweitzer, Stuart O. 1997. *Pharmaceutical Economics and Policy*. New York, Oxford University Press.

Scott, James C. 1998. *Seeing Like a State*. New Haven, Yale University Press.

Scott Morton, Fiona, Zettelmeyer, Florian, and Risso, Jorge Silva. 2000. "Internet Car Retailing." Working paper 7961, National Bureau of Economic Research, Washington, D.C.

Scully, Gerald W. 1995. *The Market Structure of Sports*. Chicago, University of Chicago Press.

Sethi, Rajiv, and Somanathan, E. 1996. "The Evolution of Social Norms in Common Property Resource Use." *American Economic Review* 86, 766–788.

Shapiro, Carl, and Varian, Hal R. 1999. *Information Rules*. Boston, Harvard Business School Press.

Sharp, David C., Ciscel, David H., and Heath, Julia A. 1998. "Back to Becker: Valuing Women's Economic Contribution from Housework with Household Production Functions." *Journal of Forensic Economics* 11, 215–235.

Shavell, Steven, and van Ypersele, Tanguy. 1999. "Rewards versus Intellectual Property Rights." Working paper 6956, National Bureau of Economic Research, Washington, D.C.

Sherwin, David. 2000. "Fraud—The Unmanaged Risk." *Financial Crime Review* 1, 67–70.

Shirk, Susan L. 1993. *The Political Logic of Economic Reform in China*. Berkeley, University of California Press.

Shleifer, Andrei, and Vishny, Robert W. 1993. "Corruption." *Quarterly Journal of Economics* 108, 599–617.

Silverstone, Brian, Bollard, Alan, and Lattimore, Ralph, eds. 1996. *A Study of Economic Reform: The Case of New Zealand*. Amsterdam, Elsevier.

Simmel, Georg. 1978. *The Philosophy of Money*. Boston, Routledge and Kegan Paul. First published in 1900.

Simon, Herbert A. 1991. "Organizations and Markets." *Journal of Economic Perspectives* 5, 25–44.

Skidelsky, Robert. 1996. *The Road from Serfdom*, London, Penguin.

Slemrod, Joel, ed. 2000. *Does Atlas Shrug? The Economic Consequences of Taxing the Rich*. Cambridge, Harvard University Press.

Smith, Adam. 1976. An *Inquiry into the Nature and Causes of the Wealth of Nations*. Chicago, University of Chicago Press. First published in 1776.

Smith, Eugene. 1975. *Minamata*, New York, Holt, Rinehart, Winston.

Smith, Vernon L. 1982. "Microeconomic Systems as an Experimental Science." *American Economic Review* 72, 923–955.

Sobel, Dava. 1996. *Longitude*. New York, Penguin.

Sobel, Joel, and Takahashi, Ichiro. 1983. "A Multistage Model of Bargaining." *Review of Economic Studies* 50, 411–426.

Sobel, Robert. 1970. *The Curbstone Brokers: The Origins of the American Stock Exchange*. New York, Macmillan.

Spence, A Michael. 1973. "Job Market Signaling." *Quarterly Journal of Economics* 87, 355–374.

Spulber, Daniel F. 1996. "Market Microstructure and Intermediation." *Journal of Economic Perspectives* 10, 135–152.

Squires, Dale, Kirkley, James, and Tisdell, Clement A. 1995. "Individual Transferable Quotas as a Fisheries Management Tool." *Reviews in Fisheries Science* 3, 141–169.

Steinbeck, John. 1996. *Sweet Thursday*. New York, Penguin.

Stigler, George J. 1961. "The Economics of Information." *Journal of Political Economy* 69, 213–225.

Stiglitz, Joseph E. 1994. *Whither Socialism?* Cambridge, MIT Press.

Swedberg, Richard. 1994. "Markets as Social Structures." In N. J. Smelser and R. Swedberg, eds., *The Handbook of Economic Sociology*. Princeton, Princeton University Press.

Szymanski, Stefan. 2001. "Income Inequality, Competitive Balance and the Attractiveness of Team Sports: Some Evidence and a Natural Experiment from English Soccer," *Economic Journal* 111, F69–F84.

Taylor, Curtis R. 1995. "Digging for Golden Carrots: An Analysis of Research Tournaments." *American Economic Review* 85, 872–890.

Temple, Jonathan. 1999. "The New Growth Evidence." *Journal of Economic Literature* 37, 112–156.

Templer, Robert. 1999. *Shadows and Wind: A View of Modern Vietnam*. New York, Penguin.

Thompson, Homer A. 1976. *The Athenian Agora: A Short Guide*, Princeton, N.J., American School of Classical Studies at Athens.

Timmer, C. Peter. 1997. "How Well Do the Poor Connect to the Growth Process?" Discussion Paper 17, Harvard Institute for International Development, Cambridge.

Trouiller, Patrice, and Olliaro, Piero. 1999. "Drug Development Output: What Proportion for Tropical Diseases?" *Lancet* 354 (July 10).

Tybout, James. 2000. "Manufacturing Firms in Developing Countries: How Well Do They Do, and Why?" *Journal of Economic Literature* 38, 11–44.

Twyman, Robert W. 1954. *History of Marshall Field & Co., 1852–1906*. Philadelphia, University of Pennsylvania Press.

Tzannatos, Zafiris. 1999. "Women and Labor Market Changes in the Global Economy." *World Development* 27, 551–569.

UNAIDS. 2000. *Report on the Global HV/AIDS Epidemic.* Geneva, United Nations, www.unaids.org.

U.S. General Accounting Office. 2000. *Foreign Assistance: International Efforts to Aid Russia's Transition Have Had Mixed Results.* Washington, D.C., GAO. (GAO)

Vatikiotis, Michael R. J. 1998. *Indonesian Politics under Suharto,* 3rd ed. London, Routledge.

Vickrey, William. 1961. "Counterspeculation, Auctions, and Sealed Tenders." *Journal of Finance* 16, 8–37.

———. 1963. "Pricing in Urban and Suburban Transport." *American Economic Review: Papers and Proceedings* 53, 452–465.

Wacziarg, Romain. 2001. "Measuring the Dynamic Gains from Trade." *World Bank Economic Review* 14.

Waller, J. Michael, and Yasmann, Victor J. 1995. "Russia's Great Criminal Revolution." *Journal of Contemporary Criminal Justice* 11, www.konanykhine.com. checkmate/yasmann.htm.

Wei, Shang Jin. 1998. "Corruption in Economic Development: Beneficial Grease, Minor Annoyance, or Major Obstacle?" Typescript, Harvard University, Cambridge.

Weiler, Paul C. 2000. *Leveling the Playing Field.* Cambridge, Harvard University Press.

Weiss, Walter M. 1998. *The Bazaar: Markets and Merchants of the Islamic World.* London, Thames and Hudson.

Welki, Andrew M., and Zlatoper, Thomas J. 1999. "U.S. Professional Football Game-Day Attendance." *Atlantic Economic Journal* 27, 285–298.

West, Mark D. 2000. "Private Ordering at the World's First Futures Exchange." *Michigan Law Review* 98, 2574–2615.

Williamson, Oliver E. 1985. *The Economic Institutions of Capitalism.* New York, Free Press.

———. 2000. "The New Institutional Economics: Taking Stock, Looking Ahead." *Journal of Economic Literature* 38, 595–613.

Wilson, Edmund. 1940. *To the Finland Station.* New York, Doubleday.

Wilson, Robert B. 1969. "Competitive Bidding with Disparate Information." *Management Science* 15, 446–448.

———. 1977. "A Bidding Model of Perfect Competition." *Review of Economic Studies* 44, 511–518.

———. 1999. "Market Architecture." Presidential address to the Econometric Society.

Wood, Ellen Meiksins. 1999, *The Origin of Capitalism.* New York, Monthly Review Press.

Woodruff, Christopher. 1998. "Contract Enforcement and Trade Liberalization in Mexico's Footwear Industry." *World Development* 26, 979–991.

Wrong, Michela. 2000. *In the Footsteps of Mr Kurtz: Living on the Brink of Disaster in the Congo*. London, Fourth Estate.

Wurgler, Jeffrey. 2000. "Financial Markets and the Allocation of Capital." *Journal of Financial Economics* 58, 187–214.

Yang, Dali L. 1996. *Calamity and Reform in China*. Stanford, Stanford University Press.

Zahavi, Amotz, and Zahavi, Avishag. 1997. *The Handicap Principle*. Oxford, U.K., Oxford University Press.

Zhou, Kate Xiao. 1997. *How the Farmers Changed China*. Boulder, Westview Press.

Zwi, Karen, Söderland, Neil, and Schneider, Helen. 2000. "Cheaper Antiretrovirals to Treat AIDS in South Africa." *British Medical Journal* 320 (June 10), 1551–1552.

INDEX